A man detained in Tulsa, 1921

THIS LAND

RACE READER

A literary chronicle of conflict
and oppression in the middle
of America

Selections from *This Land*
magazine, 2010–2016

THIS LAND

Vincent LoVoi, *Publisher*

www.ThisLandPress.com

Printed in the United States of America

First Edition

ISBN: 978-0-9962516-2-4

THIS LAND

RACE
READER

A literary chronicle of conflict
and oppression in the middle
of America

CONTENTS

COMING TO TERMS WITH RACE

Writing about race is problematic. As soon as mention of the Tulsa Race Riot of 1921 arises, difficulties unfold and multiply. The first dilemma involves the name itself. By all accounts, it wasn't a riot. "Riot" is an obtuse word and implicates rowdy participants as primary actors. Contemporary historians and writers suggest that "pogrom" is a more accurate term, because there's enough evidence to demonstrate an ethnic cleansing occurred. One famous historical record refers to the riot as the Tulsa Disaster. Lee Roy Chapman, our most impassioned contributor on race, called it "the 1921 Battle for Greenwood."

Now, nearly one hundred years later, race remains Tulsa's most divisive issue. Several areas surrounding the city's Greenwood district pay homage to a Klansman involved in the riot, Tate Brady. A political skirmish erupted in Tulsa when attempts were made to address a potential name change to a street named after Brady (the city's decision, to change the street's name to "M.B. Brady" after a Civil War photographer, drew criticism for its intellectual dishonesty). It was a missed opportunity for the city to confront its history.

Every year in Tulsa, the John Hope Franklin Center conducts a symposium that constitutes the search for the definition to another important term: reconciliation. In a literal sense, the organization is helping the city of Tulsa come to terms with its race problem. Is reconciliation achieved by means of a public park or social program? Will compensating victims or a community bring some sort of absolution or redemption? What will it take to heal Tulsa's ongoing racial divide?

Race is America's most vexing and abiding koan, a spiritual riddle whose answer requires the full force of a community to resolve. Politicians and pastors, teachers and businessmen, journalists and artists, and everyday citizens wrestle with the challenge. In the attempt to answer the questions of race and reconciliation, Tulsans are learning that the attempt itself offers hope.

Using our most courageous tool of communication—storytelling— This Land Press presents you with our own struggle to address the matter of race in America. These collected writings demonstrate our best attempts to understand our own history. Equipped with the knowledge and perspective that these stories offer, we may be more able to atone for our failings and more capable of avoiding similar disasters, pogroms, or battles ahead.

Originally published
September 2011

by Hannibal B. Johnson

EXODUST

The legacy of Oklahoma's
all-black towns

Prominently in Kansas, and then principally in Oklahoma, towns founded by black trailblazers swelled in the post-Reconstruction era. Black Southern migrants, "Exodusters," formed their own rural frontier communities. They sought economic opportunity, full citizenship rights, and self-governance: socioeconomic uplift, sprinkled with a generous measure of hope.

In addition to black homesteaders, some persons of African ancestry prospered because of Native American affiliations—through the bonds of slavery, by blood, and in affinity relations. All-black colonies populated by these "Natives" sprang up in Indian Territory, the eastern portion of modern-day Oklahoma.

Edward Preston McCabe emerged as the father of the Oklahoma all-black town movement. McCabe, a Republican, served as Kansas State Auditor in the State of Kansas from 1882 – 1886. He once lived in Nicodemus, Kansas, a seminal all-black town.

On April 22, 1889, McCabe joined 50,000 homesteaders in the Oklahoma Land Run. This was the opening of "Oklahoma Territory," Indian Country land appropriated by the federal government for general settlement. On these acres of aspiration, McCabe hoped to germinate an all-black state.

In 1890, McCabe called on President Benjamin Harrison to press the case for an all-black state. McCabe believed that a self-governing, all-black enclave would offer his people the freedom and opportunity routinely denied them elsewhere in America. In the end, his entreaties failed.

McCabe soldiered on. He founded Langston, Oklahoma, on October 22, 1890, and established the McCabe Townsite Company and the *Langston City Herald* newspaper to promote its growth and development. McCabe developed recruiting bulletins and hired agents for his Oklahoma "boosterism" efforts.

McCabe drew throngs to unspoiled Oklahoma—"land of the red people" in the Choctaw language. These pioneers founded more than 50 all-black towns in Oklahoma.

Despite an auspicious beginning, the all-black town movement crested between 1890 and 1910. Oklahoma attained statehood in 1907 and, with it, roundly embraced "Jim Crow." By 1910, the American economy had shifted from agricultural to industrial-based. These developments (*i.e.*, the rise of racism; the demise of agrarianism) doomed many of these unique, historic oases. The few that remain serve as monuments to the human spirit.

Oklahoma's pioneering black forefathers and foremothers planted the trees under whose shade we now sit. The value of their legacy to us—the likes of Boley, Clearview, Langston, Red Bird, Rentiesville, Taft, Tatums, Tullahassee—is inestimable. We owe them a tremendous debt of gratitude.

Oklahoma's all-black towns, some still viable, others long gone, represent a significant aspect of the African-American struggle for freedom, justice, and equality. This rich history should be resurrected, reclaimed, and remembered.

Originally published
November 2010

by Russell Cobb

DREAMS OF A BLACK OKLAHOMA

On the trail of the forgotten
Okies of Alberta

At some point during Coach McBride's four-week-long excursion into Oklahoma history, I figured out I could sleep on the floor. Napping at the desk was a tricky, painful proposition in a Catholic high school. I drooled on myself and woke up with neck pain. There were also the daytime nightmares of failing a test I hadn't studied for.

So it was a revelation to learn that when McBride put on some boring OETA documentary, I could simply climb down out of the desk and sprawl out on the short-pile Berber carpet of Cascia Hall. It was a wonderful arrangement for all parties: attentive students got to re-watch movies like *The Outsiders*, McBride could draw up basketball plays, and I could nap on my back, hands folded across my stomach.

One day, McBride put on a documentary about the formation of Oklahoma statehood. It involved an old reel-to-reel projector, something that was going the way of Betamax in the late 1980s. The images started to flicker, and it was as if the entire class of sophomores was transported back to pre-school. By the time McBride left for his coffee break, almost everyone was on the floor napping. When the narrator got to the role of the "Five Civilized Tribes" in the Civil War, I was asleep.

Then, out of nowhere, a swift blow came down on my head. At first, I thought it was McBride taking his revenge on the somnolent mutiny that accompanied his documentary on Oklahoma statehood. Perhaps I was having an aneurysm. The projector still flickered. Above me, the worried face of Ryan Hackler appeared. He had brought down a metal chair with full force on a spot above my left eyebrow. I touched the spot and noticed blood.

"What the hell?" I muttered, blood trickling into the eye.

Hackler had intended some harmless prank that had gone horribly wrong. He had accidentally dropped the chair on my head while attempting to throw it out a window. He gave me a dirty t-shirt to staunch the bleeding, and I sat up. My first instinct was to punch Hackler, but I was too dazed to do anything but stare at the screen.

So, there I sat, listening to the story of E.P. McCabe and waiting for the bleeding to stop. For those of you who also slept through Oklahoma History, McCabe was an obscure Kansas politician with a vision of

Oklahoma as a refuge for former slaves. McCabe had an idea that Oklahoma could become the nation's only all-black state. As the State Auditor of Kansas, he lobbied President Harrison to appoint him as territorial governor and, when that didn't work out, he headed down to Langston, which was already a haven for black settlers in 1890.

If the U.S. government wasn't going to make Oklahoma an all-black state, McCabe would take matters into his own hands. The Sac and Fox Nation opened up their lands for settlement, and McCabe recruited ex-slaves and tenant farmers from Mississippi and Arkansas to out-Sooner the Sooners. They staked their claims outside Langston but found themselves in shootouts with white cowboys. On one occasion, McCabe dodged five or six rounds of gunfire on Sac and Fox land from a group of Boomers. In the 1890s, he ran for state office and got beat by the Democrats, who soon took over the territory's political scene.

I sat there in McBride's classroom, entranced by the parallel universe in which Oklahoma was an all-black state. Tulsa—my little slice of it between Utica Square, Cascia Hall, and Riverside Drive—was so white. There was one black family in all of Maple Ridge. There were two black students in my graduating class of 1992. Cascia didn't recognize Martin Luther King Jr. Day as a holiday. And here was this story of an alternate reality that could have been: had McCabe succeeded, maybe I would be the only white kid in an all-black class right now.

Twenty years later, the question of Oklahoma identity still preoccupies me. Although I now study and teach Latin American culture and history in Canada, my pet obsession remains Oklahoma. Where is Oklahoma? The Midwest, the South, the Southwest? What does it mean to be an Okie? These are questions of vital importance to me and countless other Oklahomans, although I'm not sure why. Texans, Kansans, and Arkansans don't have this problem. We Okies, on the other hand, have no fixed identity, just a set of obsessions—football, fundamentalism, and tornadoes—that define us.

The day after the injury, fully recovered from the blow to my head, I stole a book from the classroom: *Oklahoma: The Story of its Past and Present* by Edwin C. Reynolds. I stuck it in my backpack like some sort of contraband. Being interested in Oklahoma history was, for a high schooler, possibly one of the most uncool things one could be interested in. At lunch, I opened the book to learn more about McCabe and his plan to make Oklahoma a black Promised Land. Nothing. The book—I still have it today—only mentions Langston University as one of Oklahoma's many fine institutions of higher learning.

. . .

It is an uncomfortably warm and humid evening in Clearwater, British Columbia. In a place where an August snowstorm is not uncommon, the smoke from forest fires combines with the heat to make for a smoldering afternoon. I am at the Wells Grey Diner plowing through a plate of French fries and a watery Canadian lager when Rick Jamerson comes through the door. Somehow, he knows I am the person who has been persistently dogging him via email about meeting him and his gospel-revival group, the Black Pioneer Heritage Singers. I am here to watch his group of gospel singers, descended from Oklahoma immigrants, headline a Christian music festival up the highway. This Canadian group is the living legacy of McCabe's dream.

Jamerson is a handsome man with the look of someone two decades younger in appearance than real age. He is followed by his equally striking wife, Junetta Jamerson, the lead singer of the group. I wipe off my ketchup-stained fingers to shake their hands.

We are all Okies of a sort, I tell the Jamersons. I explain to them what a weird coincidence it is that we are meeting here, in middle-of-nowhere British Columbia when we all come from Oklahoma.

But Junetta Jamerson isn't having it. Saying she comes from Oklahoma is "a bit of a misnomer," she says.

"If you flew here and changed planes in Denver, would you say you come from Denver?" she asks me. Oklahoma was just a stopover, she says, to their ultimate destination: Northern Alberta, the northernmost edge of farmland in North America. I persist.

"Everyone knows about the Okies from the Great Depression," I say. "It's part of the American national mythology. Dirt farmers pulling up stakes and heading West: *The Grapes of Wrath* and the music of Woody Guthrie."

You guys, I tell them, were the original Okies, but no one in Oklahoma knows your story! They look back at me quizzically. It occurs to me that they've probably never heard the word "Okie" before.

. . .

In the early 1900s, Oklahoma seemed like the promised land for Black Americans suffering through Jim Crow in the South. E. P. McCabe's solution, resettling former slaves on Indian lands, seemed promising. McCabe's plan was to have black settlers gather in Langston and then fan out across the state, gaining majorities in most counties. He needed to give people real incentives, so he devised a plan. In pamphlets sent out across the South, McCabe told prospective

E.P. McCabe, 1850–1920

settlers that the values of the land would soon double and massive profits could be made. More importantly, though, was the idea of a self-governance.

"At the present time," McCabe wrote in one pamphlet, "we are Republicans, but the time will soon come when we will be able to dictate the policy of this Territory, or state, and when that time comes we will have a negro state governed by negroes. We do not wish to antagonize the whites. They are necessary in the development of a new country but they owe my race homes, and my race owes to itself a governmental control of those homes."

With statehood, however, Oklahoma started repeating the tragedy of the rest of the South, only in fast-forward. Within a couple of years, Oklahoma had turned from Canaan to Egypt, and blacks lost the vote and all power in state politics. Farmers like J.D. Edwards—one of the 1,000 or so who eventually left for Canada—paid the price. Roving bands of white mobs, known as "white cappers," terrorized small towns in the early years of statehood. They rode out the entire black population of Sapulpa during a single day in 1909. They lynched a man in Henryetta from a telegraph pole and then riddled the corpse with bullets. They chased an entire all-black town to Muskogee and then burned down buildings where they thought blacks were hiding. A race riot broke out in Okmulgee.

The mobs were egged on by the editor of the *Daily Oklahoman*, Ray Stafford, an ardent racist who wanted the new state to be a part of the "Solid South." This meant purging Oklahoma of Republicans, a party that, at the time, was a biracial coalition whose platform consisted of Civil Rights and equal protection for all citizens, regardless of color, under the law. Stafford taunted Republicans for not backing Jim Crow amendments to the state constitution. For Stafford, Oklahoma had a choice: it could take the Texas road or the Kansas road toward race relations. When Oklahoma enacted laws segregating everything from street cars to schools, as well as instituting a Grandfather Clause that disenfranchised virtually every black voter, Stafford got his answer. Texas, he wrote, should be proud of Oklahoma that it didn't follow the path of Republican Kansas. In the end, he wrote, "a Republican politician cannot be separated from the nigger."

Black Americans were in a panic. McCabe disappeared from the scene. Some accused him of creating a land bubble under the guise of a black homeland. A mysterious man named "Chief Sam" arrived in Oklahoma in 1913, promising a bright future along the Gold Coast of Africa. After one ill-fated trip in 1914 in which the migrants almost died of starvation, Chief Sam disappeared as well.

Canadian immigration agents started recruiting in Oklahoma. After the many land rushes in the late 19th century, Oklahoma had become overcrowded. Western Canada, on the other hand, had nothing but land. With the continental United States settled, Canada promoted its new provinces of British Columbia and Alberta as "the last, best West." Land could be had for pennies. Pioneers were even granted subsidies for rail travel on the Canadian National. Somehow, word got out that Canada was warmer than Oklahoma and that Canadians had no racial prejudice at all. Glowing reports of Canada started appearing in the newspapers of all-black towns in Oklahoma.

Henry Sneed, a man from Clearview—one of Oklahoma's dozen or so all-black towns, decided to go scope out this place called Canada. He traveled by rail from Tulsa to Winnipeg and from there on to Edmonton. Sneed must have liked what he saw, because he returned, this time with company. Among his companions was Jefferson Davis Edwards, a cotton and tobacco farmer originally from Pine Bluff, Arkansas. Edwards, then 21 years old and single, made the trek from Tulsa to Winnipeg, where he had his first taste of whiskey at a saloon. In Edmonton, the men, in the words of one Alberta historian, "were seen more as curiosities than as threats."

Sneed again went back to Oklahoma and gathered up 194 men, women, and children. They sold their houses and their farms and filled 200 rail cars with their horses and livestock. Weeks later, they arrived in Edmonton where journalists from the local paper covered their arrival.

To a newcomer, Edmonton feels like a frontier town on the northernmost boundary of civilization. At least, that's what it feels like in 2010. One hundred years ago, it must have felt like another planet. But the Okies didn't stop in Edmonton. Canadian officials gave them land far from the city in settlements that didn't appeal to white immigrants from Britain, Germany, and the Ukraine. The most notable settlement, Amber Valley, was even farther north than Edmonton, and it took weeks to get there. Edwards landed in Amber Valley and set about clearing land, mostly by hand. In the course of a week, he later estimated, he cleared a space of land for farming that was about the size of a living room.

Despite the hardships, more black Oklahomans fled to Canada. Another group of 200 people followed Sneed's party but was detained in Emerson, on the Minnesota-Manitoba border. Canadian officials had begun to doubt whether blacks were suited to the climate of Canada and administered medical exams. When all the Okies passed the exam, the Canadians demanded a head tax. In Edmonton, where they had once been seen as curiosities, locals started to organize against further immigration. Black settlements were popping up all over Alberta, and local officials feared that Alberta would become a haven for the entire South.

A petition by the Edmonton Board of Trade was circulated throughout town addressed to the Prime Minister:

> We, the undersigned residents of the City of Edmonton, respectfully urge upon your attention and that of the Government of which you are the head, the serious menace to the future welfare of a large portion of western Canada, by reason of the alarming influx of Negro settlers. This influx commenced about four years ago in a very small way, only four or five families coming in the first season, followed by thirty or forty families the next year. Last year several hundred negroes arrived at Edmonton and settled in surrounding territory. Already this season nearly three hundred have arrived; and the statement is made, both by these arrivals and by press dispatches, that these are but an advance guard of hosts to follow. We submit that the advent of such Negroes as are now here was most unfortunate for the country, and that further arrivals would be disastrous. We cannot admit as any factor the argument that these people may be good farmers or good citizens. It is a matter of common knowledge that it has been proved in the United States that Negroes and whites cannot live in proximity without the occurrence of revolting lawlessness, and the development of bitter race hatred.

About one quarter of the city's 24,000 residents signed on. The Minister of the Interior, who happened to be from Edmonton, drafted an Order of Council and sent it to Prime Minister Wilfred Laurier for his signature. Laurier declared, "For a period of one year from and after the date hereof the landing in Canada shall be... prohibited of any immigrants belonging to the Negro race, which race is deemed unsuitable to the climate and requirements of Canada."

• • •

Before the Black Pioneer Heritage Singers take the stage on a little farm outside Clearwater, the group gathers for a prayer in a tent. They are sweating through their crisp Sunday whites, in stark contrast to the shorts-and-tanktops crowd that mills about eating popcorn. The band on stage before them serves up soft, sincere Christian pop, and the crowd seems distracted.

Junetta Jamerson doesn't seem all that thrilled about the venue, but once the group takes the stage, it's as if this bucolic farm in B.C. suddenly becomes a black Baptist church in the South. Jamerson, who mostly speaks in a lilting Canadian accent punctuated with the occasional "eh," has the entire crowd on its feet by the end of the first song, "On the Wings of Heaven."

Between songs, Jamerson's voice changes. She becomes a black preacher from the South: "We don't have to wait til we get to heaven, we can shout now!" she says to the crowd. "I've got my shouting shoes on now, so y'all better watch out."

By the second song, the Edwin Hawkins Singers classic "Oh Happy Day," the crowd is stomping and clapping, not quite in rhythm with the gospel soul of the Pioneer Singers, but enthusiastic nonetheless. It is a remarkable show, despite the fact that there was not even time for a sound check. The next morning, back at the Wells Grey Diner, Jamerson says that the group is often seen as a "curiosity" when they travel in the U.S.

"The first time I went to D.C., I spoke at an event at the Smithsonian Folkways Festival," Jamerson says. "Some black gentleman who was an African-American history professor listened to me tell our story. Later, he came up to me and said, 'Young lady, are you sure that what you're saying is true?' In all his learned studies, he had never heard of the Black One Thousand."

The Black One Thousand, Jamerson says, was a term that stuck for the Oklahoma Pioneers. Once a thousand black settlers crossed into Canada, the government went on an anti-immigration campaign, sending agents back to Oklahoma. A black physician from Chicago, C.W. Speers, was hired to tour Oklahoma and spread the bad news about life up north. In churches and newspapers, Speers told blacks that Canada was much colder than Oklahoma. So cold, in fact, that many immigrants were freezing or starving to death. Canadians, it turned out, were just as racist as Oklahomans. The land was terrible and there was no guarantee blacks could even secure a title to the land they struggled to clear and farm. By the outbreak of World War I, black immigration to Alberta had stopped completely.

Some of the Alberta pioneers went back to Oklahoma, while others moved on to greener and warmer pastures in California. Jefferson Davis Edwards, after he had carved a prosperous farm out of the pine forest, went back to Oklahoma City to visit his brother, who had become a self-made millionaire selling scrap metal during World War II. Edwards tried to get around segregation on the trains by claiming he was no longer an American and wore a Union Jack in his hatband to prove it. Quenten Brown, one of Edwards's great-grandsons and the keyboard player in the Heritage Singers, tells me that Edwards wanted to return to Oklahoma for good. "Towards the end of his life, he was talking about going back," Brown says.

Members of the Black Pioneer Heritage Singers

The exodus of African Americans from Oklahoma created a static historical memory that remained stuck in the minds of the descendants of the settlers until recently. The Oklahoma settlers gradually gained acceptance and became fully Canadian. They moved from farming settlements to cities: Edmonton, Calgary, Vancouver. But, says Junetta Jamerson, their vision became provincial. Because Canadians came to treat them like just another immigrant group, they missed out on the cultural movements of Civil Rights and Black Power. When Jamerson's father, a Californian escaping the Vietnam War, came to Alberta, he found a community that hadn't changed in its values or beliefs in half a century.

Now, as she sees it, the threat is too much assimilation.

"The new generation of African Americans here doesn't know where they come from," she says. "They don't know what kind of black they are. If you ask them where they're from, they say, 'Nowhere.'"

Part of the problem is that, despite a sizable community, there is no black neighborhood in Edmonton. For years, the community revolved around a Shiloh Baptist Church, but now even that institution is thoroughly integrated into mainstream white Canadian society.

Fearing a loss of African-American culture in Alberta, Jamerson and her husband started the Black Pioneer Heritage Singers in the early 2000s. They play Southern Black Gospel, a sound that is rarely heard in Western Canada. Gauging from their reception at the Christian music festival in Clearwater, B.C., there is a hunger among Canadian audiences for the music. Still, the Pioneer Singers are as much a cultural mission about a lost chapter in American history as they are a musical group.

Jamerson tells me that the first time she went to the South for a family reunion near Dallas, she was scared. The memories of violence had been passed down two or three generations and she still feared the worst. What she found in Texas, however, shocked her. "The infrastructure there was light years beyond what we have in Canada. We seemed like the hicks."

The older generation doesn't like to talk about what happened in the South, Paul Gardener, another member of the Black Pioneer Heritage Singers, tells me. Gardener says that, for the older generation, Oklahoma represented Egypt and Alberta was Israel. Once they were freed from bondage, they didn't look back.

"Some of them are afraid that they'll be sold back into slavery if they ever go back there," Gardener says. "This was the promised land." On their CD, the experience of the black Oklahoma pioneers is captured in a sung poem, "Amber Valley Pine":

Overcrowded wagons songs in every mouth

Out of Oklahoma and places in the South

Southern voices singing at northern windowsills

Cabins cradled in the pines 'neath the Athabasca hills

Coal oil lamps to light the way for a hungry man

Headin' home from dusty fields to biscuits in the pan

Built us a homestead your kinfolk and mine

Put down some roots in the Amber Valley Pine

I had imagined the black pioneers of Alberta as the original Okies, a group rooted in Oklahoma who set out West to improve their lives. To them, however, Oklahoma was simply a stopover from the Deep South to the Far North. But maybe this is at the heart of what it means to be an Okie, to be in constant movement toward a home that is always just over the horizon.

A parade in Greenwood, date unknown
Courtesy Greenwood Cultural Center

Originally published
September 2011

by J. Kavin Ross

A CONSPIRACY OF SILENCE

The demise of Black Wall Street

The Tulsa Race Riot of 1921 made national headlines on June 1 of this year, its 90th anniversary. Tulsa quietly commemorated the worst civil unrest on American soil since the Civil War with a candlelight vigil. A program titled "Greenwood Burned," located in the historic district, was poorly attended. The three-day conference of the John Hope Franklin Reconciliation Symposium included no riot survivors.

In the scorching summer of 1921, nearly 40 blocks of the black community of Greenwood were burned to the ground by a white mob. Thousands of Tulsans were forever affected by the destruction. Hundreds of lives were lost and many homes and businesses were destroyed. As the ashes cooled on America's "Black Wall Street," its citizens rebuilt Greenwood without the promised funds owed to them. Tulsa County commissioners denied all moneys from outside sources, vowing to take care of its own citizens, but never following through on their promise. The first commission had made plans to provide reparations to the riot victims but was quickly disbanded and reformed. The second commission sought to move blacks out of Greenwood entirely.

For decades, the events from those atrocities were kept dormant, but were tightly whispered from the lips of those who dared to tell. The white community did not talk about race war because it left a stain on the fabric of the bustling oil capital. The black community did not talk about the massacre because those who committed the unpunished crime were still alive. Additionally, and unfortunately for the residents of Greenwood, the growth of Ku Klux Klan activity increased after the so-called riot.

In this environment, a conspiracy of silence was born.

In the 1830s, many African Americans journeyed to what would later be called Oklahoma, experiencing undesirable hardships along the Trail of Tears with the "Five Civilized Tribes." Under President Andrew Jackson's administration, the Indian Removal Act relocated the tribes and their slaves to the established Twin Territories.

Of the 32 black townships that were established in America after the Civil War, 28 of them were in Oklahoma before it became a state. O.W. Gurley, one of Tulsa's earliest pioneers, named the Greenwood district. An educator and entrepreneur who made his wealth as a landowner, Gurley purchased 40 acres in Tulsa to be sold to "coloreds only." Senate Bill Number 1, the state's first piece of legislation, prevented coloreds from residing, traveling, and marrying outside their race. Gurley's property lines were Pine Street to the north, the Frisco railroad tracks to the south, Lansing Avenue to the east, and Cincinnati Avenue to the west. The still-unpaved streets would also serve as Tulsa's racial dividing lines.

After Gurley's purchase of the land, Tulsa began to grow. Black ownership was unheard of at that time, but under the state's Jim Crow laws, Greenwood was born out of necessity. The racial climate prevented coloreds from shopping anywhere but Greenwood. Among Gurley's first businesses was a boarding house located on a dirt road crossing the Frisco tracks, which would later be named Greenwood Avenue.

By 1913, more businesses followed, including the law and doctor offices of Buck Colbert Franklin and A.C. Jackson, respectively, and Dunbar and Booker T. Washington schools, Vernon AME and Mount Zion Baptist churches, Ricketts' Restaurant, The Williams' Dreamland Theater, Mann's Grocery, Stradford Hotel, and a host of haberdasheries, drug stores, cafes, barbershops, and beauty salons.

Famed educator Booker Taliaferro Washington visited Tulsa for a dedication of a small school named in his honor. Upon visiting the business district of Greenwood, he was amazed by the entrepreneurial spirit of the Greenwood residents. Washington would be credited for coining the phrase "the Negro Wall Street of America." In the turbulent era of civil rights, the tag became "Black Wall Street." The area thrived and was a source of pride in the black community— and a sore spot of envy across the tracks.

During the terrifying assault on Greenwood, many fled on foot, only to be rounded up and herded to internment camps around the city. Casualty counts varied; the dead were hastily buried in unmarked graves around the city. Funerals were forbidden. To date, the exact locations of the riot dead remain unconfirmed.

A now-legendary editorial in the June 4, 1921, editions of the *Tulsa Tribune* summed the up the sentiments of most Tulsans:

In this old Niggertown were a lot of bad niggers and a bad nigger is about the lowest thing that walks on two feet. Give a bad nigger his booze and his dope and a gun and he thinks he can shoot up the world. And all of these four things can be found in 'Niggertown'—booze, dope, bad niggers and guns. The Tulsa Tribune make no

apology to the police commissioners or to the mayor of this city for having pled with them to clean up the cesspools in this city.

Through the heat of the summer and into winter's harshness, the survivors of Greenwood lived in tents and wooden shanties supplied by the American Red Cross while the city sorted through the rubble. The county commissioners at that time proposed to buy the land for pennies on the dollar and sell the scorched lands to the highest bidders. Tulsa's power structure began to enforce various fire ordinances to prevent landowners from rebuilding. Those caught rebuilding would be arrested. Buck Colbert Franklin, father of noted historian Dr. John Hope Franklin, defended those arrested.

One such decree was that any new structure would have to be built from fireproof materials. The Acme Brick Company, located near the Booker T. Washington High School in the Greenwood district, was instructed not to sell its products, and nearby lumber yards also refused to sell to blacks. B. C. Franklin advised his clients to build with anything, even orange crates.

In an effort to expand the boundaries of downtown, the city proposed to move the Negro settlement farther north and to the east of the Greenwood district. The county offered jobs to the now-unemployed black Tulsans. However, many refused to clean up the debris left by the mob. Commissioners Tate Brady, Jeff Archer, and others created another ordinance directly at the survivors: "Notice is hereby given that all men are ordered to either get a job and go to work or if you have no job work will be furnished you by applying at the Booker T. Washington Public School on Frankfort Street. All men who have no job and who refuse to work will be arrested as vagrants," the report read. This action prompted Franklin to take the city powers all the way to the Oklahoma Supreme Court, who sided with Franklin.

Riots were prevalent throughout the country during this era. In 1905, race riots occurred in Springfield, Illinois, the land of Lincoln, and 1919 was deemed the "red summer" for its outbreaks of race wars. Rosewood, a small rural community in Florida later depicted in a feature film, was destroyed in 1923. Each riot shared similarities: A white woman accused a black man of molestation. The white mob would react by terrorizing and destroying the black community.

Of all the uprisings, Greenwood is unique in that the razed community came back, bigger, and better than before. Black residents of Greenwood during the

1940s and '50s enjoyed a peaceful but separate coexistence with the rest of the city. Separated schools were built to the north and east of the Greenwood district, including the new Booker T. Washington High School. The former BTW that survived the riot became Charles S. Johnson Elementary, which two decades later would become among the demolished inventory of Urban Renewal. The former grounds of that original BTW are now the Tulsa campus of Oklahoma State University.

The passage of the Civil Rights Bill in the 1960s allowed black dollars to be spent in white stores, and put a dent in the commerce and growth of the famed Black Wall Street. The end of an era began as Greenwood declined.

Once again, Greenwood was under attack. Not by the hands of an angry mob, but by the bulldozers of the federal government. Urban Renewal made its effects known in Tulsa 20 years after the creation of the Housing Act and the Federal-Aid Highway Act of the 1950s. Highways divided neighborhoods and urban sprawl began. The removal of large populations of the city's minority was commonplace throughout large cities across the nation.

Tulsa was the first metropolis in Oklahoma to create an urban renewal authority. Opting not to bulldoze blocks of homes, Tulsa cleared problem properties while rehabilitating others. Homes and businesses that were rebuilt after the riot were bought and torn down, and Interstate 244—renamed the Martin Luther King Jr. Expressway in the 1980s—plowed through the heart of the remaining Greenwood business district.

The University Center at Tulsa and the Greenwood Cultural Center were built in its place. Only Mount Zion Baptist Church and Vernon AME Church withstood the test of time. Also left behind was one block of buildings left standing in hopes that one day the once thriving and vibrant Negro Wall Street of America would be recognized.

In the early 1970s, a group of brothers—Robert, Ronnie, and Charlie Wilson—formed The Greenwood, Archer and Pine Street Band, by doing overtly what Senate Bill No. 1 had done deceitfully, the brothers sought to honor the boundaries of their neighborhood. Due to a lack of space on a poster, the promoter shortened the band's name to The Gap Band. The group went on to produce a string of hits in the 1980s.

Here and elsewhere, people are acknowledging the legacy of Greenwood. Underway in the nation's capital is the construction of a $500 million Smithsonian Institute Museum of African-American History and Culture. The collection will include an exhibit titled "Greenwood: Before, during and after the Tulsa Race Riot of 1921." Museum officials have made numerous visits to Tulsa to retrieve information and artifacts for the exhibit.

In Memphis, the National Civil Rights Museum is revamping its exhibits. At the Lorraine Motel—site of the assassination of civil rights leader Dr. Martin Luther King Jr.—a Greenwood exhibit will be among the highlights.

U.S. Representative John Sullivan (R) has authored a bill in the United States Congress to incorporate the Tulsa Race Riot Memorial and John Hope Franklin Reconciliation Park as a part of the inventory of the National Park Services. Also in progress is a grassroots effort to have the Greenwood district recognized on a National Preservation List of Historic Places.

With the creation of the new ONEOK Field, built on the former scorched lands of O.W. Gurley's Greenwood, the historic district is breathing new life as more patrons walk the same sidewalks from Greenwood's yesteryear. More construction in the area is planned in the future, including loft apartments.

In the spring of 2004, Bishop Desmond Tutu—who gained international attention for his role in ending racial tensions and beginning the process of reconciliation in his homeland in South Africa—visited the former oil boomtown. "Tulsa is sitting on a powder keg. Because the city refuses to acknowledge and deal with its past," Tutu said. He continued to state if Tulsa ever deals with its race relations, this magic city could become a jewel to the world.

Originally published
May 2011

by Hannibal B. Johnson

CURRICULUM COUNTS

Despite its significance as the worst so-called race riot in American history, even some Tulsans remain oblivious to the tragic events of late May 1921. Still more claim only a superficial familiarity with it.

We need to teach and learn about the Tulsa Race Riot. We need to know what happened and why. We need to hold people accountable; assign moral responsibility for the gross depredations and injustices perpetrated on Tulsa soil. If, and only if, we teach and learn about the riot will we begin the process of reconciliation in earnest, recapture a lost sense of shared humanity, and create for posterity a community more open, inclusive, and loving than the one in which we live today. We must incorporate this potent, painful, poignant legacy into the classroom in deliberate, systematic ways.

When we sanitize our past, we stifle our ability to analyze it intensively and critically.

The history surrounding the riot is but one case in point. Some believe a conspiracy of silence enveloped the community in the wake of the riot and muzzled it for decades thereafter. Tulsans scarcely spoke of this traumatic event privately, let alone publicly. Textbooks omitted references to this ugly chapter in our history.

The full dimensions of this epic tragedy have only been recently realized. Arguably, that years-long obfuscation stunted Tulsa's growth, both physically and spiritually. Our failure to come clean about Tulsa's dirty little secret undermined the ability of the community to build trust across the great chasm of race and use history as a catalyst for strategic, transformational change.

An 11-member, legislatively created 1921 Tulsa Race Riot Commission, initially convened in 1997, changed the trajectory of riot coverage and prompted a groundswell of public interest.

The state charged the Commission with conducting an investigation and further tasked it on appropriate action, including reparations. The sometimes-contentious deliberations of the Commission drew worldwide media attention and rekindled local curiosity. In 2001, the Commission issued its final report. Among the Commission's recommendations were:

- Direct payment of reparations to riot survivors and descendants
- A scholarship fund for students affected by the riot
- Economic incentives to spur development in the Greenwood district
- Construction of a riot-related memorial

Initially, the Commission's endorsement of cash reparations drew particular attention. Indeed, early media focus on money payments dwarfed coverage of the other items and, more importantly, drowned out discussion of broader philosophical questions centering on the definition of and rationale for reparations. Those foundational questions about reparations merit additional consideration.

Reparations make amends for injustices. Properly conceived, reparations help bridge divides, bolster trust, and build community.

How is it possible to satisfy the core definitional criteria for reparations—*to make amends*—and the fundamental rationale underlying reparations—*reconciliation*—without a viable effort to educate the community on the cause for which reparations are to be made? Surely, a baseline of knowledge about the event for which reparations are offered is the *sine qua non* of meaningful reparations. Broad-based support for riot reparations hinges on community awareness about our history—the events that transpired before, during, and after the fateful event we know as the 1921 Tulsa Race Riot.

The Commission's reparations wish list contained no reference to curriculum reform, arguably the most meaningful, enduring form of reparations imaginable. This stunning omission undercut its other recommendations. No matter what else we may do, we will not be whole unless and until we own our past, process it, and integrate its lessons in the classroom.

In recent years, there has been a growing recognition of the centrality of curriculum in addressing the riot and its legacy. On October 12, 2008, the Tulsa City Council passed a riot-inspired resolution supporting, among other things, the teaching of an appropriate curriculum to ensure the riot is adequately covered in Oklahoma's educational institutions as an historical event. It was a call for reparations. It was a call to action, and a moment of hope.

Teaching about the riot is now part of the state's "Priority Academic Student Skills," proficiency expectations for various subjects and grade levels. Some ninth-grade Oklahoma History textbooks now include a discussion of the riot. Creative teachers have supplemented regular curricula with riot-related materials and experiential activities. The John Hope Franklin Center for Reconciliation compiled supplementary curricular materials on riot history, and is working with Tulsa Public Schools to make them widely available to educators. The Franklin Center's annual *Reconciliation in America* symposium brings together scholars and practitioners in an effort to spur racial reconciliation efforts. Curriculum reform is a core piece of the puzzle. While these are encouraging developments, much work remains to be done.

Why not be honest and transparent? Why not infuse interdisciplinary teachings about the riot into our schools? Why not ask the provocative questions that expose the present manifestations of past horrors?

With a sense of purpose and a dose of creativity, riot-related history may be woven into our curricular fabric. The consequences will be powerful, positive, and generation-spanning.

TULSA RACE RIOT EDUCATIONAL SURVEY

In April of 2011, This Land Press conducted an online survey asking people about their educational experiences involving the 1921 Tulsa Race Riot. We received 168 responses with the following results:

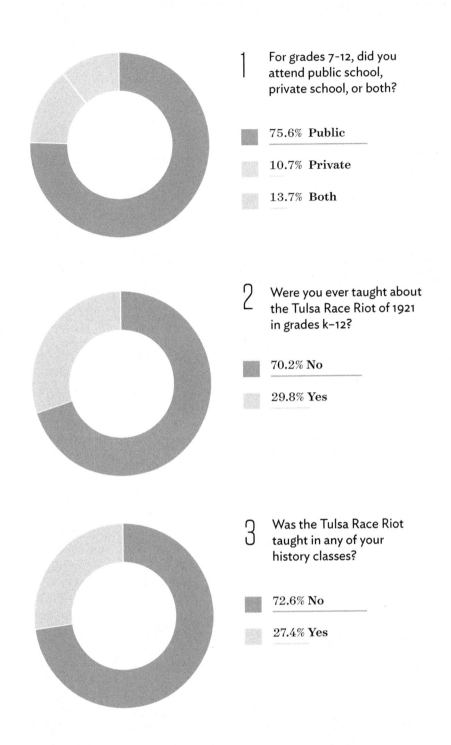

1 For grades 7-12, did you attend public school, private school, or both?

- 75.6% Public
- 10.7% Private
- 13.7% Both

2 Were you ever taught about the Tulsa Race Riot of 1921 in grades k–12?

- 70.2% No
- 29.8% Yes

3 Was the Tulsa Race Riot taught in any of your history classes?

- 72.6% No
- 27.4% Yes

4 Was your Oklahoma History teacher a coach?

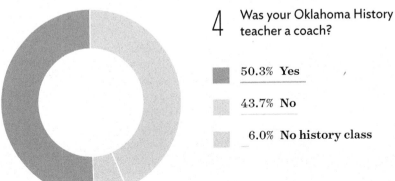

- 50.3% Yes
- 43.7% No
- 6.0% No history class

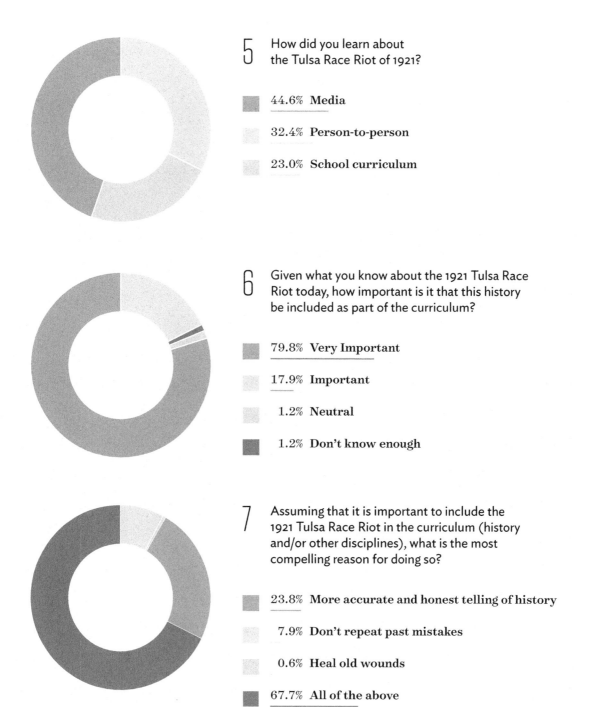

5 How did you learn about the Tulsa Race Riot of 1921?

44.6% Media

32.4% Person-to-person

23.0% School curriculum

6 Given what you know about the 1921 Tulsa Race Riot today, how important is it that this history be included as part of the curriculum?

79.8% Very Important

17.9% Important

1.2% Neutral

1.2% Don't know enough

7 Assuming that it is important to include the 1921 Tulsa Race Riot in the curriculum (history and/or other disciplines), what is the most compelling reason for doing so?

23.8% More accurate and honest telling of history

7.9% Don't repeat past mistakes

0.6% Heal old wounds

67.7% All of the above

H.H. Brady and family. The young W. Tate Brady is pictured seated at center. Both father and son were members of the Ku Klux Klan.
© 2011 The Eugene B. Adkins Collection Archive at the Fred Jones Jr. Museum of Art, the University of Oklahoma, Norman, Oklahoma and the Philbrook Museum of Art, Tulsa, Oklahoma. Used by permission.

Originally published
September 2011

by Lee Roy Chapman

THE NIGHTMARE OF DREAMLAND

Tate Brady and the battle for Greenwood

The 17 men were terrified, and with good reason. They stood shivering in the November midnight air, their bare chests lit by the headlights of the parked cars surrounding them. In the dark, they could barely make out their captors, a group of about 50 men dressed in black hoods and robes.

Two hours earlier, during a special session of night court, Tulsa judge T.D. Evans had declared them all guilty of the crime of not owning a war bond—a conviction that smacked of political and ideological retaliation. All defendants but one were members of the Industrial Workers of the World (IWW), a workers union. The "Wobblies," as they were commonly called, were opponents of the war effort and of capitalism. None of the men had a criminal record, but all men were fined a hundred dollars.[1]

They weren't expected to pay for their crimes, at least not in money. Once the trial ended, policemen rounded up the 17 and loaded them up in squad cars. Instead of jailing them, the police delivered the convicted men into the custody of the black-robed Knights of Liberty,[2] who were waiting for the Wobblies at the railroad tracks near Convention Hall.[3] The Knights kidnapped the Wobblies at gunpoint, tied them up, threw them into their cars, and drove them into the area west of town.[4]

"We were ordered out of the autos, told to get in line in front of these gunmen, and another bunch of men with automatics and pistols," Joe French, one of the Wobblies, would later testify. One by one, they were pulled from the lineup and tied to a tree. A Knight then approached each man with a

---

1. Five men present were witnesses for the defense. Judge Evans convicted these men, along with the men charged, stating, "These are no ordinary times."

2. Referred to as a "faction" of the Klan, the Knights of Liberty were a short-lived secret order with cells throughout the nation. In Oklahoma, they carried out extralegal action on behalf of the Tulsa Chamber of Commerce and its Council of Defense, in the tradition of the reconstruction-era Ku Klux Klan, the "Invisible Empire." After the end of the war, the Knights of Liberty, in some areas of the country, turned against the Klan.

3. The Convention Hall building is now known as the Brady Theater.

4. The area where the Tulsa Outrage tortures occurred was then known as Irving Place Editions, an area today understood as a combination of the Crosby Heights and Owen Park neighborhoods.

double piece of hemp rope and whipped the victim's back until blood draped his skin. Another man stepped forward and slathered boiling tar on the victim's back with a paint brush, coating him from head to seat. In a final act of humiliation, the Knight then padded the victim's back with feathers from a down pillow.[5]

"I've lived here for 18 years, and have raised a large family," pleaded an older man in the group. "I am not an IWW, I am as patriotic as any man here."

The man's cries were ignored; every man was whipped, tarred, and feathered. The incident became known "The Tulsa Outrage," and was reported in the national press. According to multiple interviews conducted by National Civil Liberties Bureau investigator L.A. Brown, two men were repeatedly identified as perpetrating the torture: Tulsa's Chief of Police, Ed Lucas, and W. Tate Brady, one of Tulsa's founders. That's Tate Brady, as in Brady Theater, Brady Arts District, and Brady Heights.[6]

The following day, November 10, 1917, the front page of the *Tulsa Daily World* would make an announcement to the city regarding the flogging of the Wobblies: "Modern Ku Klux Klan Comes into Being: Seventeen First Victims;[7] Black Robed 'Knights of Liberty' Take Prisoners from Police to Lonely Ravine."

THE SEGREGATION OF HISTORY

According to the Oklahoma Historical Society's *Encyclopedia of Oklahoma*, Tate Brady was a "pioneer, entrepreneur, member of the Oklahoma Bar, politician, and early booster of Tulsa." The Brady Heights Historic District website calls him "a pioneer Tulsa developer and entrepreneur, who was a powerful political force in the state's early years. He was Oklahoma's first Democratic National committeeman, and he built the Cain's Ballroom and the now extinct Brady Hotel." *Tulsa World* wrote: "Brady, a pioneer merchant, was an incorporator of the city, as well as a political leader at the time of statehood."

All of these accounts exclude any direct mention of Brady's less-than-honorable traits: his violent behavior, his attempts to segregate Tulsa, his deep involvement with the Klan and affiliated organizations, and his abuse of power.

"Well, it's political," one employee of the Oklahoma Historical Society said, when asked about the gaps in Brady's biography.

Despite the widespread segregation of memory surrounding Brady, a rounder, more accurate portrait of the man emerges when all of the history is taken into account.

THE MAKING OF COMRADE TATE

Wyatt Tate Brady was born in Forest City, Missouri, in 1870, and moved to Nevada, Missouri, when he was 12. By the time he was 17, he had taken up work at W.F. Lewis' shoe store, where he encountered his first brush with real terror—as a victim.

In the early morning hours of March 3, 1887, a customer unfamiliar to Brady entered the store. The stranger asked to see samples of shoes and offered to pay for them. Suspicious of the customer, Brady slipped his revolver from under the counter into his pocket. When Brady went to the safe for change, the stranger rushed Brady and shot at him, sending a bullet through Brady's left ear. Brady fired a shot back, missing the robber. A disoriented Brady was then pistol-whipped and the robber made his getaway.

Undeterred by the assault, Brady set out for a new frontier.

Three years later, in 1890, the young bachelor headed toward the Creek Nation, Indian Territory, to make his mark as a merchant, providing goods for the established cattle trade and railroad. By Brady's arrival, Tulsa had a cemetery,[8] a Masonic lodge, a post office, a lumberyard, and a coal mine.

Five years after his arrival in Tulsa, on April 18, 1895, Brady married Rachel Cassandra Davis, who came from a prominent Claremore family. She was 1/64th Cherokee, which gave her new husband special

---

5. The act of tarring and feathering is a medieval form of torture, dating back to the 12th century. The application of hot tar burned the skin; the inclusion of the feathers added insult to injury. The most recent case of tarring and feathering occurred in 2007 in Ireland.

6. The L.A. Brown Papers were acquired by This Land Press from the New York State Archives. L.A. Brown was the investigator of the Tulsa Outrage for the National Civil Liberties Bureau (now the ACLU).

7. According to the Oklahoma Historical Society, the Klan did not officially arrive in Oklahoma until 1920 when the Invisible Knights of the Ku Klux Klan, Inc. registered in the state. However, as far back as 1907 there were reported incidents of extralegal activities by "white cappers." The existence of a Ku Klux Klan prior to 1920 is well-documented. For instance, Altus organized its own KKK in 1917, around the time of the Tulsa Outrage.

8. The cemetery was located at 2nd Street and Frisco Avenue—underneath the western half of the BOK Center.

CLOCKWISE
Glenn Condon, Managing Editor,
Tulsa Daily World

Cover of the September 1918 issue of
Tulsa Spirit, published by the Tulsa Chamber
of Commerce

Tate Brady and Davis Brady (seated)
© 2011 The Eugene B. Adkins Collection
Archive at the Fred Jones Jr. Museum of
Art, the University of Oklahoma, Norman,
Oklahoma and the Philbrook Museum of Art,
Tulsa, Oklahoma. Used by permission.

privileges among the Cherokee tribe.[9] Together, the Bradys had four children: Ruth, Bessie,[10] Henry, and John. Three years later, January 18, 1898, Brady and other prominent businessmen signed the charter that established Tulsa as an officially incorporated city. Tate Brady was now a founding father of Tulsa.

"Indian and white man, Jew and Gentile, Catholic and Protestant, we worked together side by side, and shoulder to shoulder, and under these conditions, the 'Tulsa Spirit'[11] was born, and has lived, and God grant that it never dies," Brady wrote in a *Tulsa Tribune* article.

Brady was operating a storefront by this point and preparing to expand his operation when an event occurred that would forever change Tulsa's history.

In 1901, the Red Fork oil field was discovered, which catapulted Tulsa onto the scene of world commerce. As the city began to swell with oil-minded entrepreneurs and workers, Brady saw an opportunity: the visitors needed a place to stay. In 1903, he opened the Brady Hotel, located at Archer and Main street, just a short walk from the railroad tracks. It was the first hotel in Tulsa with baths. By 1905, with the discovery of more oil in the Glenn Pool south of town, the Brady Hotel found itself with a rush of clientele.[12]

With his hotel and mercantile businesses thriving, Brady began broadening his scope of influence. He lent financial support to an early paper called the *Tulsa Democrat*, and he began to buy and develop land near his businesses.[13] Along the way, Brady became a true Tulsa booster. In March of 1905, he, along with a hundred civic leaders, a 20-piece band, and "the Indian" Will Rogers, hired a train and toured the country to promote Tulsa as a city with unbound potential.

Brady's Confederate sympathies ran deep— sympathies that would steer his actions in later life. His father, H.H. Brady, had fought as a Confederate soldier in the Civil War. By 1912, Tate Brady's name had already appeared in Volume 20 of the *Confederate Veteran*. The magazine listed him as the commander of the Oklahoma Division of the Sons of Confederate Veterans. In 1915, Nathan Bedford Forrest, General Secretary of the Sons of Confederate

Veterans, visited Tulsa. In the *Confederate Veteran*, Forrest wrote that he consulted with "Comrade Tate Brady," and together they made plans for "an active campaign throughout Oklahoma."

Forrest, it should be noted, was the grandson of General Nathan Bedford Forrest, a pioneering leader of the Ku Klux Klan.

THE TULSA OUTRAGE

Tulsa's oil was an important national resource during World War I. By 1917, the city was selling a tremendous amount of Liberty Bonds, a type of war bond that helped bolster the USA's financial position during the war. Because the war effort consumed so much oil, however, Tulsa stood to gain massive economic benefits. Any opposition to the war was viewed as a threat to personal prosperity and success.

To help support the war effort, the national defense act established the state Councils of Defense. In Tulsa, the Tulsa Chamber of Commerce fulfilled that role. Its members were asked to report any seditious activities, including statements of dissent, acts of industrial sabotage, or "slackerism" (the refusal to participate in work or war). In Tulsa, this essentially put business leaders in charge of finding and reporting anything or anyone they found threatening to the war effort.

No group was more hated or feared in Tulsa than the IWW. As individuals publicly opposed to the war effort, Wobblies felt compelled to dampen industrial productivity by encouraging workers to strike. If such a strike were to occur, it could impact oil production and threaten the supply of oil to the military campaign. Tulsa's economy was vulnerable to an act of worker sabotage.

On August 2, 1917, a sharecropper's uprising in southeastern Oklahoma resulted in the arrest of several hundred people. The Green Corn Rebellion, as it came to be called, essentially ended the socialist movement in Oklahoma. It also proved that anti-war sentiments had not only reached a wide level of social acceptance among working-class Oklahomans, but had escalated to the point that many were willing to take up arms in opposition to the war.

---

9. Brady served as the General Chairman of the Executive Committee of the Cherokee Nation. According to Kiowa County's Mountain Park Herald, Brady sought to recover lands and money given to Cherokee Freedmen since 1866, which were then valued at $30 million.

10. Bessie Brady would eventually marry Eugene Sloan Adkins, father of art collector Eugene Brady Adkins. Philbrook Museum of Art and the Fred Jones Jr. Museum of Art share the $50 million Eugene Brady Adkins Collection.

11. This term was adopted by the Tulsa Chamber of Commerce and can be seen in use today on Tulsa Police Department patrol cars.

12. Not all of the clientele were oil-based. The Hotel Brady also served as a meeting place for Democrats. According to *A Century of African American Experience* (Don Ross, 2003), the hotel was "where Democrats headquartered, laid plans to control the Constitutional Convention leading to statehood that barred blacks, and also designed plots for segregation after statehood."

13. Around this time period, in 1908, Brady sustained a serious—perhaps life-threatening—injury when he fell from a streetcar. It's unknown whether he sustained any ongoing complications from that injury.

Brady held a particularly strong antipathy for the Wobblies. Just a few days before the Tulsa Outrage, on November 6, 1917, Brady saw a rival hotel owner, E.L. Fox standing at the corner of Main and Brady streets. A year prior, Fox had leased an office to the IWW, unaware of the Wobblies' mission. Their presence in the neighborhood infuriated Brady.

"When are you going to move those IWW out of your building?" Brady yelled at him.

"There's no North Side Improvement Association anymore," Fox replied, implying that Brady had no authority over Fox's business affairs.[14]

An aggravated Brady punched Fox, knocking him to the ground and beating him into the gutter. dozens of people witnessed the assault, which was reported in the *Tulsa Daily World* the following day.

The Council of Defense had no better ally or mouthpiece than the *Tulsa Daily World*, Tulsa's largest newspaper. Historian Nigel Sellars called the *World* "the most pro-oil industry, pro-war, racist, anti-foreigner and anti-labor paper of them all."[15] Throughout 1917, most of the paper's vitriol was aimed at the IWW, whom the *World* accused of being a German-controlled organization.

In what is arguably one of the lowest points in the paper's history, *Tulsa Daily World* published an editorial titled, "Get Out the Hemp."[16] Glenn Condon, a managing editor for the *World*, wrote that "the first step in whipping Germany is to strangle the I.W.W.'s [sic]. Kill 'em as you would any other snake. Don't scotch 'em; kill 'em. And kill 'em dead."

The day after the article was published, the 17 Wobblies were convicted of a minor charge and handed to the Knights of Liberty by Tulsa's own police. Brady was a ringleader in the kidnapping and ensuing torture in the woods west of town. Only two people in the mob were not robed—a reporter and his wife. The reporter was Glenn Condon,[17] who at the time was also serving as a member of the Council of Defense.

A month after the incident, in the December issue of their magazine *Tulsa Spirit*, the Tulsa Chamber of Commerce included this note:

> The Tulsa social event of November to attract the most national attention was the coming out party of the Knights of Liberty with about seventeen I.W.W. in the receiving line. As is usual in such social functions, a pleasant time was not had by some of those fortunate enough to be present.

DIXIELAND

Terrible as it was, the Tulsa Outrage foreshadowed an event that would soon eclipse it in violence and notoriety. By 1918, extralegal violence, including lynchings, had spread throughout the state and had appeared to gain a quiet acceptance and collaboration among law enforcement, politicians, and business leaders. during this heated period of racial tension, Tate Brady and the Tulsa Chamber of Commerce brought the Sons of Confederate Veterans 28th Annual Reunion to town.[18]

Back then, the Sons of Confederate Veterans wasn't merely a benign Civil War re-enactment club, as it is so often portrayed in today's media. One of its organizing principles was, and remains, "the emulation of [the Confederate veteran's] virtues, and the perpetuation of those principles he loved."

As the largest gathering of Confederate veterans since the Civil war (more than 40,000 attended), the 1918 Tulsa convention celebrated Southern nostalgia and ideologies. Tulsa leaders banded together to raise over $100,000 to cover the cost of the event. Reunion visitors were treated to the best of Tulsa's marvels: tours to the oil fields, free trolley tickets, and lodging with modern-day heated quarters. Although Tate Brady was the primary organizer of the reunion, its committee members included judges, ministers, and influential names that are still widely recognized in Tulsa: R. M. McFarlin, S. R. Lewis, Earl P. Harwell,

14. According to the *Tulsa Daily World*, Brady founded the North Side Improvement Association, which "combined some of the functions of Civic Club and Chamber of Commerce on the north side." Brady wanted Tulsa to develop toward the north into the Cherokee Nation.

15. *Oil, Wheat and Wobblies: The Industrial, Workers of the World in Oklahoma*, 1905-1930.

16. The editorial "Get Out the Hemp" appeared without a byline on the op-ed pages. The managing editor at the time was Glenn Condon. According to Sellars, the editorial may have been written by editor Eugene Lorton.

17. The year following the Outrage, Condon left Tulsa on a secret mission on behalf of the Council of Defense. He eventually settled in Tulsa in 1926, becoming a founder of the radio station KOME, "The Magic Empire." He was also a well-known radio personality for KAKC and later KRMG. Condon was an early member, then president of the Tulsa Press Club and Benevolent Association. He died in 1968.

18. Merritt Glass and Tate Brady founded the Tulsa Chapter of Sons of Confederate Veterans in 1908, at the Hotel Brady. During the convention of 1918, the Tulsa Chamber of Commerce provided meeting rooms for Forrest, who was headquartered at Convention Hall. Following the reunion, the Chamber of Commerce wrote that Tulsans had raised a considerable amount of money toward the event, and that it was "the best investment in friendship and hospitality ever made by any city in the South."

Charles Page, W. A. Vandever, Eugene Lorton, and J. H. McBirney.

The event was so popular that it took up several columns on the front pages of the *Tulsa Daily World*, which helped promote a number of other ancillary events happening across the city. While the reunion was largely received as an economic boost of Civic Pride, history won't excuse the darker attitudes that motivated the organization and its leaders.

The reunion's figurehead, Nathan Bedford Forrest, served as the KKK's Grand Dragon of Georgia, and an "Imperial Klokann" for the national Klan.[19] The Klan actively recruited its members from the Sons of Confederate Veterans. A few years after the convention, Forrest served as the business manager of Lanier College, the first KKK college in Alanta. "Our institution will teach pure, 100 percent Americanism," Forrest told the *New York Times*.

The 28th annual Sons of Confederate Veterans Convention demonstrated that Tulsa's most powerful and influential leaders at the very least tolerated— and at the most promulgated—the beliefs and biases that primed Tulsa for its most violent display of racial tension, the Tulsa Race Riot of 1921. Publicly, there was no dissenting voice, no expressed opposition to the Tulsa Outrage or the reunion.

BRADY AND THE RIOT

Tate Brady's prominence and wealth increased with each passing year. In their tenure, his retail stores sold some $5 million worth of goods ($60 million in today's dollars), and the Hotel Brady did $3 million in business. He began to invest in coal-mining operations and farming interests. In the early '20s he began expanding his property holdings, spending $1 million in property acquisitions—some of which was in Greenwood.

In 1920, Brady built a mansion overlooking the city and modeled it after the Arlington, Virginia, home of one of his personal heroes, General Robert E. Lee.

The home contained murals of famous Civil War battle scenes favorable to the Confederacy. Brady and his wife held galas celebrating Lee's birthday.

By 1921, Brady was a recognized city leader and a tireless booster of "Tulsa Spirit," a term he coined. Yet despite his position at the top of the town's social circles, he managed to find time to volunteer when civic duty called.

When the Tulsa Race Riot occurred on May 31, 1921, mayhem broke out in Greenwood, with buildings catching fire just two blocks from the Hotel Brady. During the early morning hours of June 1, white mobs numbering in the thousands were spotted on each major corner of the Brady district.[20] They headed eastward, invading Greenwood.

Brady and a number of other white men volunteered for guard duty on the night of May 31. During his watch, Brady reported "five dead negroes." One victim had been dragged behind a car through the business district, a rope tied around his neck.

The following week Brady was appointed to the Tulsa Real Estate Exchange Commission. The Exchange, created by the Tulsa Chamber of Commerce, was tasked with assessing the property damage.[21] The loss was estimated at $1.5 million. In conjunction with the City Commission, the Real Estate Exchange planned to relocate black Tulsans further north and east, and to expand the railroad's property over the damaged lands.

"We further believe that the two races being divided by an industrial section will draw more distinctive lines between them and thereby eliminate the intermingling of the lower elements of the two races," the Exchange told the *Tulsa Tribune*.

The Exchange then created new building requirements that made rebuilding in the area difficult. The Exchange reasoned that if residential property could be inhibited, commercial property would take its place, increasing its value by over three times its original cost. Greenwood's property value could skyrocket, and the races could be separated.

---

19. An "Imperial Klokann" was one of four positions known as an auditor; together with other administrators of the KKK, the Klokanns acted as an advisory cabinet to the Klan. Grand Dragons were leaders of state Klan organizations that were supported by 11 cabinet members. At the time of Forrest's leadership, Georgia had about 156,000 members in the Klan, which earned Forrest an estimated 2.5 million annually in today's dollars.

20. The pogrom consisted of Oklahoma National Guard units, Tulsa home Guard units under the command of Patrick J. Hurley, and various whites who were armed.

21. The real estate exchange was established by the Tulsa Chamber of Commerce.

To the Exchange commission, it must have seemed like an ideal plan.

Accusations of land-grabbing tormented Brady so much that he publicly issued a $1,000 reward to anyone who could prove that he benefitted from the Tulsa Race Riot. Brady, incidentally, owned rental properties that were destroyed in the riot, and tried to collect insurance on them, but did not succeed.

Despite the Exchange's efforts, Oklahoma's Supreme Court overruled the proposed ordinances, allowing Greenwood citizens to rebuild.[22] Black Tulsans were left to rebuild their homes without any aid from the city or from insurance companies.[23]

BRADY'S CURSE

Following the riot, Klan activity increased. A large parade of Klansmen, women and youth was organized in the months following the riot. In 1923, the Klan, established as the Tulsa Benevolent Society, paid $200,000 for the construction of a large "Klavern" or gathering hall that could seat 3,000 members. Beno Hall, as it was known, was located at 503 N. Main St., on land owned by Brady.[24]

Brady's prominence in Oklahoma politics suffered a setback when Oklahoma Governor John C. Walton targeted the Klan. In August of 1923, Walton put Tulsa under martial law to investigate Klan activity.

During a related Oklahoma military tribunal in September 1923, Brady admitted his membership in the Klan.[25]

"I was a member of the Klan here at one time, " Brady said, claiming he resigned his membership by October of 1922. "I have in my home the original records, some of my father's membership in the original Klan, and I think that you [the current Klan] are a disgrace." he didn't like the Klan telling him how to vote, he explained.[26]

Brady's testimony hinted at a larger social predicament. Oklahoma's Democratic Party was losing its dominance to the republicans, putting Brady, a committed democrat, in a weaker position politically. Nevertheless, he still appeared outwardly hopeful.

"As I look about me during this my thirty-fourth year in Tulsa, I see locks, once raven, sprinkled with snow, and life's fires burning low in the eyes of pioneers once bright," Brady wrote. "As we start this new year of 1924 may the spirit of the pioneer—the spirit that built Tulsa—prevail as of yore. Cursed be he, or they, who on any pretext try to divide our citizenship and destroy this spirit."

While he saw a sunny future for Tulsa, Brady's own situation did not appear as golden. By 1925, his considerable holdings had been reduced to about $600,000, according to a *Tulsa Daily World* estimation, which also suggested that he was indebted on those holdings.[27] In the spring of that year, his son John Davis Brady—a promising law student at the University of Virginia—died in a car accident.

Lacking the political power he once held through both the Democratic Party and his Klan affiliations, diminished in his fortune, and aggrieved by his son's death, Brady began to fall apart. Tulsans reported seeing him dining at his hotel alone, staring into space and leaving his meals untouched. Gone was the steeley-eyed entrepreneur. A portrait published in the *Tulsa Daily World* around this time shows an aged Brady looking weary and morose.

In the early morning hours of August 29, 1925, Brady walked into his kitchen and sat down at the breakfast table. He propped a pillow in the nook of one arm, and rested his head upon it. With his right arm, he took a .44 caliber pistol, pointed it at his temple, and pulled the trigger.[28] Brady, who worked to divide Tulsa along racial lines, died a victim of his own curse.

THE BRADY DISTRICT TODAY

Today, the Brady Arts District is the focal point of multi-million-dollar developments involving local organizations such as the George Kaiser Family Foundation, the Oklahoma Museum of Music and Popular Culture, the University of Tulsa, Gilcrease Museum, Philbrook Museum, and the Arts and Humanities Council of Tulsa. Local businesses also thrive in the district: numerous bars and restaurants,[29] the family-owned Cain's Ballroom (which once served as Brady's garage), and the Tulsa Violin Shop, to

---

22. The ordinance was overturned by the efforts of B.C. Franklin, father of noted historian John Hope Franklin.

23. By the summer of 1922 an estimated 85 percent of the Greenwood area was rebuilt.

24. Today, the location is an empty lot owned by the Oklahoma State Department of Highways.

25. The Klan played a role in impeaching Walton.

26. John C. Walton Papers, Box 14, folder 27, Proceedings of the Oklahoma Military Commission in the Matter of Klan Activity of Tulsa, Oklahoma, Western History Collections, University of Oklahoma Libraries, Norman, Oklahoma.

27. A former owner of Brady's mansion, Tim Lannom, told *Tulsa World* that Brady "committed suicide so his wife could collect a million dollar insurance policy ... That was back in the days when you could get away with that." In a follow up editorial, Lannom apologized for the statement, writing that he had done research and could not substantiate the rumor, and added that he could not find any evidence linking Brady to the Klan. Lannom died in 2007, the victim of a gunshot wound to the neck.

name a few. A large new ballpark separates the Brady district and the Greenwood area.[30]

In 2005, the National Park Service/US Department of Interior published *The Final 1921 Race Riot Reconnaissance Survey* commissioned in 2003 by the Oklahoma Historical Society and the 1921 Tulsa Race Riot Memorial of Reconciliation Design Committee. The purpose was to determine if Greenwood possessed enough "extant resources" to merit national significance. The survey concluded that the Tulsa Race Riot is significant because it is "an outstanding example of a particular type of resource," and "possesses exceptional value or quality in illustrating or interpreting the natural or cultural themes of our national heritage." In addition to the findings, the report explained Brady's role in

segregating not only Tulsa, but Oklahoma.[31] Despite these findings, the Tulsa Race Riot area, including Greenwood, remains unregistered.

Preservation consultant Cathy Ambler stated, in a February 2010 PLANiTULSA proposal: "Today, there is a faction of Tulsans who take issue with some of the associations and choices that Tate Brady was involved with, but there is no denying that he was a huge supporter of Tulsa and played a very big part in its early development."

In September 2010, the Brady Arts District was placed on the National Register of Historic Places, owing to its significance as a place of commerce. It enjoys the full benefits allotted under the designation.

---

28. Tate Brady was laid to rest in Oaklawn Cemetery. Dr. Clyde Snow, a forensic anthropologist who consulted for the Tulsa Race Riot Commission in 1999, believes that a mass grave of race riot victims is located at Oaklawn. The City of Tulsa prohibited the Commission from excavating the site.

29. Disclaimer: Vincent LoVoi, publisher of This Land Press, is a partner in the McNellie's Group, which operates The Brady Tavern restaurant.

30. The ballpark was originally to be located at 3rd Street and Greenwood Avenue, outside the areas identified in the report. It was relocated to its current location, which rests upon those lands designated as historically significant.

31. The report stated "a Tulsa city incorporator, and one of its first alderman, Brady built the first hotel in the city in 1903, where Democrats headquartered and laid plans to control the constitutional convention leading to statehood that provided the legal foundation for segregation."

Originally published
September 2011

by Alfred L. Brophy

TATE BRADY, THE MAGIC CITY, AND THE DREAMLAND

Tate Brady, as Lee Roy Chapman points out, did a lot of good for Tulsa, but the positives came with lots of negatives. It is the tragedy of this story that building the city of Tulsa involved violence. In Brady's case, it was violence against workers and African Americans. Therein lies a story we hear much about in American history at this time.

The "magic city's" development was linked, as Tulsa boosters told themselves, with episodes of violence, such as running the International Workers of the World out of town. On May 29, 1921, the *Tulsa Daily World* ran an article suggesting that Oklahoma hire a press agent to tell the rest of America that Oklahoma is a place where "people are civilized and refined... where there are metropolitan cities with miles of paved streets and many towering skyscrapers... And where IWW's anarchists are tarred and feathered whenever they become obstreperous." Tulsa's booster linked a modern state and violence together. Two days after that article appeared, there was again violence in the city. This time thousands of African Americans were left homeless, and many others were left dead. On the evening of May 31, 1921, amidst sensational stories of a young African-American man assaulting a young white woman in a downtown building, white Tulsans armed themselves and went to the courthouse to see what would happen—and perhaps participate in the lynching of that young man. Meanwhile, African Americans in Tulsa's segregated Greenwood section—many of them veterans of the recently ended "Great War," which we know as World War I—armed themselves to stop the expected lynching. When those two groups clashed at the courthouse late that evening, a riot began, which led to the destruction of blocks of Greenwood and the deaths of dozens. One person trying to interpret how the Tulsa riot occurred focused on the desire of African Americans to stop the lynching. He said that one of the leaders of the Greenwood community had "come back from France with exaggerated ideas about equality and thinking he can whip the world." Indeed, W.E.B. Du Bois editorialized after the war that African Americans would not return to their status before the war. Du Bois wrote in May 1919 that the soldiers were returning home "fighting." Thus, Tulsa was primed for a clash between African Americans and white residents.

Brady was a key player in the policing of that old order. But Tate Brady was not unique. As African-Americans' aspirations increased, many communities turned to violence to put them back in their place. Thus, we hear of "negro drives," where towns and counties used violence, or threats of violence, to drive out their African-American residents. Lee Roy Chapman provides a case study of what happened in many places at this time.

What is important about Tate Brady's story is that we have obtained the details of it—and that he was a leader of the local community. We know a lot about this because in 1923 the governor of Oklahoma declared martial law to help wrest control of the state back from the Ku Klux Klan—and also to boost his falling political fortunes. During martial law, military tribunals took extensive testimony about the Klan's activities; many of the records of those secret tribunals are now in the library at the University of Oklahoma. From them we learn details about the Klan's operation and their violence; those materials are available for no other states.

The final, haunting end of Brady's life, after his son's tragic death, invites questions about how the violence in early Tulsa injured those who were the perpetrators as well as the victims. Though we will never know, perhaps Brady's suicide was partly a result of his conscience's turmoil over the violence he had seen and committed.

Originally published
May 2013

by Steve Gerkin

DIAMOND IN THE ROUGH

On the trail of the man at the center of
the Tulsa Race Riot of 1921

Scenes from the Tulsa Race Riot
Courtesy Ruth Avery Collection

Secreted out the alley door of the Tulsa County Jail into an awaiting car provided by Sheriff McCollough, Diamond Dick Roland took in the smoldering midday air, while 30 square blocks of Tulsa's Greenwood district burned to the ground. It was June 1, 1921, and Roland was bound for a suspect destination in Kansas City intended to keep him safe from a vigilante lynch mob. He hid in the backseat. Then, he disappeared forever.

In his absence days later, Roland was represented pro bono by court-appointed attorney Wash Hudson, who was a member of Tulsa's Ku Klux Klan. Roland was formally charged by a grand jury with intent to rape a 17-year-old white woman named Sarah Page. Newspapers, and many following historical accounts, suggest that Roland's arrest triggered the Tulsa Race Riot of 1921. The perfumed and dapper Mr. Hudson ventured into the charred remains of Greenwood to advise Dick's mother, Damie Roland Jones, of the situation.

Damie lived in a tent provided by the Tulsa Chamber of Commerce, pitched where her family's boarding house and Roland's home once stood at 505 E. Archer in downtown Tulsa, which is a concession stand and centerfield entrance to the Drillers baseball park now. Several months before her death in 1972, the 87-year-old survivor told interviewer Ruth Avery that she saw Dick one more time following his disappearance. There are no certifiable accounts of him returning to Tulsa. Damie claimed he had gained weight from the jail food, and had the stench of a man who had hitched a ride in a train car. She said he cried to her, "Look what I have done," and left before dawn to avoid detection by angry survivors.

Roland was rumored to have moved north. Possibly working at Unity Bindery and living in an industrial neighborhood just east of downtown, a "Richard Roland" vanished from the Kansas City, Missouri, public records in 1926. Damie stated Dick wrote that Page was still "bumming around Kansas City," suggesting that Roland not only knew Sarah Page, but that they were familiar. There is no census or directory information that Page actually lived in the metropolis. The Great Depression was on the horizon and work was drying up. Damie says that Roland wrote of an interest to see the shores of Oregon, seeking employment in the shipyards.

A "Richard Rowland" appeared in the Portland directory in that time period, working in a mattress factory. Living in the black community of Albina, a segregated community on the outskirts of downtown, Rowland would have felt the full force of the Jim Crow environment so prevalent in Oregon. Sundown laws made it illegal for blacks to be in Portland after sundown, so they formed their own community, now known as the Albina district of Portland. Later census data proved this Richard Rowland was a white man. Yet thousands of nameless blacks lived along the Columbia River supporting the shipbuilding industry.

Shipbuilding outside Portland was a huge industry in the '20s and '30s. The Henry Kaiser Shipyards expanded in anticipation of WWII needs and conducted nationwide advertisements for jobs. A hundred thousand people flocked to Oregon—many of them blacks. Kaiser built an entire community including a housing development, schools, and a hospital for 6,000 of his black workers who were not wanted in Portland. This settlement became Vanport. On Memorial Day, 1948, the Columbia River swelled 15 feet above flood level, wiping out the complex. Lives were lost, swallowed up by the torrents. Maybe that Rowland was among the nameless swept towards the Pacific.

The only Richard Rowland on the Oregon death rolls turned out to be a six-year-old boy, who lived his life in the Fairview Home (formerly known as the Oregon State Institute for Feeble Minded), and after his tragic death was buried in a state cemetery in Marion County south of Portland. Evidence has since surfaced that places another Richard Rowland closer to Tulsa.

He may be resting in an all-black cemetery in Topeka, Kansas. Enforced segregation caused the creation of Mount Auburn Cemetery, which was also the burial ground for impoverished whites. Black veterans from seven different wars lie in proximity to a Richard Rowland. The records of Hall-Diffenderfer Funeral Home show him to be in the Crittenton lot. Born Richard Dean Rowland in the black Florence Crittenton Home, this child died at birth on June 3, 1936. The Dick Roland of Tulsa remained missing without a trace.

Although history books often refer to him as "Dick Rowland," the man at the center of the riot had several names. He was first called "Jimmie Jones" and, per census records, became "John Roland" when he and Damie moved in with her parents, Dave and Ollie Roland, after 1910. Their name is misspelled as "Rolland" and "Rowland" in various census and Tulsa directories. In most news reports following the riot, Dick's last name was spelled "Rowland." According to Damie, when Jimmie entered Booker T. Washington High School he changed his first name to Dick because he liked the name. Roland was a classmate of well-known educator W.D. Williams, who told legislator Don Ross in his publication *Impact*, June 1971,

that Roland's friends called him Johnny. Yet, the 1921 Booker T. Washington yearbook shows him as "James Jones" and "J. W. Jones."

Dick Roland may be close by. In Tulsa's Oaklawn Cemetery at 11th and Peoria, the Roland family plot has headstones for everyone but Dick: his uncle Clarence, Clarence's daughter Earlene Roland Morris, and his grandparents Dave and Ollie, along with Damie Roland Ford and her husband Clifford Ford. According to *Shadows of the Past: Tombstone Inscriptions*, in an adjacent section is a small headstone cryptically inscribed "James Jones (18 years old), 1921," curiously matching Jimmy's age and year he vanished and the year of the riot. That James Jones, however, died in March of 1921—two months before Roland would've been arrested. According to the headstone located a mere 10 yards from the Roland plot, James Jones was "Gone But Not Forgotten."

After the riot, the media gave him the derogatory name of Diamond Dick, stemming from the small diamond ring he wore—a birthday present given to himself from tips earned at his bootblack job near the Drexel Building in downtown Tulsa. The Drexel had a jerky elevator, where Roland once tripped, nearly fell, and grabbed the arm of the operator, Sarah Page, who was by then a good and intimate friend, according to Tulsa Race Riot historian Eddie Faye Gates. The discomfort from Dick's hand, reportedly, caused the feisty dishwater blonde to shriek and yell at Roland, which alarmed a Renberg's clothing store salesman. The salesman fabricated a wrongful tale passed onto authorities and yellow journalists.

The charge against Roland was thrown out due to County Attorney William Seaver's wrongful inclusion of assault in the charge and an alleged victim who never considered herself to be one. The demurer of his charges in September 1921 and its signature, spelled "Dick Roland," was signed either in absentia or by the real man—no way to tell; there is no record of him being in Tulsa. Maybe he was already dead.

Perhaps Roland was in a "safe" jail at an undocumented location or became just another dead black man floating in the Arkansas River. Or perhaps he was placed on a flat bed truck alongside other corpses, or he may have been disposed in a rural setting towards Kansas City. Maybe he was hung in the gallows on his county jail cell floor and was carried out the alley door to his final resting place. Whatever happened to the man, when the riot started, Roland was no longer on Tulsa's mind. Maybe his mother's dementia-like ramblings to interviewer Ruth Avery were just a mother's fantasy that kept her son alive, creating a peaceful memory in her last days.

"I have lost my only boy," lamented Damie.

IS THIS THE FACE OF THE MAN AT THE CENTER OF THE TULSA RACE RIOT?

A wealth of clues suggest that newly discovered images may reveal the young man whose arrest sparked the 1921 Tulsa Race Riot

In 1921, a young black man rode in an elevator with a young white woman. When the elevator doors opened, she screamed, and the young man was arrested. In Oklahoma at that time, young black men were sometimes lynched, often soon after their arrests. So, a group of black men congregated at the Tulsa County Jail to protect this young man, whose name was reported as "Dick Rowland." His arrest is often referred to as the incident that sparked the 1921 Tulsa Race Riot. Since the riot, however, his whereabouts and his identity have largely remained a mystery.

For many years, one of the most sought-after records pertaining to the Tulsa Race Riot was the 1921 yearbook for Booker T. Washington High School in Tulsa, because it was rumored to contain a photo of the never-before-seen "Dick Rowland." The yearbook had been missing for so long that many research-ers had stopped looking. Suddenly, about a year ago, two copies appeared, one at Rudisill Library in Tulsa, and the other at Booker T. Washington High School's media center. Researcher and *This Land* contributing editor Steve Gerkin scoured the yearbook in search for the young man at the center of the riot.

Here's what Gerkin discovered: In the 1921 year-book for Booker T. Washington High School, a student named James Jones appears twice—once in a basketball team photo, the other in a "Sophomore-A" class photo.

Damie Roland Jones claims that her adopted son Dick Roland had been named Jimmie Jones, and that at some point during his school years, her son changed his name to Roland, out of respect for his grandparents Dave and Ollie Roland, who helped raise him in their home. Later, he chose Dick because he

1921 Booker T. Washington Sophomore "A" Class, where Jones (second from right, bottom row) is listed as "James Jones," and next to his name a description reads, "I Can't Help it Because I am Tall." Dick Roland, it was reported, was 5'10."

liked the name. There's a Damie Jones, by the way, who appears in the 1910 census records for Bristow Township, Oklahoma, as a daughter of Dave and Ollie Roland. There's also a John Roland, aged 16, listed in the 1920 census for Tulsa.

In newspaper articles following the riot, Dick Roland became reported as "Diamond Dick Rowland," the "Diamond" being a flourish added by Roland himself, and the "w" in "Rowland" being added by inaccurate reporters.

Booker T. Washington graduate W.D. Williams recalled attending high school with Roland, and claimed that Roland went by the name "Johnny." Both Williams and Jones appear in the 1921 yearbook—Williams as a junior, and Jones as a sophomore. Williams later made the claim that Roland had dropped out of high school to take a job shining shoes,

which suggests that maybe Roland shouldn't be listed in the 1921 yearbook. But Damie Roland claimed her son dropped out of school and returned to school on several occasions.

James Jones the student shared the same name, age, and school as Dick Roland, and yet, unfortunately, there is no direct evidence that connects Jones to Roland with absolute certainty. We don't know if James Jones was, in fact, Dick Roland. There's a grave in Tulsa's Oaklawn Cemetery that reads "James Jones," and gives a date of birth similar to that of the Booker T. Washington student—but the Jones at Oaklawn died two months before the riot took place. Until a new bit of information appears—and a new trove of riot records has recently been recovered—the fate of Dick Roland remains a mystery.

1921 Booker T. Washington football squad, where Jones is listed as "J.W. Jones"

1921 Booker T. Washington
basketball team

According to a hand-inscribed photocopy, Jones is pictured at the
center, holding the ball. The player to the right is listed as W. D.
Williams, who would later state that he attended school with Dick
Roland. The coach pictured at far left is S.E. Williams, the namesake
for the football stadium at Booker T. Washington High School.

Originally published
February 2014

by Steve Gerkin

FIRST CHARGED, LAST FREED

The exonerated
czar of Greenwood

Greenwood in ruins. From the collection
of I. Marc Carlson, Tulsa Race Riot
Photographs. Courtesy Greenwood
Cultural Center.

John the Baptist moved to Tulsa in 1899. The Stradford family called him J. B.[1] He was a former Kentucky slave who was not afraid to preach the gospel of equal treatment and racial solidarity for black Americans. College-educated in Ohio at Oberlin College, Stradford received his law degree from Indiana University, practicing in Indianapolis and yearning to influence black equality. Tulsa became his destiny. Leaders of the local white community yearned for his demise.

In America, the late 1800s provided an unpainted canvas of opportunity for post-emancipation blacks. They were free to relocate, joining up with other freshly freed blacks and Freedmen from Creek enslavement to start communities separate from the white population. While racial distrust remained, their new beginnings were sites of burgeoning entrepreneurship.

Over 60 percent of the U.S. black population served whites as domestics, restaurant cooks, bootblacks, and laborers. Wages were brought back to their new settlements and spent with black grocers, black lumberyards, black saloons and gambling enterprises, black theaters, and a cadre of like-skinned businesses.

Oklahoma's future looked bright for blacks. Led by the vision of Edwin McCabe, founder of the first black community of Langston in 1890, the state became a mecca for black towns and self-reliant communities—50 by 1920.[2] The *New York Times* warned on March 1, 1890, that a "Negro settlement" is "a camp of savages." McCabe sent recruiters to the South, appealing to racial pride, and hoped to recruit enough blacks to become the majority race and force the whites to turn over the region to them.

McCabe's dream of a politically powerful, black-friendly state lured Stradford from Indianapolis to the dirt streets of Tulsa's undeveloped Greenwood area.

---

1 The slave master named his slaves, calling J. B.'s father Julius Caesar or J. C., but he had no legitimate last name until J.C. forged his master's name on a pass and escaped to Stratford, Ontario. Changing one letter, he adopted the surname of Stradford, earned enough money to return to Kentucky prior to emancipation, and secured legal documents declaring his family free. Many blacks used initials during that time period so that whites would not be able to disrespect them by using their first names.

2 Census numbers show that the black population in 1890 of 250,000 ballooned to more than 2 million by 1920.

Buying up large tracts of undeveloped land northeast of the tracks that bordered downtown, 39-year-old J. B. Stradford sold his Greenwood parcels to blacks only. O.W. Gurley, the acknowledged founder of the new community, did the same as Black Tulsa took shape.

Yet, Stradford was not a real estate man by trade. He was a University of Indiana-educated attorney who used his investment profits to aggressively litigate for black social justice. Never shy to voice his outrage, he occasionally declared, "The day a member of our group was mobbed (lynched) in Tulsa, the streets would be bathed in blood." The activist put himself on the line to prevent lynchings. In 1918 he turned back

J.B. Stradford, date unknown

a lynch mob in Bristow, Oklahoma. When Stradford suffered Jim Crow discrimination, he did not sit idly.

Walking along Greenwood Avenue, a white deliveryman made a racist remark about Stradford's skin color. After nearly beating him to death, friends pulled Stradford off the bloodied iceman. They told him that if he killed the white man, he would be lynched. Later, he was acquitted for violating Oklahoma Jim Crow laws.

Riding a train from Kansas to Tulsa in 1912, nearly 50 years after the end of the Civil War, J. B. experienced the continuation of slave law in Oklahoma. When the locomotive reached the Oklahoma border, the conductor stopped the train and Stradford

was forcibly removed from the black luxury car, even though he had paid the higher fare. Oklahoma exempted railroads from the expense of such cars if it did not make economic sense. Stradford sued Midland Valley Railroad in state and federal courts for false imprisonment. All courts ruled against his demand for justice by law, angering Greenwood residents.

In 1916, Stradford railed the Tulsa City Commission for its segregation ordinance that he claimed casts "a stigma upon the colored race in the eyes of the world; and to sap the spirit of hope for justice before the law from the race itself." The upside of segregation was the "white" dollars earned by black Tulsans stayed in the district, giving Deep Greenwood merchants the spoils of their neighbors, while the black print media continued to pull no punches.

The most militant black voice in America and a founder of the NAACP fanned the embers during a Greenwood speech. Brought to the community by Stradford and newspaperman A. J. Smitherman in March of 1921, the first black Harvard Ph.D., W. E. B. Du Bois, lectured the throngs that the hatred in the white man's heart was still strong. At times, the professor proposed that the only solution to hate is hate.

Du Bois argued in those times, "We have suffered and cowered... When the armed lynchers come, we too must gather armed. When the mob moves, we propose to meet it with sticks and clubs and guns." There was a rising tide of passion in Greenwood. They were ready to forcefully defend the promise of equality under the law.

White Tulsa became less enchanted with the likes of J.B. Stradford. Although Stradford was respected as a legitimate businessman, many Tulsans despised him.

Stradford and his close friend Andrew J. Smitherman, the owner/publisher of the black newspaper *Tulsa Star,* situated on Greenwood Avenue, spoke out against the trio of leading causes of civil rights in Oklahoma—lynching, voting rights, and the railroad segregation policy. *The Black Dispatch*, a black Oklahoma City newspaper published by Roscoe Dunjee, regularly fired up Greenwood residents, declaring the courts were full of dead men's bones, denied enforcement of the United States Supreme Court decision guaranteeing black Oklahomans' right to vote, and validated Oklahoma's railroad segregation statute.

During vaudeville shows at the famed Dreamland Theater on Greenwood, a frequently bantered slogan was "Don't let any white man run it over on you, but fight." Racial rhetoric primed Tulsa.

While inflammatory verbiage continued in district tabloids and on street corners, business was good. J. B. Stradford amassed a sizeable bank account. With 15 rental houses, including a 16-room brick apartment building, he earned a real estate income of nearly $8,000 a month in 2013 dollars.

Stradford decided it was time that black travelers of means should have accommodations as swank as downtown's Hotel Tulsa. He envisioned his hotel as the pinnacle of his dreams, remarking, "The Stradford would be a monument to the thrift, energy, and business tact of the race in Tulsa [and] to the race in the state of Oklahoma." The exuberant opening of his eponymous hotel on June 1, 1918, signified the realization of his promised land, adding credence to Booker T. Washington's description of this district as Black Wall Street.

The three-story edifice of pressed brick above the windows and stone slabs below cost a glitzy $50,000. The segregated Stradford, serving blacks only, was perhaps the largest black-owned and operated hotel in America. While it fulfilled his dream, the construction of the hotel created financial difficulties. Stradford ran out of money. Borrowing $20,000 helped, yet, when a boxcar of beds, rugs, and chandeliers rolled into the station, the new hotelier could not pay the $5,000 bill.

Within eyeshot of the hotel, the furnishings for the 54 modern "living rooms," gambling hall, dining hall, and saloon languished on the rails. Stradford negotiated paying a quarter of the total and the remainder in monthly payments. The Stradford Hotel at 301 N. Greenwood was open for business.

It was a lively time. A new form of music ricocheted up Greenwood Avenue from the dancehalls. Jazz, with its gyrating rhythms and freedom to improvise, stimulated the dancers and frightened the white community, who considered the music style as vibrations for the half-savage. The piano in the Stradford Hotel pounded out jazz for its distinguished clientele who tripped the fantastic toe.

Amid the glamour of the Stradford, the racial tension in Greenwood and the region was superficially suppressed. Desperate events stoked emotions.

. . .

In April 1921, Greenwood celebrated the success of a group of Muskogee black men that stormed the city jail, liberated a black man (John McShane), and shot a white deputy sheriff in the process. The local black community justified the action, claiming they prevented a lynching. Their defiance energized Greenwood.

Stradford and Smitherman agreed that a community must be vigilant if a black man was in danger of being lynched. It was justice—a legal right, they reckoned, to take aggressive action, encouraging their community to support armed militancy towards lynching.

On the afternoon of May 30, 1921, the *Tulsa Tribune* ran a front-page story announced a "negro will be lynched tonight." The following day, a Greenwood teenager, Dick Roland, was arrested under the allegations that he attempted to rape a 17-year-old white girl, Sarah Page, in an elevator. Although a grand jury indictment against him was rendered several days later and then dismissed within three months for lack of a prosecution witness (Sarah, according to oral histories from Greenwood survivors, was his taboo lover), the yellow-journalism article fomented the deadliest and most destructive "riot" in the history of the United States—an event that would forever be referred to as the Tulsa Race Riot of 1921.

A. J. Smitherman's office of the *Tulsa Star* was the center of activity the night before the battle. Several carloads of passionate armed veterans made repeated trips from the newspaper's curb to the jail holding Roland, where they confronted a growing white mob. Dedicated to stop a lynching, J. B. held court with the gathering crowd, repeating his often used statement about "blood in the streets." He recalled in his memoirs that he declared to the nervous onlookers what he would do if there were a lynching: "If I can't get anyone to go with me, I will go single-handed and empty my automatic into the mob and, then, resign myself to my fate." His comments encouraged men, including a tall, light-skinned veteran named O. B. Mann, to continue making trips to the courthouse.

Mann, a successful Greenwood grocer, returned from the war with inflated ideas about equality and sure he could take on the world, according to O. W. Gurley. He continued, during court testimony on an insurance claim relating to property damage from the riot, that it was the inadvertent discharge of Mann's handgun when grabbed by a white man that activated the fatal chain of events.

. . .

At dawn, the sound of an air horn commanded the heavily armed white armada, loaded with Klansmen, to step over the tracks and attack an underarmed band of black veterans in uniform and frightened Greenwood resident's intent to defend their families and homes. Within a matter of hours, hundreds were murdered and homes and businesses were looted and burned as thousands of black Tulsans were arrested

Greenwood in ruins. From the collection of
I. Marc Carlson, Tulsa Race Riot Photographs.
Courtesy Greenwood Cultural Center.

and herded into detention.

Dick Roland was a forgotten man. Sheriff McCollough claims Dick spent a safe evening in the county jail and was secreted out of town by 8 a.m. amidst the gunfire of the massacre, never, according to most, to return to Tulsa. The carnage would continue through the day.

The June 1, 1921, evening edition of the *Tulsa Tribune* wrote that "a motley procession of negroes wended its way down Main Street to the baseball park with hands held high above their heads, their hats in one hand, a token of their submission to the white man's authority." The reporter continued, "They will return, not to their homes, but to heaps of ashes, the angry reprisal for the wrong inflicted on him by the inferior race." Some of that race-under-siege resisted the roundup.

Attempting to hold the mobsters from advancing, Stradford and others fired from the second-story porch that fronted the hotel. The building represented black equality to him and he preferred death rather than to lose it. The west-facing windows on the third-floor had been smashed by a machine gun. Six men were wounded and one was dead.

The hotel became a haven for black families. Most left, surrendering to the militia. A sobbing Augusta, Stradford's wife, pleaded with him, "Oh, Papa, let us go, too."

"If you want to go with the crowd, then go," he said.

"I intend to protect my hotel."

Augusta stayed. Others returned with a message of hope. The militia had promised to keep the hotel from further destruction, if Stradford surrendered. He agreed.

A short, slightly rotund man with a pencil-thin mustache perched above his squared chin, the now 60-year-old Stradford was reportedly the wealthiest man in Greenwood with over $1.6 million dollars of investments in today's currency. He stood with his gun in the doorway of his hotel, waiting for the car of his captors. His dark, piercing eyes surveyed the burning buildings in Deep Greenwood. Hundreds of the 8,000 Greenwood residents ran through the street before him. Some with raised hands were marshaled to detention centers, shots fired at their feet and hopelessness on their faces.

A man described by descendants as having the strength of a Mandingo warrior, watched mobsters enter his building. They took him to the Convention Center where city officials took $2,000 of his money. There is no mention of Augusta's whereabouts. Stradford was not detained long, but he was still in harm's way.

One day later, an order asked for the arrest of Stradford so he could face a grand jury. The contention was he had encouraged carloads of armed blacks who organized and left from the Stradford Hotel. Without his presence, he was indicted for inciting a riot. The penalty for the charge was death or life imprisonment. The white community needed a definable villain and they decided on Stradford.

His name was well known in the Tulsa white community. His railroad segregation lawsuit as well as his defiance towards the segregation ordinance put him squarely in opposition to their values. He named a hotel after himself, so they knew he was a man of ambition. As Greenwood's Republican Party leader, the local papers named him a "henchman." Since the media labeled the riot a "Negro uprising," they reasoned that the wealthiest, most defiant and outspoken man must be the ringleader—and, he fled, so he must be guilty.

With authorities on his heels, Stradford leaned back in a segregated railroad car headed for Independence, Kansas. Through a gentle rain, Stradford gazed up Greenwood Avenue spying his symbol of black pride, reduced to smoldering ashes and charred brick. Oklahoma was no longer the Promised Land.

Along with hundreds of black Americans who died on June 1, 1921, and thousands who had homes, businesses, and possessions stolen or burned, the Stradford Hotel laid in ruins, never to be reconstructed. The crown jewel of Black Tulsa shined a scant three years to the day.

On June 6, J. B. Stradford became the first person formally charged with inciting a riot. To be proven guilty, the county district attorney only needed to show he abetted the riot that resulted in murder, looting, and theft. Never mind those crimes were committed by the white mob.

Shortly after arriving at his brother's house in Independence, local police, at the request of Tulsa authorities, paid a visit to Stradford. Asked if he would turn himself in, he replied, "Hell, no." Arrested and booked, he called his son in Chicago. Cornelius Stradford, a graduate of Columbia University Law School, took the first train to Kansas and posted the $6,500 (2013 value) bond. J. B. was told to stay put and appear in court on June 10. Convinced he would not get a fair trial if returned to Tulsa, Stradford and his son boarded the next train to Chicago. Incensed Tulsa litigators vowed to extradite and try him for the charge of inciting a riot.

. . .

Wrangling successfully against the extradition attempts, the aging Stradford settled into Chicago life with his wife, son, and numerous grandchildren. Trying to re-create his success in Tulsa, he practiced law and filed a suit in September against the American Central Insurance Company, trying to recover some of his real estate losses. Stradford did not appear at the hearing. Due to the riot exclusion clause in insurance policies and local leaders defining the travesty as a "riot,"

all riot victims' claims, including the one by the gentleman considered by some as an outlaw, were knocked out in legal fights.

Desiring to re-create his real estate prowess, he formed a group of investors to build a luxury hotel like the Stradford. Regrettably, the project ran out of money and the building was not completed. He did, however, construct a candy store, barbershop, and a small pool hall. His modest business holdings in Chicago reminded him of what once was.

Stradford lost more than money in the Tulsa Race Riot of 1921. He lost his black sense of place. In his unpublished memoirs, he wrote, "It is incredible to believe that in this civilized age that a white man could be so void of humanity." He continued, "My soul cried for revenge and prayed for the day to come when I could personally avenge the wrongs which had been perpetrated against me." He died in 1935 at the age of 74. Sixty years later, family members extracted his atonement.

. . .

Cornelius E. Toole was a former NAACP lawyer and a Cook County, Illinois, circuit court judge. He was also a great-grandson of J. B. Stradford. Toole harbored resentment for the smearing of his relative's name, the destroying of his properties and his dreams. Through impassioned communications with Mayor Susan Savage and local black leader Don Ross in 1996, the 63-year-old former judge insisted that the charges against Stradford be dismissed. The decision rested on the shoulders of first-year District Attorney Bill LaFortune, who needed to render an opinion on a strict legal question—did evidence support the notion that Stradford incited a riot?

Nancy Little was assigned the investigation. Her detailed inspection revealed innocent black families suffered a ruthless attack. She was shocked. While it was undeniable Stradford violated law by jumping bail and refusing extradition, Little concluded he was innocent of inciting a riot. LaFortune vacated the charges.

In October of 1996, Stradfords from Texas, Illinois, Ohio, and New York set foot in Oklahoma—the first time since June of 1921. The vindication ceremony at the Greenwood Cultural Center featured moving statements from Governor Frank Keating. Quite simply, District Attorney Bill LaFortune presented the motion to dismiss and Judge Jesse Harris accepted it.

John the Baptist Stradford was the first riot victim indicted and the last alleged outlaw exonerated—first charged, last freed.

Originally published
March 2015

by Steve Gerkin

THE UNLIKELY BARONESS

The life of Oklahoma's
youngest black millionaire

Sarah Rector, date unknown

The young black girl poses in a common, patterned dress by an ordinary side chair. Her shadow creates a ghostly presence on the light-colored wall behind her. The pigtails of the 10-year-old Sarah Rector sprout opposite her ears, like antennas on a Flash Gordon space helmet.

Historical records conflict over the issue of the first black female millionaire, though Sarah was the first black adolescent to achieve millionaire status, hands down. Her road to riches involved mandated endowment, racial triumph, and good fortune.

Long before the births of Sarah and her three siblings, the Creek Nation agreed with the federal government to emancipate their 16,000 slaves, giving them citizenship in their nation and entitling them to equal interest in soil and national funds. They became known as Freedmen.

The efforts to totally assimilate the Five Tribes of Oklahoma Territory into white America continued with the passage of the Dawes Allotment Act of 1887. This legislation forced the tribes to disband their centuries-old communal lifestyle and assigned roll members individually owned lots of land.

The Creek Nation was sliced up into 160-acre squares, "more or less," and doled out to the Natives and former slaves; each received 120 acres for agriculture and 40 acres for homesteading. In an attempt to maintain a semblance of community, the Freedmen collectively chose allotments in an area known as Black Jack, 10 miles west of the county seat of Muskogee (eastern present-day Oklahoma), and formed the settlement Twine, honoring the newspaperman and resident William Henry Twine, who was nicknamed "Black Tiger" for his print-battle to ensure racial justice.

Born March 3, 1904, into a former Creek slave family of Joseph and Rosa Rector of Twine, Sarah and her clan moved down the dirt road to the newly created town of Taft, one of two-dozen black towns in the Indian Territory. Joseph farmed corn and cotton on Rosa's acres, while the kids watched the trains come and go from the Midland Valley Railroad station. Sarah lived poorly in the pre-statehood territory. Yet, she had her allotment.

The landmark Dawes decision provided nearly 600 black children, or Creek Freedmen minors, with an inheritance of land, which was, generally, not fit for farming. The bulk of Sarah's allotment was on rocky banks either side of a horseshoe bend in the Cimarron River, in another county near Tulsa, 50 miles from her home.

Since taxes were due on the allotted lands, Joseph Rector sold his acres to avoid debt and generate revenue for basic living. Black parents were not automatically considered the guardians of their children. They were required to petition the county court for permission to manage their children's affairs. Joseph was granted legal guardianship on Christmas Eve 1909. He promptly sold the land of his oldest child, Rebecca, for $1,700.

Sarah's land had a value of $556.50, but the annual tax burden of $30 created a financial dilemma. Postponing the crisis, her father leased Sarah's Cimarron land to Devonian Oil Company for $160, or $1 per acre. They did not renew, and Joseph asked the court for permission to sell. Good fortune stepped into Sarah's life in the form of a lease by people working for Tom Slick, the man who would become the "King of Wildcatters." Prior to his deal for Sarah's mineral rights, Slick struck oil just five miles south of her land. He cut telephone lines to stymie word getting out before he could snatch up all the nearby leases. Sarah's lease changed hands in 1918 with the receipt of a $300,000 signing bonus. Her property became the domain of Prairie Oil and Gas, a subsidiary of Standard Oil (John D. Rockefeller), originally recruited to capitalize oil ventures in Kansas by Harry Sinclair, a Tulsa resident and the founder of Sinclair Oil Company.

Sarah received the typical royalty deal of 12.5 percent. If oil came in, she would be set. One hundred forty-three Freedmen minors had similar opportunities, but, according to the *Muskogee Times-Democrat* in the spring of 1910, these children ended up in orphanages, dumped there by guardians who filched their wealth. When poor kids became "plute" (plutocrats/wealthy), courts assigned them guardians, usually whites with sway; many billed for false expenses and kept profits from the sale of their land. These "grafters," comprised of whites, blacks, and parents, were prosecuted. Murder became a byproduct of greed.

In a scheme to claim the wealth of two Creek Freedmen, 12-year-old Herbert and 10-year-old Stella Sells, two men—one black and one white—were sentenced to life in the Oklahoma State Penitentiary for placing dynamite under the children's bedroom in the early hours of March 23, 1911, and causing their murders from the explosion. Likely, in such a small locale, Sarah knew them.

Sarah's first oil well came in August 1913, producing 105,000 gallons of oil each day. In a time when a nickel bought an ice cream soda, she netted more than $300 a day ($7,000 in 2015 currency). Published drilling updates reported Sarah ended up with over 50 completed wells on her property and the area exceeded the famed Glenn Pool production.

The *Times-Democrat* broadcast that Sarah owned one of the greatest gushers in the Belt, producing 4,800 barrels or 200,000 gallons of oil the first day. With limited mass communication, newspapers relied on each other to cobble together their national stories. Reporters were seldom sent into the field to get the scoop. It was often cut-and-paste.

Major newspapers around the country, as well as international news sources in Germany, Australia, and Amsterdam, sensationalized Sarah's situation with bold headlines and mistaken text. From *Chicago Defender* (the leading black-owned paper in the U.S.):

- November 1913: "Richest Colored Girl Forced to Live in Shack" claimed the white guardian made "a fabulous sum of money a year," doling out only a "few dollars a month" for Sarah's care; insisted she would be better with a black guardian; berated her parents as "ignorant" and "too ignorant to insist on a good education and befitting comfort for her."

- November 1913: "Brown Skinned Colored Girl Made White" has a dateline of Guthrie, Oklahoma. The text says, "Oklahoma passed a law declaring all Indians white and is about to make an Afro-American young lady the same hue on account of her millions. She would be given special privilege to ride across the state in a Pullman car where it is denied others of her race." It continues, "White People Alarmed" and "... They do not like such wealth belonging to a girl of Afro-American blood so Oklahoma is passing a law to the effect that this brown girl will be white."

- March 1914: The paper asked, "Where Is Sarah Rector?" and responded, "Not in Alabama! Not in Oklahoma!" The article claimed her disappearance was a kidnapping, or a "trick" by (white guardian) T.J. Porter designed to hide and offset the call for a black guardian or she was murdered. They implored Sarah be found.

- March 1914: "Find Sarah Rector," text by John A. Melby, included: "Little Sarah Rector cannot be hid. She is of too much importance to her race."

- April 1914: "Little Sarah Rector Found" included: the "Afro-American girl with the $15,000 income per month is found at home in good health."

Elsewhere, *Washington Post*, in January 1914, proclaimed, "Oil Made Pickaninny[1] Rich." The article claimed Sarah was "ignorant, with apparently little mental capacity." It did show she had a new home and Judge Thomas Leahy had to approve "every nickel spent on her welfare."

The Salt Lake Telegram, The Oregonian, and *American Magazine*, in 1914 and 1915, profiled Sarah as the "bewildered little ten-year-old girl" who had a "big income" but still wore tattered dresses and slept each night in a big armchair beside her six siblings in a two-room prairie house in Muskogee, Oklahoma. The accounts of her mother dying of tuberculosis prior to 1913 and her father passing in prison in 1914, orphaning 10-year-old Sarah, also proved false. Joseph died in 1922 just months before Sarah's first marriage, and Rosa lived a long life, passing away in Kansas City, Missouri, with Sarah and the remaining family close at hand.

Historian Tonya Bolden, author of *Searching for Sarah Rector,* a winner of the Coretta Scott King Honor, sat in her New York City office and warned that "we need discernment with 'first drafts' of history—the farther the periodicals, both black and white, from Oklahoma, the more distorted the picture of Sarah they painted." The articulate writer added that it is "better to rest on research and reason than on scuttlebutt." Yet, emotions ran high in the early awakening of American racial justice.

All of the media attention alarmed the NAACP in New York City, especially their special agent, attorney James C. Waters Jr., and one of the NAACP found-

---

1 The origin of "pickaninny" may be derived from the Portuguese *pequenino,* meaning "little one." Once a term used in an affectionate way among slaves in the West Indies, "pickaninny" is now considered prerogative/insulting.

ers who was the publisher/editor of their publication, *Crisis*. The editor was the famed social justice advocate W.E.B. Du Bois, the first black Ph.D. graduate of Harvard University. Oklahoma Governor Lee Cruce wrote to Waters that Sarah "has been exceptionally well-managed" and, essentially, to mind his own business. In contrast, Muskogee County Judge Leahy proved to be a more gracious recipient of numerous Du Bois interrogatories. The activist implored the judge give him the "facts." Leahy responded that the information he gave to him was his to use at his discretion, "as I have no desire for it to be treated confidential."

A weekly, billed as "the oldest colored paper in Oklahoma," Twine's *Muskogee Cimeter*, cheered, "It takes an awful big man to give the Negro a square deal and Muskogee's judge is such a man."

Among Du Bois' concerns were allegations by the *Defender* of Sarah's guardian gouging her funds, actual oil revenues she received, her education, her standard of living, and if her guardian was white.

Leahy wrote the allowed guardian fees were between 2–6 percent and her guardian, T.J. Porter, received $900 to date, much less than 2 percent of Sarah's income. He explained Porter had negotiated $40,000 in first-mortgage loans at 8 percent—twice her possible returns from a bank deposit account. Leahy continued she did not receive $15,000 a month from her oil wells, but rather for the eight months since the first payment in October 1913. She had deposits totaling $54,490, or less than $7,000 ($170,000 in 2015 dollars) a month.

The judge's report related that Sarah and her sister were set to attend a prestigious school in Tuskegee, Alabama, in the fall of that year, 1914. Regarding accommodations, Sarah and her family lived in a new five-room cottage with a well, outbuildings, and other improvements. The judge had approved every expense for the construction and furnishing of the $1,700 home. Leahy's documents emphasized his insistence that Sarah own her home and the land beneath it.

Mr. Thomas Jefferson Porter was her guardian and he was white; "It is true," Leahy confirmed. He continued, "The parents themselves selected him. T.J. Porter had been the family's benefactor for years and long before there was any probability of them ever having money."

Like most of the Freedmen, Joseph Rector was not an educated man, and he suffered to provide for his family. T.J. Porter was officially made guardian by a request from Joseph that was granted by the court in July 1913, one month before Sarah's first oil strike.

Sarah had income from loans, savings bonds, Muskogee real estate that included rental income from several stores and the Busy Bee Hotel and Cafe, leasing income for 2,000 acres of valuable river-bottom farmland, as well as the oil royalties. She had a double-barreled sentry—a white guardian who was not a "grafter" and a white judge who oversaw all her financial transactions.

Asked about Sarah's black-white situation, regarding her treatment in a negative environment, Ms. Bolden offered, "The roles that Porter and Leahy played in Sarah's life remind us that we really do need to avoid generalizations and that even during racially charged times, there have been and are cases of trust across the color line." She continued, "Greed knows no color." The education-oriented scholar reported Sarah went to Tuskegee Institute.

Indeed, in the fall of 1914, at the urging of Judge Leahy, 12-year-old Sarah and her older sister, Rebecca, enrolled at Tuskegee Institute's elementary school, called the Children's House. The young Rector girls studied at the famed institution for several years, away from the antics of ambitious detractors in Muskogee who continued battling for her war chest.

Court documents show Sarah and Rebecca were preparatory students at a black university, Fisk University in Nashville, in 1917. Porter requested the court in a May document for $350 to cover school expenses and railroad fare to bring them home for the summer.

T.J. Porter was the kingpin of Sarah's fortune. In August of 1917, he stepped down "under fire" amid legal accusations that he and his attorney had taken more than their fair share of Sarah's assets. Although the disgraced Porter was found innocent, his attorney, Edward Curd Jr., received a guilty verdict for taking "secret commissions" or kickbacks from real estate deals totaling $8,500 and lost his license to lawyer. Perhaps, motivated to distance themselves from these events and those still grabbing at the 13-year-old's fortune, the entire Rector family moved to Kansas City, Missouri, in the fall 1917.

· · ·

Sarah Rector arrived in Kansas City with the spotlight still shining. Local headlines trumpeted her arrival.

The Kansas City Sun, a black-owned newspaper, under the headline "The Richest Negro Girl in the World Now Lives Here," noted that Sarah and her three siblings attended the Attucks[2] School and all were "quiet, mannerly and neat in their appearance and deportment." The story mentioned her income of $700 a day, as well as a summary of Sarah's holdings. Due to extreme modesty, it said, the paper was unable to obtain a photograph.

The Rectors moved into a temporary residence along one of the grand boulevards of Kansas City, The Paseo. This grand street, divided by heavily treed islands, contrasted with their rustic road in Muskogee. The corner house abutted the two-square-block park called The Parade, the site of a pond, swimming pool, parade grounds, ball fields, and, in the winter, a huge skating rink. While they attended school and played in the park, Sarah's empire grew.

During 1921, Sarah paid $20,000 cash for a brick-and-stone mansion in the black district at 2000 East 12th Street (12th and Euclid), just six blocks from The Parade. The family lived in this house that became known as the "Rector Mansion." Her youngest brother, Roy, was squired from this residence to school in a chauffer-driven Rolls-Royce. At one time, Sarah owned the entire block. Yet, she still faced the onslaught of greedy, legal wranglers who claimed she was not fit to handle her financial affairs.

With her worth estimated at $11 million, Sarah reached the legal milestone of 18 in March 1922, officially freed of guardian oversight. At last, able to manage her own empire, she was free of the shackles and protection created by the court system.

She bought real estate in Kansas City, drove expensive cars, and dressed in fine clothing, jewels, and furs. The stock market was rocketing skyward and oil was still flowing. This was the decade of living the high life.

With the roaring '20s in full swing, Sarah was ready to breathe in the gusto of life; the nucleus of the Kansas City Jazz Age and roaring dance halls, filled with attractive revelers, was just round the corner at 18th and Vine.

She was a looker. According to her brother Roy, she was "very beautiful and of average height and weight and she had beautiful hair." Her appearance attracted attention.

She met Kenneth Campbell, a 19-year-old black student who had just graduated from the district's Lincoln High School. He was on the University of Kansas football team. On November 3, 1922, *The Kansas City Sun* announced, "High School Boy Marries Miss Rector: Kenneth Campbell, Graduate of Lincoln, Wed to Rich Girl During September." The writer tells of the September 16 wedding in Lawrence, Kansas, witnessed only by Sarah's mother and the bridegroom's grandmother. The announcement of the wedding was made by Miss Rector's attorney, C.H. Calloway.

The article mentions Mr. and Mrs. Campbell were involved in a serious car accident in late October after attending a football game in Sedalia, Missouri, involving Kenneth's former high school team.

Another newspaper, *The Kansas City Call,* a black-owned newspaper, reported that the accident occurred as they attempted to turn a corner—the car skidded and turned "turtle," injuring Sarah and a passenger while fracturing three of Kenneth's ribs.

Further, the publication called for the white newspaper, *The Kansas City Star*, to either "prove or retract their allegations" in their account that attempted to "besmirch" Sarah's character.

Apparently, the injured Campbells were taken to the "colored" General Hospital #2, also known as the Wheatley-Provident Hospital, where they recovered in the facility for several days before returning to the mansion to convalesce and attend to business.

In addition to buying local real estate, Kenneth and Sarah opened a Hupmobile[3] car dealership in the heart of the black entertainment district at 19th and Vine. The racial climate made it difficult for blacks to own a car dealership and some white Kansas City dealerships did not allow blacks to test drive their cars.

Some recount that Sarah loved to drive her big cars, perhaps her silver-plated Lincoln, around town at a high rate of speed, resulting in traffic stops. The cops would be confronted with the question, "Do you know who I am?" Often, there was no ticket.

Flaunting downtown Kansas City department stores' segregation and Jim Crow laws that barred African Americans from upper-end, white establishments, Sarah routinely strolled through Jacquard's,

---

2 Crispus Attucks was born into slavery in Framingham, Massachusetts, around 1723, to a mother who was a Native American and an African-American father. He joined a crowd who protested the British presence in Boston and became the first casualty of the Boston Massacre in America's fight for independence.

3 The Hupp Motor Company began production in 1909. In 1912, Hupp became the first U.S. automaker to use all-steel bodies. The company closed in 1940.

choosing expensive diamonds and other jewelry. Defying 1920s racial guidelines, Sarah used fitting rooms to try on clothing before purchasing. She paraded around big-name stores. Her money seemed to eliminate barriers.

Stories account for the twosome becoming local royalty. They entertained famous African-American legends in their mansion on East 12th. Duke Ellington and Count Basie rubbed elbows with Sarah and Kenneth. Sports figures like Heavyweight Champions of the World Joe Louis and Jack Johnson went a few rounds in their home.

They had three boys: Kenneth Jr. and Leonard preceded the birth of Clarence in August 1929. Clarence Rector told a *Kansas City Call* reporter his mother wore a "beautiful, full-length, black-fur coat" and drove a green and black Cadillac. He added, "She had rich tastes."

The stock market crash began in late October 1929. Sarah's investments took a sudden turn south; her fortune nearly disappeared. Speculation is that Kenneth had used family funds to invest in a number of enterprises that became losses. One source hints there may have been a connection with the local "mafia." The marriage dissolved around 1930. Kenneth headed to Chicago to open a Hupmobile dealership with Kansas Citian Homer B. Roberts and took the older two boys to live with him in Chicago.[4] Sarah sold the mansion to the Adkins Funeral Home and moved to a more modest home at 2440 Brooklyn Avenue and, subsequently, 2418 Campbell, according to Clarence. The mansion sold again, this time to C.K. Kerford Funeral home. Sarah's mother, Rosa, and the rest of her children lived nearby on Wabash Street. The reduction of her real estate holdings continued.

By 1933, Sarah's Oklahoma real estate had been sold or suffered foreclosure, and she sold her allotment in 1932 to Herman Epstein for $100.

In 1934, Sarah married Williams A. Crawford, a baker, who owned a restaurant at 18th and Vine. The 1940 Federal Census shows them still living with Clarence on 12th and Euclid. But, unfortunately, an extended period of uneventful living would end violently.

Tragedy struck Sarah's family when Kenneth Jr. was gunned down and killed in Kansas City during the 1940s. Though, amid the darkness, a bright spot appeared.

Beginning in 1946, the Indian Claims Commission held hearings regarding possible misuse and fraud of government-taken tribal lands. Restitution was ordered and Sarah received a settlement, although, the finances of the agreement is unknown. Records sought by Clarence from the Bureau of Indian Affairs were denied.

Sarah bought a small farm east of Overland Park, Kansas, at 4800 Riverside Drive, a few miles from Kansas City, Missouri. Family spent weekend time with her there, and she maintained her stable of Cadillacs and Lincolns.

Eventually, Sarah Rector Campbell Crawford suffered a stroke. Rushed by family members from her rural setting on July 22, 1967, she died in the General Hospital, at the age of 63. Her wake was held at the Kerford Funeral Home, the building formerly known as the Rector Mansion. Her relatives escorted her to Muskogee for a proper church funeral and internment in Taft's Black Jack Cemetery.

She returned home to Oklahoma, this time resting next to her paternal guardians.

---

4 According to the *Kansas City Call*, Kenneth was a retired lieutenant colonel, a Chicago alderman, and the right-hand-man of Mayor Daley. Clarence visited him in Chicago and remembered that his father was "the best dresser in city office."

Originally published
February 2011

by Hannibal B. Johnson

THE LIMITS OF THE LAW

Justice Thurgood Marshall in Oklahoma

The words "law" and "justice" fit together like handmaidens.

Historically and strategically, African Americans have been true believers in the marriage of these concepts. From abolition to civil rights, African-American liberation movements viewed changes in the law as the primary means by which to achieve our ultimate end, justice. Over time, we successfully challenged many of the laws that oppressed us. Whether our concerted push toward equality before the law has led to justice is, at best, an open question.

Is our continued faith in law as the chosen vehicle for social change and, ultimately, justice, misplaced? Stated differently, does the law, even when neutrally applied, lead inexorably to justice?

One of our great American heroes and a shining star in the legal pantheon, the late United States Supreme Court Justice Thurgood Marshall, pondered those questions. On June 29, 1991, on the occasion of his retirement from the Court, he noted:

> The legal system can force open doors, and sometimes, even knock down walls. But it cannot build bridges. That job belongs to you and me.
>
> We can run from each other, but we cannot escape each other. We will only attain freedom if we learn to appreciate what is different and muster the courage to discover what is fundamentally the same.
>
> Take a chance, won't you? Knock down the fences that divide, tear apart the walls that imprison. Reach out, freedom lies just on the other side.

Justice Marshall, a stalwart soldier in the battle for African-American equality before the law, came to realize that justice requires more than the law alone can afford. Justice demands both legislative and spiritual awakening.

In his early career, Thurgood Marshall, a crackerjack lawyer trained at Howard University Law School, led a frontal assault on segregation on behalf of the National Association for the Advancement of Colored People (NAACP). He worked the legal system from within, deftly challenging discriminatory practices on Constitutional and other grounds. Marshall had strong Oklahoma ties.

In 1941, the NAACP dispatched Marshall to Hugo, Oklahoma, to defend W.D. Lyons, an African American who stood accused of three counts of capital murder and arson. Upon his arrest, law enforcement officers viciously beat Lyons and forced him to handle the bones and teeth of the murder victims. Lyons confessed. Marshall sought to suppress the confession on account of coercion.

A state convict on temporary and unsupervised prison release had previously confessed to the December 31, 1939, crimes for which Lyons stood accused. Marshall, convinced of Lyons' innocence, concluded that Oklahoma Governor Leon C. Phillips squelched the convict's confession for political reasons, and then sought and found a scapegoat, Lyons.

The heinous nature of the case, coupled with the curiosity of, in Marshall's own description of comments he overheard, "a nigger lawyer from New York," made the case inescapably attractive. Townsfolk by the hundreds filled the courthouse. Teachers even brought their students in to see the spectacle that the judge called a "gala day."

The judge allowed Lyons' confession into evidence, and the jury convicted him. Lyons, however, was sentenced to life imprisonment instead of death, as sought by the prosecution. Given the circumstances, Marshall viewed the sparing of Lyons' life as a partial victory. He also saw the appeal of the decision as a viable vehicle through which to build the NAACP's legal defense fund. The United States Supreme Court, in a 1944 decision, *Lyons v. Oklahoma*, upheld Lyons' conviction.

Years later, Marshall returned to Oklahoma to represent a young woman from Chickasha, Ada Lois Sipuel, in her quest to integrate the University of Oklahoma College of Law. In cases like *Sipuel v. Board of Regents of University of Oklahoma* (1948) and, later, *Brown v. Board of Education of Topeka* (1954), Marshall tore down America's wall of de jure segregation, brick by brick. Later, as Judge on the United States Court of Appeals for the Second Circuit, United States Solicitor General, and United States Supreme Court Justice, Marshall continued to give voice to the voiceless as an unwavering advocate of legal egalitarianism.

Thurgood Marshall devoted his life to equality under the law, ostensibly for African Americans, but, in reality, for all Americans. He recognized that changing the legal system was necessary, but not sufficient, to make America a land of "liberty and justice for all." Experimentally, he tested the limits of the law. Beyond those outskirts lies, broadly speaking, a spiritual realm.

Today, African Americans are over-represented in prisons, on welfare, and among the unemployed and uninsured. The educational achievement gap shows no sign of abating. On virtually all socioeconomic indicia of well-being, African Americans lag behind. Where is the justice—fairness, equity, moral rightness—in that?

While every American shares responsibility for this perilous state, individuals acting alone cannot rectify this ugly reality. The true test of a society is how it treats the least of those in its midst. It is about the interconnectedness and shared fate of which Justice Marshall spoke. If we are to extricate ourselves from this morass, we will do it with the support of forward-thinking people of all persuasions who understand the folly of doing nothing. We will have to do more than make changes to our laws. We will have to change hearts and minds, too.

What might you do to better incorporate diversity and inclusion into your own life? How might you help build a more inclusive community where you are? A few simple steps follow:

- Expand your mind. Learn about your own diversity dimensions (e.g., your racial, ethnic, and cultural heritage) as well as that of others. Broaden your horizons by discovering your own history and that of the world around you.

- Know yourself. Get in touch with your feelings, preconceptions, and stereotypes. Know your biases and work to eliminate them.

- Reach out. Step outside your comfort zone. Reach out to "the other"—people from different backgrounds.

- Listen. Pay attention to what others say about their experiences around diversity and inclusion issues. Incorporate the lessons you learn into your life.

- Engage. Get involved with clubs and organizations, initiatives, and issues that embrace and foster diversity and inclusion.

We do honor to the memory and legacy of Justice Marshall when we run with the baton he handed off to us. We have to stride beyond mere equality under the law. If we want "justice," then we must be willing to round the track as long as necessary to make the human connections that will ultimately win the race.

Originally published
September 2011

by Steve Gerkin

BENO HALL

Tulsa's den of terror

The monstrous three-story, steel-reinforced, stucco building towered along the western edge of Greenwood. It dominated the landscape at the foot of Standpipe Hill, sporting a bright whitewash, the favorite color of its primary residents. Inside, its members vowed to protect their notion of "100% Americanism." To become a guardian of liberty, they reasoned, you had to swear to secrecy and seclusion. And you had to embrace intimidation and violence as a way to assert your values.

In January of 1922, the Tulsa Benevolent Association of Oklahoma was officially formed as a holding company for the Knights of the Ku Klux Klan, Incorporated. Among its founding members was Washington E. Hudson, the attorney for Dick Rowland—the young black man who was a scapegoat for the 1921 Tulsa Race Riot. They provided the financing and leadership to begin building their Klan temple, or Klavern, known as Beno Hall. Locals jokingly called it "Be No Hall," as in "Be No Nigger, Be No Jew, Be No Catholic, Be No Immigrant."

Six months after its inception and bolstered by a raffle of 13 Ford automobiles netting nearly half of the $60,000 purchase price, the Benevolent Association bought the Centenary Methodist Church, at Main and Easton streets. The organization quickly outgrew this facility and the church was razed, making way for the future monument of white supremacy. Beno Hall was built for $200,000 ($1.5 million in today's currency). Financing of the construction was kept quiet, but the land for the building was owned by the entrepreneur, politician, and early booster of Tulsa, Tate Brady, and his wife, Rachel Brady, who received a large parcel of land as a Cherokee allotment in 1910. When Beno Hall was completed, it was one of the largest auditoriums in the Southwest, holding 3,000 people. Its size alone provided Tulsa with a visual reminder of the Invisible Empire's power, passion, and presence.

Abundant evidence points the finger at the Klan for fanning the sociological tinderbox that was 1920s Tulsa. Yearning for a spark, if even an invented one, a fired-up mob of whites took the bait and burned Greenwood to the ground in the Memorial Day 1921 Race Riot. Two months later, a national Klan official, Caleb Ridley, who was also a Baptist minister, lectured at the Tulsa Convention Hall on the principles

of the Klan, calling the riot a complete success, adding that it "was the best thing to ever happen to Tulsa and that judging from the way strange Negroes were coming to Tulsa we might have to do it all over again."

Under the watchful eye of its Tulsa leader, Exalted Cyclops William Shelley Rogers, membership grew to include all civic and social levels: from law enforcement to welders, bankers, dry cleaners, judges, commissioners, and oil field workers. All partook in the Beno Hall sessions that focused on increasing membership and efforts to keep Tulsa free from moral corruption and centered on family values.

Barely three months after the riot, some 300 Tulsans, supported by a throng of 1,500 onlookers, were initiated as the first class of the Tulsa Klan No. 2. A year later, in a field north of Owasso, a nighttime "naturalization" ceremony initiated 1,020 Tulsa Klavern members before a fiery, 70-by-20-foot cross.

Recruiters known as Kleagles "capitalized upon the emotions in the wake of the race riot to propagandize the white community of Tulsa," writes Carter Blue Clark in his 1976 dissertation, *A History of the Ku Klux Klan in Oklahoma*. While the Oklahoma Klan boasted over 150,000 hooded devotees in the early 1920s, the Tulsa Klavern—a reference to the smallest local unit of the organizational structure, wherein ritual ceremonies and Klan Khoral Klub rehearsals were held—swelled to 3,000 members. Hence the need for a permanent structure—a very large, secure structure.

Nestled near the two-year-old ashes of upperclass black homes that once sprawled up the slopes of Sunset and Standpipe hills, overlooking the industry that was Greenwood, Beno Hall towered over nearly 2,000 black Tulsans as they huddled in makeshift tents. They lived within earshot of the member revelry. From the halls of Beno sprung midnight parades, cross burnings along the boundaries of Greenwood, night-riding terrors, meetings determining political candidates' success or failure, plans to squash the proliferation of filthy people with filthy morals who bootlegged, gambled, consorted with whores, or were unfaithful husbands—all of which conflicted with the Klan's version of white, Protestant ideology.

The Klan loved parades. The most spectacular occurred in August of 1922, while the wounds of the 1921 riot were still fresh. The parade featured 1,741 white-robed members marching silently through downtown Tulsa before an estimated crowd of 15,000. The Women of the Klan provided extra pizzazz, carrying signs with various slogans such as, "Kiss the flag or cross the pond," a reminder that immigrants were not Americans, therefore, there should "Be None" on American soil, certainly not in Oklahoma.

The Knights had nothing against what they deemed "good niggers." They were also morally incensed by the behavior of white men—especially the oil field workers who used the trolley system to come to downtown Tulsa, where they spent their cash on booze, dames, and pounds of cocaine, morphine, and heroin. In *Tulsa, Biography of the American City*, Danney Goble wrote, "Kluxers meted out rough justice to those that lived beyond the law's bounds"—justice that predominantly involved acts against white Protestants.

The Klan wasn't just for older white men, either. The Tulsa Klavern vigorously promoted the Women of the Klan society and an adolescent male branch called the Junior Ku Klux Klan, which recruited boys aged 12 to 18.

According to an invitation on Junior Ku Klux Klan stationery of the Tulsa Benevolent Association, a Junior KKK "Open Air Initiation" at the Lynch Farm north of Rose Hill Cemetery began at 7:30 p.m. Friday, September 18, 1924. It promised a ride to the event, if needed, and "lots of fireworks."

When the seasons turned chilly, Beno Hall became the Juniors' initiation site. On January 22, 1925: "All members were expected to be there, members received $.50 for each candidate they bring and new initiates must pay at least $2 on his initiation." Further, it announced the "Final Plans for the Big Weiner and Marshmallow Roast on Thursday night, January 29, when you can bring your girl." The attraction of the evening proved to be a talk by the assistant to the Exalted Cyclops and "ice cream sandwiches—O Boy!"

Beno Hall supplied new recruits with official Klan gear. For a premium price, reportedly pocketed by national officials, the home office in Atlanta regularly shipped cheap white sheets and pointed hats all with the tightly sewn-on patch of the organization. Yet, a Tulsa Knight's trappings were incomplete without the Klan weapon of choice, the official KKK whipping strap.

The strap was a piece of top-grain leather four inches wide and three feet long, the handle wrapped in industrial tape, its last six inches cut into ten slits, effective for slicing through skin. Hundreds of these prized weapons arrived in Tulsa.

During the Oklahoma Klan heyday years between 1921 and 1924, officials knew of 102 Klan floggings, three killings, three mutilations (including castrations), and numerous tar-and-featherings that, as a rule, followed whippings of the victims' backs. Official but incomplete tallies showed Tulsa County provided the most violations with 74, Okmulgee County chalked up 20, while the rest of the state totaled 37.

At the time, lawlessness prevailed in Tulsa. A local reporter witnessed the flogging of J.E. Fletcher, an alleged car thief and bootlegger, on a remote Sand Springs road in September 1921. County Attorney John Seaver said no inquiry would be made, that Fletcher had gotten what he deserved and an investigation would just lead to criticism of the investigators. This gave carte blanche to extralegal marauding.

During that same month, a statement by H.O. McClure, president of the Tulsa Chamber of Commerce, put the writing on the wall in a *Tulsa World* article: "In Tulsa our courthouse and city hall are practically filled with Klan members, elected to office with Klan support." It wouldn't be long before an Oklahoma governor would step in to throttle the free hand of Tulsa's hooded fraternity.

After local Klansmen used their whipping straps to mutilate the genitalia of accused drug-peddler Nathan Hantaman, the already unpopular Governor Jack Walton, on August 14, 1923, declared martial law in the city and county of Tulsa. The results of the military court investigation drew statewide attention to the horror of the Oklahoma extremists as 12 locals were hauled away. The Oklahoma legislature passed an anti-mask bill hoping to stem vigilante violence.

The flamboyant Walton, aiming squarely at the Tulsa Klavern, even calling them by name, went on the attack, saying, "I don't care if you burst right into them with a double-barreled shot gun. I'll promise you a pardon in advance." Additional irresponsible statements, the suspension of the writ of habeas corpus, censorship of the press, an effective Klan defense and counter-attack, and the extension of military rule to include the entire state, further weakened public sentiment toward the state's leader.

Governor Walton's declaration of war on the Order exposed their reign of terror, but they would get the last laugh. The Klan influenced the impeachment of "Jazz Band Jack" Walton, who served but 10 months as governor. The boys in white cheered the demise of their nemesis in their newly dedicated Beno Hall that had earlier been the site of the Tri-State Klan convention.

The next few years saw a healthy Klavern using their north Tulsa facility for holiday dances, ice cream socials, and political plotting. The outer foliage appeared robust, but inside, the society was withering from internal disagreements, greed, and graft. By 1928, the Oklahoma Klan had negligible power.

The Tulsa Benevolent Association sold the storied building to the Temple Baptist Church in 1930. During the Depression, the building housed a speakeasy, then a skating rink, then a lumberyard, and finally a dance hall before radio evangelist Steve Pringle turned it into the Evangelistic Temple of the First Pentecostal Church. In his first revival meeting, Pringle introduced a little-known Enid preacher by the name of Oral Roberts, who worked his animated, faith-healing magic on the bare lot next door. Roberts impressed in the tent atmosphere and preached with his cohort inside the vast auditorium once known as Beno Hall. His fire and brimstone was a fitting bookend to the fiery crusades of the Klan.

Throughout the '70s, Beno Hall became a Main Street blight where vagrants gambled, drug transactions took place, and sex was exchanged for money. It was destroyed in 1976, and the empty lot now belongs to the Oklahoma Department of Highways.

Originally published
May 2011

by Steve Gerkin

THE MAN IN THE BOX, REVEALED

Call it a death parade.

A white-draped car floated quietly down the warm streets of Copan, Oklahoma. Inside the vehicle, a man held a fiery cross. Behind the car marched 15 white-robed members of the Ku Klux Klan, their presence sending a clear message—a message that appeared on signs declaring "America for Americans." Upon reaching the Copan Undertaking Parlor, the column of Kluxers silently entered the front door of the establishment.

A flowery aroma filled the parlor where the dead man lay, his casket surrounded with arrangements from his Masonic affiliations, the Copan High School, and many others. The eye-grabbing centerpiece was a large floral pillow sent by his brethren of the Invisible Empire, the KKK, which boasted 20,000 members in Oklahoma at the time.

The Klan had a habit of interrupting ordinary affairs; intrusion was their modus operandi. Although the funeral service for Joseph C. Sheets was already underway, the hooded mourners "filed by the coffin, silently dropping a red rose on the heap of floral offerings," according to a newspaper account. Joseph C. Sheets belonged to the De Molay, the Scottish Rite and the Masonic Temple, and he had the flowers to prove it. In small towns, however, being a Mason often implied a connection to the Klan. If Sheets was ever a secret member of the Klan, his cover was blown by the large floral bouquet placed before his casket.

On September 5, 1922, the *Tulsa Daily World* noted that the Masonic Rose Croix service for Joe Sheets was "probably the most impressive funeral ceremony ever held in Copan." Over 1,500 Masons and friends gathered at Sheets' stately home. The story left out the bit about the parade.

· · ·

Sheets got his first job in oil and gas at the age of 16. During his career, he established himself as one of the shrewdest oil operators in the state. He was involved in management positions with the Swastika Oil and Gas Company, the Alamo Oil Company, the Collis and Jackson oil companies and Georgia Oil and Gas Company.

In 1902, at age 26, Sheets moved from his native West Virginia to Independence, Kansas, then onto

Joseph C. Sheets' casket surrounded by arrangements from his Masonic affiliations, Copan High School and the Ku Klux Klan, among others.

Editor's note: *For years, this photo of a KKK funeral has circulated among several photography collections in Tulsa, but the identity of the person in the casket has remained a mystery. In this article, writer Steve Gerkin uncovers the identity of the man in the box.*

Bartlesville. He, along with his brother Earl, formed Sheets Brothers Oil and Gas. By 1905, Sheets was successful enough to move his family into a newly constructed Copan home. The prodigious structure stood out above the tent city along the railroad tracks.

Riding on the find of the Copan Oil Field discovery of 1907, the Sheets family had 300 oil and gas wells in production within a decade. A year earlier, Sheets had donated 10 acres for the establishment of the Copan school district. A standalone arch structure was located at the entrance. It was called the Copan Unkwa Arch in homage to the Cherokee word for "red man."

The booming town of Copan featured four hotels for house oil laborers, plus a pool hall, a lumberyard, and a grocery store where fights tended to break out. As a longtime member of the Copan School District Board and devoted husband to Millicent and father to daughter Alice, Sheets served his community and family but shied away from political office, though he did serve on the Washington County Council of Defense. The Kleagles, the Klan's recruiting unit, aggressively pursued the leaders of Oklahoma wartime councils.

In addition to black gold, he had interests in farm and timber tracts, and owned an insurance agency for The Northern Assurance Company Limited of London, specializing in coverage for fire, tornado, automobiles, and sprinkler leakage. His local influence grew with his holdings.

The Bank of Copan opened its doors in 1910, and, by 1915, Sheets was its president and principal stockholder. But all work and no play makes a dull good ol' boy, so for fun Sheets joined the Copan Red Cross baseball team and participated in Copan wild-game suppers where the men would hunt for anything moving, large or small, even crows. The animals were cooked together in large iron kettles set up on Main Street as cheering spectators watched wrestling matches conducted in the mud hole in the center of the street.

· · ·

Given the secrecy of the Klan, Sheets' exact position was not known. There was no evidence of him participating in the Klan whipping teams that flogged residents who, in the Klan's opinion, were immoral. Some whippings were exercised on prisoners turned over by local law enforcement.

Ninety-year-old Perlie Moreland knew the Sheets family well. Her parents arrived via covered wagon in Copan in 1905. Ultimately moving next door to the Sheets, she became fast friends with Millicent and Alice after Joe passed.

"Mr. Sheets was involved with the Klan—always heard about that," she comments.

She eases out of the over-stuffed chair in her family room to retrieve a three-ring notebook brimming with clips and photos from the now-defunct Copan Leader newspaper. Plastic sleeves protect the dogged and yellowed pages with their bold-faced headlines and grainy images. Perlie has turned the screen of an old television set into a pasteboard for Scotch-taped photos of her grand- and great-grandchildren. Atop the old TV, a new flat-screen model balances.

Returning to her favorite chair, struggling with hip pain, Perlie settles in and opens the binder, the cover of which displays a photo of the former Bank of Copan, now a knitting supply store. Putting on her plastic-framed glasses that she needs only for reading, she begins turning the proud pages. A self-described "old, white-haired gal, getting shorter all the time," Perlie spins stories of Copan and Joe Sheets, who kept a Klan robe in a remote closet. Yet the Copan that Joe knew had changed.

Perlie catalogues old buildings with her camera to save at least their memories for posterity. The structures—neglected and disfigured, like an old town dog—succumb with regularity: Perlie's portraits reflect a Copan out of time. Two joints—Jessie's Café and the Truck Stop, Perlie's personal favorite—were not part of the eatery scene during the town's heyday. The vanishing memories and the new arrivals add up to a kind of empty.

Perlie acknowledges that the Klan was active in the Copan area during her youth. She'd always heard that Joe Sheets was involved in the organization, in some way. She spent hours with his widow, who knitted incessantly and loved to reminisce. According to Perlie, "Millicent had a hard time talking about it." She let all of her husband rest in peace.

Originally published
May 2014

by Michael D. Bates

STEPS TO NOWHERE

The undevelopment of
Tulsa's Near Northside

Just north of downtown Tulsa there is a vast empty area, about a half-mile long by a third of a mile wide. This wasteland is punctuated only by the Salvation Army's compound on the south end and a 1970s vintage elementary school at the north end. The Oklahoma State University-Tulsa campus borders it on the east.

Superimposed on the empty, green space is a grid of seldom-used streets, each one paralleled by a pair of buckled or overgrown sidewalks, interrupted periodically by the stub of a driveway. Where there is a steep enough incline from the sidewalk to the middle of the block, there are sets of stone or concrete steps, leading up the rise to bare ground. At the steepest inclines, tilting, buckling walls try to keep the hill from spilling out onto the street.

MISTAKEN IDENTITY

The observer notes that this place is north of downtown and remembers that it was north of downtown in 1921 that a white mob invaded, looted, and burned an African-American neighborhood to the ground.

Ethiopian artist Eyakem Gulilat photographed this empty land and the concrete steps to nowhere, intending his installation to be a record of the physical legacy of the 1921 Race Riot. "Using photography as a constant witness, I observe the changes that took place in this location through the last 100 years and how the place holds memory of this great tragedy. The land is an unbiased witness to the lives and events from the past..."

The land is an unbiased witness, but the steps and sidewalks tell us only that once there were homes here—not when they were built, what they looked like, when they went away, or why they went away.

The regularity of the boundary and the thorough cleansing that took place within does not suggest the chaotic destruction of an inflamed mob. The land bears the mark of an officially planned and methodically executed purge—more *Kelo v. New London* than Kristallnacht.

There are other unbiased witnesses: federal census records, annual city directories, fire insurance maps showing the shape, height, and material of every building, aerial photos, title deeds, subdivision plats.

RACE READER

Created at the time for various practical purposes, these records combine as an unintentional documentary of a neighborhood's history, providing a context for these ruins on a hill overlooking downtown.

There are also living witnesses whose fond memories and precious photographs put flesh on the bones of the official records. They are senior citizens now, but as children in the middle of the 20th century, they bounded down these steps heading to school or church or summertime explorations with their pals. They rode their bikes down these streets in the pre-dawn darkness delivering the morning paper. Walking these sidewalks, they carried groceries home from the corner store. Where there is now only a treeless stretch of grass, they drank chocolate shakes at a drugstore soda fountain.

These witnesses tell a story. Until 25 years ago, there was a neighborhood here. Until 10 years ago, a few buildings remained.

The story of the steps

The story of the steps to nowhere is not a tragedy on the order of the 1921 looting and burning of the African-American community down the hill and a half-mile to the east. It is not a tragedy on the order of the City of Tulsa's federally funded demolition of the neighborhood that the African-American community had rebuilt from the ashes of 1921.

It is a tragedy of relentless bureaucracy, faulty projections, and bad urban design. Even as cities across America were rediscovering the value of the traditional neighborhood with jobs, shops, schools, and churches within walking distance of homes, Tulsa was destroying one of the few traditional mixed-use neighborhoods still in its possession, for the sake of a goal that vanished before the destruction was even complete.

At the beginning of the 20th century, Tulsa grew from sleepy whistle-stop to oil-fired boomtown. The population, 50 times bigger in just 20 years, spilled out into new neighborhoods in every direction.

On the highlands to the north, past the Frisco and the Katy tracks, seven new subdivisions were laid out, their streets forming a seamless grid and a single neighborhood. Asked where they lived, the residents of this new neighborhood would simply say "the Northside" or "up on the hill."

The Northside wasn't downtown, wasn't Owen Park, off to the west, and it especially wasn't the district down the hill to the east, known variously as the East End, Greenwood, Little Africa, or more derogatory names. The Northside spanned from Easton Street on the south to Marshall Street on the north to Osage Drive and the Tulsa Country Club on the west. The eastern border came up Detroit Avenue as far as Haskell Street (known today as John Hope Franklin Boulevard), then traced around the crest of Sunset Hill.

Early city directories documented Tulsa's racial geography by marking certain residents' names with a "(c)" for "colored." The Northside was a white neighborhood, with the exception of a few residents of servants' quarters over the detached garages of the grander homes. In the 1920 directory, every name on the east, odd-numbered side of Detroit Avenue is followed by a (c); on the west, even-numbered side, none are.

The 1918 "Aero View of Tulsa" shows most of our Northside neighborhood in the foreground, and captures it in a state of near-complete development, filled with one- and two-story frame houses, mainly of the craftsman and foursquare styles. Standing atop its namesake hill between Easton and Fairview is the city's standpipe, or water tower, and, on the hill's western flank at Boston Avenue, the impressive two-story Sequoyah School with its domed bell tower, opened as Northside School in 1906. A block further west, at Main and Easton, is Tigert Memorial Methodist Church, the first church in the neighborhood; in just six years it would be replaced by the Ku Klux Klan's Beno Hall. Next to Tigert Church on the north is Fire Station No. 2, built in 1909.

At the five-points intersection where Boulder, Main, and Haskell come together, where downtown's railroad-tilted grid meets the compass-aligned streets that dominate the rest of the city, the picture shows a scattering of brick apartment buildings and stores. There are two hospitals—infirmaries, really—on Boulder between Easton and Fairview: Cinnabar, in a large house across from two-story brick Morningside, forerunner of Hillcrest.

On the right-hand side (south and west) there are the first few buildings of Osage School, one of the first built to Tulsa's innovative, incremental "unit plan," opened in 1913. (Lee School and the former Lincoln School are surviving examples of the type.)

The school is flanked by the grand mansions of the country-club district, with the open space of Owen Park and the Tulsa Country Club beyond. The tracks running down the center of Cheyenne belong to the Tulsa Street Railway, connecting the Northside to downtown via Cameron Street and Main Street with a trolley car every seven-and-a-half minutes from early morning until late at night.

Off the edge of the picture to the north is another new unit-plan school: Emerson, between King and Latimer on the east side of Boston Avenue, had opened its doors on January 5, 1916.

Around this time C.W. "Doc" Medlock established his home and his optometry practice just north of Standpipe Hill at 618 N. Cincinnati. (N. Cincinnati was renamed Martin Luther King Jr. Boulevard in 2012.) Doc made glasses for his white neighbors on the hill and the African-American residents of the valley to his east.

On June 1, 1921, Detroit Avenue, the dividing line between the races, became the front line of the battle, just a block east of Doc Medlock's place. Years later, his wife, Ollie, would tell their grandson Chris (who would grow up to be a Tulsa city councilor) how Doc sat up all night on the front porch with a shotgun, prepared to defend his home against anyone who might try to attack.

But the 1921 Race Riot barely grazed the Northside. National Guardsmen were called to the north edge of Sunset Hill, west of the present-day Pioneer Plaza tower, to deal with a report of black riflemen at the base of the hill firing up into the white-owned homes on the crest of the hill. The guardsmen had heard a rumor that the shots had killed a white woman, and two guardsmen who came to investigate were slightly wounded under fire. The guardsmen returned fire with a few shots from a decrepit machine gun and then moved down hill in pursuit of the riflemen.

That is the only report of riot violence reaching the neighborhood of steps to nowhere; all of the buildings "up on the hill" survived the riot. Down the hill, the Greenwood residents successfully fought a city plan to convert the burned-out district to an industrial center, and then rebuilt their homes, stores, and churches. They weren't able, half a century later, to stop a city plan that leveled all but a handful of buildings in the name of "slum clearance" and "urban renewal."

DECADES OF STABILITY

New neighborhoods sprang up further north, so our neighborhood is better described from this point forward as the Near Northside. The Near Northside changed over the next 50 years, but redevelopment happened gradually, one lot at a time. Small apartment buildings, filling stations, and mom-and-pop stores mixed in with the homes and schools. The neighborhood had a few churches, a Jewish community center, and a couple of beer joints.

Tulsans who spent their childhoods in the Near Northside during the 1940s, 1950s, and early 1960s remember it as an idyllic place.

As a five-year-old, Bill Leighty (today a realtor and former planning commissioner) walked on his own to Curry Drug at Main and Latimer, where he could browse comic books or enjoy a cherry Coke at the fountain. A striped pole on a small house behind Curry's marked Bert Daniels' barber shop.

The 50-foot-deep pits that the brick factory had dug into the side of Sunset Hill, declared off-limits by responsible parents, were magnets for the adventurous young person, where Martin Reidy (the last homeowner to leave in 2004) hunted for scorpions, tarantulas, and horny toads.

For spending money, a kid could mow lawns or deliver handbills for the corner grocery. If you shopped at Romney's on Main and needed help getting your groceries home, Johnnie Cherblanc (a real estate executive nowadays) would carry your bags for a quarter tip.

A kid didn't depend on grown-ups to get around. Mike Littrell, who lived near Boulder and Fairview in the early '60s, would walk to the Page-Glencliff dairy store at Boston and Haskell for a 10-cent scoop of banana nut, ride his bike downtown, or take the bus to see the Oilers play ball.

But this beloved neighborhood was doomed. At mid-century, the experts believed that government could and must reorganize America's cities. The science was settled: Traditional neighborhoods, with their mixture of homes and shops and jobs, small lots, old homes, and dense street grids, were insalubrious and a cause of poverty. New neighborhoods on the edge of the city would be designed in accordance with modern, scientific planning theories. Residential areas would be uncontaminated by nearby businesses. Expressways, modeled after Hitler's autobahns, would speed residents between their shiny new suburbs and downtown jobs and shopping.

A new tool called "urban renewal" would be used to level and redevelop obsolete neighborhoods that didn't match the scientific model. Uncle Sam generously offered $9 to match every local dollar toward urban renewal and expressway construction. States authorized cities to create the planning commissions and urban renewal authorities required to receive Washington's largesse.

For some local leaders, it was a happy coincidence that free money from Washington gave them the power and resources to shunt lucrative demolition and construction contracts to political allies, to boost demand for new homes and shopping centers in the suburbs for their developer friends, and to relocate undesirable ethnicities away from the city center. The Germans kept their autobahns away from their cities and towns; city leaders in America saw that they could be used to eliminate outdated neighborhoods or at least wall them off from the central business district.

About the time that Jane Jacobs and her allies were successfully defending New York's traditional neighborhoods, Tulsa was pushing ahead with modern, scientific planning, as fast as state law would

allow, forming the Tulsa Metropolitan Area Planning Commission in 1955 and the Tulsa Urban Renewal Authority in 1959.

TMAPC's 1957 Comprehensive Plan defined the model suburban square mile: a school surrounded by houses on large lots, connected by winding streets and cul-de-sacs. Shopping centers on the periphery, carefully segregated from the houses, had plenty of parking spaces and needed them because there was no direct path from home to store.

The map of "blight, sprawl, and renewal areas" in TMAPC's Preliminary Land Use Plan claimed that over 30 percent of the buildings on nearly every block of the Near Northside were "dilapidated," and the neighborhood was "needing treatment."

The 1957 expressway plan connected an "Inner Dispersal Loop" hub around downtown to distant, growing suburban neighborhoods, the spokes cutting through older, inner neighborhoods.

Oklahoma law authorized cities to condemn property for "blight," a condition so expansively defined that it could apply to any building that wasn't brand new. An entire neighborhood could be condemned as blighted, no matter how well-kept each individual property might be, if their arrangement didn't fit the new suburban standard.

The grand metropolitan plans began to nibble away at the neighborhood in the late '60s, when the state began clearing land to make way for I-244. Cincinnati was widened and cut through the middle of Standpipe Hill to connect to the new freeway. In the '70s, the western fringe of the neighborhood was cleared and Osage Elementary School was demolished to make way for the Osage (now L. L. Tisdale) Expressway.

Now out of sight and out of mind for city leaders downtown, the area headed into a decline. Stores that sold new items became resale shops. Drug dealers and prostitutes roamed the streets.

In 1975, Emerson Elementary was demolished and replaced with a new building, part of the school district's "magnet school" desegregation strategy. TURA cleared four whole blocks—46 single-family homes, four duplexes, seven apartment buildings, and a beer joint—and the city closed Boston and King through the new school's "superblock" campus.

Urban renewal plans of this period called for the clearance of nearly all non-residential uses and multi-family housing, with commercial uses permitted only along Denver, south of Fairview. The city's policy was to eliminate the mixed-use quality that set the Near Northside apart from other neighborhoods. Given time, those former commercial sites might have been filled with single-family homes.

Tulsa's pursuit of state-funded higher education would change everything for the Near Northside. In 1982, the dream of a free-standing Tulsa State University gave way to an awkward compromise called the University Center at Tulsa (UCAT). Langston University, Oklahoma State University, University of Oklahoma, and Northeastern State University would offer graduate and upper-level undergraduate courses toward a degree from one of the four schools, on a 200-acre campus to be provided by the city.

The city chose the Greenwood District, north of I-244 and east of Detroit, as the heart of the new campus. The 84.6 acres had been home, in 1960, to about 2,200 people and dozens of businesses, but it had been leveled by the Model Cities urban renewal program and sat empty save for two churches, and a house. The plan to replace Greenwood with high-intensity residential and commercial development had gone nowhere.

In 1985, the City of Tulsa established the University Center at Tulsa Authority (UCATA) to acquire, improve, and maintain a campus on behalf of the four colleges. A firm drew up a master plan, and City of Tulsa voters approved funds for the first academic buildings, which opened in 1988. In 1986, the Tulsa Development Authority, successor to TURA, had signed a lengthy development agreement with UCATA, requiring the land be used for a public university and for development to occur in a timely fashion, and transferred the initial campus area to UCATA.

The remaining 115 acres would come from the Near Northside neighborhood. The homes east of Cincinnati atop Sunset Hill had already been cleared. Urban renewal plans were updated in the late '80s to reflect the new direction. East Haskell (now John Hope Franklin Boulevard) would be connected to West Fairview as a peripheral road, and every other street in the acquisition area (Jasper south to the IDL) would be closed. Pedestrians would be given a tunnel under the new road east of the former site of Boulder Avenue. In the early '90s, the Tulsa Development Authority, successor to TURA, began voluntary buyouts of Near Northside homes.

Two parts of the Near Northside would be spared. On the west fringe, Denver and Cheyenne avenues had been added to the National Register of Historic Places in 1980 as the Brady Heights Historic District. Emerson School's superblock protected the homes and the Boydell Apartments to its north; the commercial buildings were cleared in accordance with the earlier plan.

A 1990 historic preservation report recommended adding the rest of the Near Northside to the Brady Heights Historic District. City authorities had already sealed the area's fate; the report was shelved.

UCAT becomes OSU-Tulsa

While TDA was relentlessly bulldozing homes for UCAT, UCAT was mutating into something very different from a campus that boosters confidently projected would have 20,000 students by 2000.

The consortium blew apart in 1998. OU-Tulsa moved to 41st Street and Yale Avenue. Broken Arrow built a campus for NSU. Langston wanted its own building in the UCAT acquisition area. OSU-Tulsa was all that remained of UCAT.

In 1999, OSU-Tulsa unveiled a grandiose master plan. With only 4,200 students enrolled, the 20,000-student target was rescheduled from 2000 to 2020. The plan, still on display in an upstairs lounge, shows the campus sprawling across all 200 acres. Academic buildings would sit on a series of five terraces leading from the original campus buildings up Sunset Hill to a new campus library on the summit, replacing Pioneer Plaza and Sunset Plaza Apartments.

Campus housing and a wellness center would go west of Cincinnati. The urban grid would be replaced with winding suburban streets and cul-de-sacs. For the complete college experience, OSU-Tulsa even planned to build houses for fraternities and sororities.

In April 2004, TDA demolished the last three homes in the neighborhood. By the end of 2005, Fire Station No. 2 and a few nearby industrial buildings were gone, the final step to nowhere.

OSU-Tulsa's latest master plan, from 2011, a Google map superimposed with Arial type and shaded polygons, has already been overtaken by events.

The Oklahoma School for the Visual and Performing Arts will be at the former Roosevelt Junior High and won't need eight acres south of Emerson School. The Tulsa City-County Library is renovating Central Library, rather than relocate to the western half of Standpipe Hill. Vision2's defeat in November 2012 eliminated funding for a new classroom building and student center. The future of the Millennium Center, a demonstration site for sustainability concepts, is up in the air. OSU-Tulsa caters to commuting locals; on-campus housing won't be needed. The Salvation Army, Pioneer Plaza, and Sunset Plaza Apartments won't be moving. OSU-Tulsa doesn't need the land to move forward with its plans, and there are no funds for relocation.

A technology and research park on Sunset Hill between MLK and Pioneer Plaza is still on the table. OSU-Tulsa would build and lease office and lab space to high-tech companies.

Only the "Hill Top Gateway" on Standpipe Hill has been realized. Without stairs or windows, the tower, which stirs uncomfortable memories of snipers firing into Greenwood from that same hill, serves only as a big sign to alert I-244 drivers to OSU-Tulsa's existence.

Steps back to somewhere

In the 15 years since OSU-Tulsa's first and most elaborate master plan, enrollment has shrunk from about 4,200 to 2,842 for spring 2014. Langston-Tulsa has 356 students. That's a long way from 20,000 by 2020.

The demand for higher ed in Tulsa may be as great as UCAT boosters expected, but students have found more convenient and cost-effective means to meet their goals. Tulsa branches of private and for-profit colleges and dozens of online options cater to the needs of non-traditional students.

Even OSU's own online course options are competing with OSU-Tulsa. For the fall 2013 semester, the school offered the "Get Here" tuition waiver—$250 for students who took all their courses on campus. A poster promoting the plan pointed out that on-campus students would also avoid extra online class fees.

The wasteland was created for a university, but it isn't owned by a university. The Oklahoma A&M Regents own the north academic building and the auditorium (but not the administrative building), and they own the site of the Technology Center west of Elgin. As Langston's governing body, they also own the Langston-Tulsa campus. The remainder of the 200 acres—including the Near Northside wasteland and OSU-Tulsa's massive parking lots—still belongs to UCATA, a trust of the City of Tulsa governed by six trustees who are appointed by the mayor and confirmed by the City Council to five-year terms.

The terms of the land's transfer from TDA to UCATA allow for the land to revert if it's not needed for higher ed.

Despite its total destruction, the Near Northside's wasteland has never been replatted. The grid of streets and parcels that served as the womb for its development 100 years ago could be the matrix for its regeneration, one lot at a time. Tulsa's new comprehensive plan calls for zoning tools that could be used to recreate the style of homes and mixture of uses that characterized the neighborhood in its heyday.

Perhaps someday, the steps to nowhere will lead somewhere once again.

Originally published
September 2012

by Anne Barajas Harp

THE TROUBLE WITH HENRY

Mary Popkess marched into the Sand Springs football stadium under a full head of steam. She made straight for the visitor's sideline where Homer Hill was watching his undefeated Dewey Bulldoggers line up for kickoff in the 1938 Verdigris Valley playoffs. Hill, the wiry, electric coach one sportswriter tagged "The Real Little Napoleon of the Bench," had won 50 of his last 55 games and two conference titles. This night could be his third.

Popkess leaned into the coach. "They won't let Henry in," she said urgently over the noise of the crowd.

Hill walked to the line where players tensed for the whistle and pulled his team captain Carl Burget aside. Words were exchanged. Burget huddled with the other team seniors, leather helmets close together, then the rest of the players were gathered. Game officials were called in and more words were exchanged.

Minutes later, the officials and 4,000 eager football fans looked on in stunned bewilderment as the Dewey Bulldoggers walked off the field. They would understand why soon enough.

• • •

The only written history of Henry Kemps' existence is his obituary. His life has been forgotten by all but a handful of family and friends. On paper, Henry was no one of particular importance—a deliveryman, a janitor, a colored man in a world that was starkly black and white. But he also was a man whose friendship and dignity inspired 30 boys to make an astounding act of loyalty, the memory of which is all but lost.

My dad was one of the boys on that field, and the first to tell me Henry's story. He knew the good parts. But it took his older brother, my Uncle Louis, to point me toward the hard parts.

One Sunday, Uncle Louis climbed into my car and directed me to drive into Dewey's west side, which had once been filled with black families. We circled the waning neighborhood and my uncle showed me where the unthinkable had happened in the town my family had called home for nearly a century.

Henry, you see, had lousy timing.

When he came to Oklahoma in 1916, whippings and lynchings were at an all-time high and state legislators were working hard to ensure blacks couldn't vote. Economic pressures, a world war, and paranoia that black communities would take over the state fed the fear and violence.

Two years after Henry arrived, a black man named Aaron Wardlow shot and killed Dewey's police chief, Walter L. Mull, on the night of August 11, 1918. A band of enraged white citizens went to the county jail in Bartlesville to lynch Wardlow. They were too late. He had been moved to safety and the mob unleashed their venom on Dewey's west side.

"The crime aroused the people of Dewey to such a state of anger that they proceeded to wipe out the Negro settlement in west Dewey," the *Bartlesville Daily Enterprise* reported two days later. It was an exaggeration, but the truth was bad enough. Twenty-one homes and the Antioch Baptist Church had been burned to the ground. Dozens of black families fled during the night and into the next day when unknown persons went house to house telling them they had to leave Dewey by sundown.

Wardlow was convicted of murder. Thanks to the involvement of *Tulsa Star* publisher and black activist A.J. Smitherman and Oklahoma Governor Robert Lee Williams, 36 members of the white community—including Dewey's own mayor—were arrested and charged with the race riot crimes. But the damage was done. A generation of black people had learned the hard way to be wary and quiet, and to keep to themselves on the west side.

Henry Kemps never learned that lesson. Maybe it was because he knew most white people in Dewey were ashamed to the point of silence by what had happened. Perhaps it was because his employer and the town's most prominent doctor, L.D. Hudson, had driven into the middle of a burning neighborhood to get Henry and his new bride, Willie, out of harm's way.

Or maybe that's just who Henry was.

• • •

It has been almost 70 years since Willa Mae Ross last saw Henry Kemps, but when she talks about him her face lights up like she's still a little girl watching from her front porch.

"Mr. Kemps would pass our house, just smiling," says the puckish 83-year-old, who has lived on Dewey's west side her whole life. "His teeth were pearly white and he wore a tie all the time. I admired him and I liked him so much because he smiled all the time. He would have waved at a cat, if a cat could wave back."

Ross saw Henry leave his and Willie's spotless, large property each morning in a Model T truck with a two-by-four holding up the front bumper. The entrepreneur would be on his way to several jobs he had cobbled together into a business: carrying patients to and from doctors' offices, running errands, delivering for two different pharmacies, and cleaning office buildings.

Dewey was a small town of 2,000 people, flanked by the smoke-blue Osage Hills on one side and the gray dust of the Portland Cement Company on the other. Those four blocks between made up Main Street and were Henry's territory. This alone set him apart from almost every other black man in town.

If you worked in Dewey in the 1930s, you were probably one of hundreds of whites, blacks, Native Americans, and Hispanics churning out 3,500 barrels of Portland Cement each day. The town's well-to-do white families owned grocery and drug stores, banks, a dry cleaner, a candy store, and movie theater. Black people shopped in these places. They didn't work in them.

"In that time, black people stayed in their part of town," says Charlotte Thaxton, an 86-year-old Dewey native who remembers the rules of a segregated Oklahoma with chagrin. "They couldn't eat in the restaurants. They couldn't use the restrooms, they couldn't drink out of the water fountains. We didn't have anything to do with black kids. We didn't see them because they didn't go to school with us."

In fact, Henry Kemps was the only black person many white children really knew.

"I didn't know anybody who didn't like Henry," Thaxton says. "He was so friendly, he was always smiling. I can just see him. He would run across the street to one of those stores and be a-waving."

George "Pete" Morrison, a retired Phillips Petroleum Company executive, retains a sharp image of Henry Kemps, even at 93.

"I remember Henry as a small man with a lot of energy and enthusiasm. He was one of us, and that was before colored people were accepted," Morrison says frankly. "The fact was that he knew everybody and he could call your name, and everybody knew him."

Henry was usually seen around town in a pressed shirt, pants, and a tie. If working for a doctor or pharmacy, he would don a white lab coat. That made an impact in Depression-era Dewey, where most men went to work in dungarees or worn overalls.

"The people who worked at the cement plant, boy, they'd get off work and you couldn't tell what color they were. They were covered in cement," Morrison says wryly.

The issues surrounding color and race weren't as easy to cover. Thaxton recalls that her father worked at Dewey Portland alongside many African Americans. Yet, he still managed to rationalize the color bar that kept them apart.

"My dad was prejudiced, but he thought the world of all those black men he worked with," she says with a touch of irony.

The same topsy-turvy, ingrained thinking allowed an entire town to openly adore Henry Kemps while referring to him as "Nigger Henry" without a trace of ill will. I cringed the first time the name came from my own father's lips. He responded by lifting his shoulders in a sign that was less an apology than a no-nonsense admission that the world he had grown up in was vastly different.

"My kids can't believe it, but that was what they called him," Thaxton says. "We didn't disrespect Henry, we loved him. We just loved him to pieces."

Contradictions weren't limited to the white community. Henry's wife, Willie Ogans Kemps, was a reserved, proper woman who carried herself with great poise. She also was a mulatto so light-skinned that she could easily have passed for white. Willie's older sister had left Dewey. One day she and Willie met by chance in a local grocery store. Willie greeted her sister with delight, only to be rejected.

"She said, 'Never, never acknowledge me again.' She was passing for white and had married a white man," says Janet Ogans Shirley, Willie's great-niece. "It was very painful for my aunt."

Willie and Henry also experienced the pain of being childless. But they had Willie's nephews and the children of the west side to spoil. Willa Mae Ross and her playmates would watch for Henry, who kept pigs and calves on a family acreage near the edge of town. He would go there after work with vegetable scraps he had salvaged from behind Dewey's grocery stores and cafes.

"Sometimes, he'd stop and he'd have candy and gum. A treat for the kids," Ross says. "We'd all be lined up on the porch. I can just hear that little Model T turning the corner."

Soon, Henry would aim his truck toward his true passion: high school football. He never missed a game, home or away, and rarely a practice. Henry was a one-man pep squad for the Dewey Bulldoggers. George Morrison was a member of the team throughout high school. "Henry knew the players, he could call them by name. He knew football," he says.

The team would be working from the moment school let out on a field surrounded by a towering, 7,000-seat grandstand. It had once been home to the Dewey Roundup, one of the world's top three rodeos, where Henry took his first local job as a horse groom.

He would be with the team until dark. "There used to be a track in front of the field in the old stadium," remembers Carl Ropp, who was on the squad in the 1940s. "He'd always meet us as we came across there and give us chewing gum."

Henry could be found in the same spot at the end of each home game. One rare photo shows him in a suit, topcoat, tie, and fedora outside the stadium. He is beaming, and at the bottom is written in white ink, "Henry says, 'We may have lost, but that sure was a good game.'"

Ropp laughs. "After the game, if we got beat, he'd say, 'Them old boys were sure big and tough.' The truth was that we just weren't as good as some of them that beat us."

There weren't many teams that could boast they beat Dewey in the 1930s. During the entire decade, the Bulldoggers lost only 17 times.

"Dewey had a history of being a powerhouse team," Morrison says. "There wasn't anything to do in Dewey except football, softball, basketball. That was it. That was the entertainment. People came there to see Dewey play football, and they always expected Dewey to win."

Expectations were mixed on the eve of the 1938 Sand Springs game. Dewey's undefeated team was described as "a gang of powerful boys with versatility and shrewdness" who had only one tied game to their debt. But Sand Springs had no losses or ties on their record and were the team to beat in the conference. Sportswriters at *Bartlesville Daily Enterprise* put the odds on Sand Springs, writing, "Two of the best high school teams in this section of the state will meet in a game that may decide the football championship of the Verdigris Valley."

More would be decided in that game than just a championship.

• • •

Under the floodlights in Sand Springs, the Dewey Bulldoggers turned their backs on 4,000 waiting fans and walked to the bench. The choice was clear: If their friend Henry Kemps could not enter the stadium, they would not play.

Henry was totally unaware 30 boys had taken a stand that could cost them everything they had worked for. He was still sitting alone in his Model T, where Mary Popkess had found him while crossing the parking lot. He had told his pharmacy employer that he had been turned away at the stadium gate because of his color. But he wasn't leaving.

"He was going to sit there and wait until the game was over so he could get the score before he went back home," says Wilbur King, who was a member of the Dewey High School marching band that night.

Henry had never been denied entrance to a game, and he had not missed watching his team play in 18 years. Oklahoma's state code segregated everything from coalmines to telephone booths, but stadiums went unmentioned. Henry had likely come across a local ordinance or custom. In the world of November 11, 1938—the 20th anniversary of Armistice Day and the night Kate Smith introduced "God Bless America" on NBC Radio—barring a black man from a high school football game had no consequence.

There were consequences for the Dewey Bulldoggers. The team had won every game that season and

held five of their competitors scoreless. Football was a lifetime highlight for those who often had only a cement plant job in their future. Nationwide, boys wearing leather helmets and pads literally lived and died to play. An article in the same week's paper touted a decrease in football-related fatalities; only 14 boys had died in the previous three months.

Coach Homer Hill, the slight man whose voice carried across an entire school, had not been defeated in conference play for five years. His record and reputation as an innovator who designed plays other coaches never dreamed of would be stained if the Bulldoggers forfeited the conference championship. In spite of that, he sat with his team on November 11 and waited.

Exactly how long they waited is unclear. Accounts vary. Some don't remember at all. My dad, a sophomore on the team, estimated that the sit-in lasted as long as 30 to 45 minutes. Watch a minute tick away. Think of boys, ages 14 to 18, refusing to surrender to thousands of anxious fans and the mounting, sour pressure of game officials. Does it matter if it was 20 minutes, or 30? What does it say about the character of those boys when the only thing standing between them and ending that pressure was loyalty to a man who couldn't even drink from the same water fountain? More important, what does it say about Henry?

Finally, someone yielded, and the power of segregation bowed to 30 high-school boys and Henry Kemps. The crowd must have heaved a sigh of relief, expecting the team to take the field. Instead, the Dewey Bulldoggers turned and ran.

"They literally took Henry out of the car, put him up on their shoulders, carried him in and set him on the players' bench," Wilbur King remembers. Henry, after all, was one of them.

On the field, the game went nowhere fast, with two experienced defenses battling it out under the lights. The game remained scoreless until the third quarter, when Sand Springs received the ball at the 80-yard line and drove the length of the field and scored. The extra point was kicked—and blocked. Sand Springs had six points on the board.

Dewey took the following kickoff at their 35-yard line and ran it to the Sand Springs 19. On the second play from scrimmage, Walter Scott—whom the quarterback writers called a "miniature tornado"—threw a 15-yard pass to fullback John Hill. He caught the ball at the three-yard line, spun and jogged in to tie the game.

Zeke Scott, the quarterback's brother and himself a small, speedy running back who doubled as Dewey's kicker, came to the line for the crucial extra point. Just two weeks before he had been a hero when his kick had made the difference against archrival Bartlesville. If he made this kick, Dewey would win the game and the conference championship. If not, the game would end in a tie, Dewey's second of the

season, and Sand Springs would take the title for their flawless record.

The stadium grew quiet. Zeke stepped back and awaited the snap. The ball went down and his kick went up, and missed. The Sands Springs crowd erupted, realizing that Dewey had just lost the Verdigris Valley Conference championship.

While the Sands Springs fans celebrated, the Bulldoggers headed toward their buses, and Henry toward his car.

A few hours later, a nine-year-old Willa Mae Ross was in her home on the west side of Dewey. She recalls a sudden confusion, loud noises and shouts, adults exchanging worried glances. What they heard was a victory rally. As soon as the Bulldoggers had arrived back in town, they had loaded up in cars and driven into the west side to circle Henry's home.

"It was such a cheering and an ovation," Ross says. "You would have thought that it was New Year's Eve. They were blowing their car horns. You could hear them all over the neighborhood and we thought, 'What's going on, what's happened?'

"I only found out when I went to school the next morning. The principal, Professor Wardell MacNamee, said that Mr. Kemps had had a celebration. They were celebrating Henry Kemps because he had opened up the barrier.

"We asked, 'What barrier?' and he said, 'The color barrier.'"

. . .

Before they all could graduate, a third of the 1938 Dewey Bulldoggers would have a new battle to fight. Two of them—Bud Shull and Gene Stead—would not come home from World War II alive.

Henry grew ill the same year that the war began. People recall seeing him use a cane around town, and he quit travelling with the team. Still, his smiling face was at every home game. In mid-December of 1943, when ads were filled with ribbons, bells and "cheery good wishes," an obituary four times larger than any other was published in Dewey's paper, the *Washington Countian*.

"This community was shocked to learn that Henry Lee Kemps had passed away," the editor wrote. "Henry Kemps was an exceptional colored man, he was a good citizen, a good provider for his home which he owned, was thrifty in his dealings and was always looking to the future.

"It was about 23 years that he did not miss a Dewey High School football game at home or on a road trip." Then he added, "To show the respect the Dewey Bulldoggers had for Henry, they attended the funeral to a body."

A new team had crossed the color line for their friend.

Originally published
April 2016

by Jimmy Maxwell

DOWN THROUGH THERE

A member of the United Aryan Brotherhood reflects on his time behind bars

I'd been sweating. The nights leading up to my release were sleepless, haunted by turbulent dreams that something would go wrong again. I finally laid down on that last evening, trying to will myself to sleep so I would wake up and it would be time to go. Finally, there it was: daybreak.

"Maxwell, bunk and junk," the guard said when he came by. Four words of freedom.

I took a moment to see all my friends and Brothers one last time, then I was off to the laundry. My closest Brothers helped me haul my Bureau of Prisons-issued bedding, clothing, and personal property up the hill. There, the laundry officer checked off my belongings from when I had first arrived and signed me out. We then walked to the administration building, where I said my last goodbyes to the Bros who were left on the yard after the last incident. I had some good Brothers and some good friends there, so a bit of my spirit would remain and I would carry with me a little of theirs. After a few final hugs and a wave, I turned and went through the Admin doors on my last round to the business office to get my check. Over the course of 16 years, I had accrued a total of $232.85 to begin my future with. From there, I went to the warden's secretary for my release papers and, finally, the last stop: Property. That's where they have you change out of your prison khakis into street clothes, which your friends or family should provide. That, or some Salvation Army crap the prison kept on hand.

Every step I took my pulse quickened. I worried that an officer would holler, *Maxwell, there has been a mistake. Your release has been cancelled!* Each breath I took, I silently prayed not to hear those words, mad at myself for even thinking them.

I understand people want things to be black or white, but the truth is that life is a lot of grays. The Aryan Brotherhood has never been a racial thing with me, just a prison thing. It's that way for a lot of people. Unfortunately, people want to hate something, and I guess I'll always be a stereotype. I didn't break away from the Brotherhood for racial reasons or any big epiphany that I all of a sudden didn't hate people of others races, because I never hated them in the first place. My first wife and mother of my children is even half Korean. I'm laying it out how it really is for most Caucasian people in prison, or in low-income housing projects. I broke free of the hood because the hood *is*

RACE READER

prison. I am at a place in my life that I don't want to be in prison, physically or mentally. I don't want to be involved in drugs or crime or the pain of others in any way, shape, or form anymore, or with people who believe living in prison is an acceptable way of life. That is why I stepped away. That doesn't mean I don't have memories.

· · ·

Six months leading up to my scheduled release, every member of my little band of Universal Aryan Brotherhood [UAB] pals and I went to lock-up for stomping all the Oklahoma Skinheads off the yard. There are differences within the Aryan Brotherhood. Almost every state has its own branch and its own leadership: Skinheads, KKK, Dirty White Boys, and groups like the Aryan Circle. Each are independent of the rest, but bound by the code that governs the overall white brother-hooded community—with severe consequences when it is broken. In this case, the Skinheads had an unholy arrangement going on with the prison's Captain of Security. Apparently, one of them had a "give and take" relationship with the Captain, which had carried over from another yard, where he'd been his stool pigeon. When the Captain asked that skinhead's Brothers to cover for him, they agreed. They sold out for promises of favor, breaking the cardinal convict prescript, and in doing so ensured their own destruction. My impending discharge almost derailed when several of them ended up in the hospital. We lost Ricky to the surveillance camera tapes. Thank God they were too grainy to identify anyone else.

Not long after that, around 30 pounds of tobacco were found behind the toilet paper roll holder in the bathroom wall of the dental lab where I worked. Ever since they made all federal and most state prison yards tobacco-free environments, a single small cigarette goes for five or six dollars and a one-ounce pouch can bring $150. Tobacco in that quantity equals a significant amount of money, about $20,000–$30,000. An officer obviously brought it in, which makes it, in the minds of security and the administration, a big deal.

They rounded up all of the dental lab workers, about 15 including myself, and put us in the Secure Housing Unit, or SHU (pronounced "shoe"). We spent a couple of weeks in the hole, until someone broke and told them what they wanted to know. The rat turned out to be the only one they kept locked up and let the rest of us out. The officer got scared and wouldn't return to work, so the police got a warrant, went to his house, and caught him with more tobacco, weed, and heroin packaged to be brought into the yard. They fired us all and shut down the dental lab program.

A few weeks later, about a month before I was to be released to 90 days of halfway house, Darold "D.K." Ellsworth—a good friend who'd celled with three of the four years I'd been there—approached me during a chow call.

"I don't know if you've already heard this, or if it's even true, but I figure if it is, you'll want to know about it…" He hesitated, rubbing his stubby fingers back over his bald dome, as if he was fixing to tell me something he'd rather not.

D.K. made the decisions for his particular group of A.B.Ts, the Aryan Brotherhood of Texas; I called everything for Oklahoma. We trusted and had backed each other, more than once.

I took in the demeanor of the short, stocky con, and I could see something was bothering him. "I'm listening," I replied.

D.K. said some Oklahoma independent whiteboys had sold a little white Okie kid to a black Puerto Rican on A-Unit. "Independent," in these circumstances, refers to people who have no gang/family affiliations. However, they are still beholden to adhere to the same ethical standard as the rest of us, with similar consequences when failing to do so. This is regardless of whether they are a patch-holder or not and bartering off some young white boy to be a sex slave, especially to another race, was definitely a violation of that standard.

"That can't be true!" I said, shooting him a sideways glance out of my narrowed eyes. "But you can bet I'll look into it, to be sure."

I was more or less just assuming it was some bullshit story. I had people up in A-Unit who were supposed to ensure things like that didn't happen. Not to mention, on this yard, the UAB strictly enforced racial respect and racial boundaries. Separatism reigns in prison. Every race governs their own people, and if something happens between different skin tones, it is discussed by those calling the shots and the outcome is handled. White or black, Mexican or Indian, we all tried to keep the operation of the prison running smooth because we were all involved in different (some quite lucrative) money making hustles, which directly depended upon it.

Hell, when new people arrive on a unit, they are met by a committee of representatives from their own race who check their paperwork, meaning court documents to show they were not government collaborators, and their gang affiliations, and if *not* affiliated, hook them up with people from their state who would then give them a care package if need be and help them find a cell with their own people. Or sometimes, if there's a problem, e.g.: their paperwork doesn't check out, or they are from a rival gang, send them out on a stretcher.

Occasionally, prison administrators send new people in when there were no cells of their race available. The "committee" will then tell the new guy, if he's not smart enough to do it on his own, that he must refuse housing and sit in lock-up until things get shifted around.

I marked D.K.'s account as something that needed to be clarified.

When our unit was finally called, D.K. and I walked to chow together. We discussed the recent tornados and my wife's fearful trip down from Guymon through the thunderstorms with her cat, Cricket, and her little Pomeranian, Ruby.

After reaching the mess hall and getting our trays, we went our separate ways—D.K. to go sit at one of the ABT tables and me to sit at one of the UAB tables. It was just a sign of respect that the rest of the population would leave our tables and a couple of other families' tables, such as the Aryan Circle and the Dirty White Boys, empty for us. There were a couple of U-abs (slang for a member of the UAB) seated at two of our tables, men from different units who had already eaten.

I noticed Drew sitting at a table by himself. Drew is a 6'5", bald-headed 33-year-old with a pile of time. He had the job of handling his Brothers, our business ventures, and whatever else needed to be watched over on A-Unit. He looked up when I sat down.

"Hey, Brother, how's your wife doing? Did she make it alright through that tornado?" he asked. I told him she had, even though she and her freaked-out animals had to take cover under an overpass at one point.

"Man, you sure got a good woman," Drew finished.

"She should be up to visit tomorrow," I said. Then I told him what I'd heard, even though I couldn't imagine it to be true.

"Well, if it did happen, it would be Shannon Fry and his bunch." Drew went on to tell me they had some slow-witted youngster down on Shannon's end of the building that they tormented on a regular basis. Rumor had it that they even had been molesting the kid and torturing him with hot metal objects that they'd held over an open flame.

I could feel my blood turn to molten lava as anger came surging up through my throat into my head.

"How could you not know if this is true or not?" I asked.

"Look, Brother, I don't mess around with those people down there," he said. "But, we can go find out." We got up and threw our uneaten trays in the slop window and headed toward A-Unit, a red wave of rage threatening to overwhelm me as we stormed up the sidewalk.

Suddenly, Drew pointed, "Shit, bro, there's that kid right there." I looked and saw a youngster in his early 20s walking up the sidewalk. He had dishwater-col-ored hair that sat on his head like seaweed, and it was clear that he wasn't well-hinged by the slack look in his face.

"Hey!" I yelled at him. He froze in the middle of the walk, looking like a cornered rabbit.

"Is it true someone sold you to a Puerto Rican?!"

"Y-y-yes," he timidly replied. Trapped in the intensity of my growing anger.

"Who the hell did that to you?" I gritted, feeling my face get flush.

The kid was trembling. He was afraid to tell me and afraid not to tell me.

"I'd rather not say," he said, pleading with his eyes.

"You don't have to," I exploded. "I already know!!"

I did know. It was Drew who had said it probably was Shannon Fry. Shannon was a big ol' corn-fed peckerwood from McAlester, Oklahoma. He was strong as a draft horse with a head on him like a gator-mouth pit, and was someone I already didn't like.

He and his brother had written to us from jail the year before and told us they were Okies who wanted to stay in Oklahoma, close to their families. However, the guy who testified on them was on the El Reno yard. They asked if we would help them out because the BOP would not send them to a yard that housed someone with an obvious sepratee against them. (A "sepratee" is paperwork an official files to make sure two people who cannot exist peacefully, for whatever reason, on the same prison yard do not end up on the same yard.)

We discussed the Frys' letter as a group since this involved putting our own people at risk for non-patch holders. It was my opinion that I would rather have solid people on the yard than a known snitch who could become a potential problem for us in the future. Besides, we had a couple of prospects who needed to put some work in anyway. In this case, "putting in work" is an act—violent or otherwise—that a member or a prospective member of a brotherhood performs strictly for that faction. As a matter of fact, one of the prospects knew the Frys and spoke up for them—and volunteered for the job. The vote was unanimous in favor of the Frys, so we sent our volunteer and another prospect to handle it. It was handled. Ace, the little Brother with the mask on, got away with it. Cole, our volunteer, ran right out in front of the surveillance camera and went to lock-up.

The rat was gone, and one of the Fry brothers, Shannon, made it to El Reno. Considering the next closest federal prison they could have went to was in either Leavenworth, Kansas, or Beaumont, Texas, it was a pretty good favor.

Cole was still in jail for the assault when Shannon showed up. The Fry brother was grateful and thanked us for helping him and looked out for Cole until he got out of lock-up. They stuck together like wet toilet paper until Cole discharged. Cole finally got his patch right before he left.

No sooner than Cole was gone, it reached me that Shannon was up on A-block running him down about something supposedly out of their past. I took Shannon out on the ballfield and asked him what kind of guy waits until their friends are gone to talk about them behind their backs. He denied the accusation and tried to explain it away as a misunderstanding. I told him I would stand in the gap for any of my Brothers in their absence and even though he was a big ol' boy, if anything else came up, we were going to go down through there, meaning we were going to fight.

My taste for him was already soured when this latest insult to the dignity of the people of our state came up; the audacity and shame was more than I could stand. I had spent all my time there looking out for the white Oklahomans, securing a safe environment for them by pushing all the other gangs out of Oklahoman affairs. To have one do this to another weaker one, one with clear mental health issues at that, caused me to blow my shit.

Enraged, I made a beeline straight for Shannon's building. By the time I got to the doors of his unit, I wasn't concerned about losing my halfway-house date.

Drew was working to keep up behind me, stress etched in his face. He tried to remind me that my wife expected me to come home to her and told me he and the others would handle it. I was just too furious to hear any of it. Somewhere in the back of my mind was a vision of Jenna in tears, but I couldn't stop.

I stormed into A-Unit and saw Shannon leaning against a pillar outside of his room. He was listening to his Walkman and took the headphones off his closely cropped blond head when he saw me coming. "Hit the cell," I snarled. This was it. I was tired of messing with the man. I told my other Brothers who were gathering to stay out of it, and he and I rolled up in his room for war.

Now, Shannon is about 6'3" and around 250 pounds, but I am not a little man myself. I'm real close to 6'2" and about 240 pounds, so it was a heavyweight battle. That big catfish head of his could take a punch, and I'm fairly infamous for how hard I hit. I never did drop him, but by the time the look-out reported guards heading to our side of the building, Shannon's head was twice its normal size.

When I got out of his unit and back to my cell, I found out I had a few contusions as well. However, nothing noticeable that would catch the attention of the staff. Somehow I had made it through my momentary loss of control without tricking everything off.

As my adrenalin subsided and with my anger and indignation expended on Shannon's head, my thoughts turned to Jenna and what a close call I'd just had.

She'd be upset if I had gotten caught and lost my halfway house and good time. I forgot all that as soon as one of my bros and D.K. came through my door and told me Shannon's head was all swollen up and he wanted a re-match before he went to jail. I told them to tell him to bring his ass down on my unit this time. We would clear out the TV room and box until one of us couldn't walk out, but Shannon was afraid there were too many of us down on my unit and wanted a more neutral spot, like the ballfield. *Is he shitting me?* I thought. I probably should have just stood my ground and sent word to either come to me or suck it up, but I was still mad, and to have that piece of crap call me out made me madder still.

D.K. and Mize, another of my Brothers, were standing there with me.

"The cocksucker is just trying to save some face and make sure I'm going to lock-up with him," I said. "If I wasn't going home in a month, I'd stab him full of holes for this."

Whether it stopped me from going home or not, I wasn't going to hesitate to at least rip into him again, so I headed out to the ballfield. It was a nice spring day. *As good a day as any to fuck-off everything I'd worked so long for,* I thought. He finally showed up, wary of the possibility I had brought a shank

To minimize the risk of getting caught, D.K. and I told our guys to keep everyone except Shannon back away from the ballfield so we wouldn't draw a crowd. They told him I would wait for him, by myself, out in the field, where, hopefully, the police would really have to be looking to see a couple dudes out there banging it out. It wasn't a bad plan, except for the gawker factor—everyone on the yard is drawn to a fight like bees on honey. All the prisoners stopped what they were doing, stood and stared from where they were. When the guard finally looked out the window, he saw everybody looking up the hill. He looked to see what the attraction was, and there we were, two big bulls in a field duking it out like something out of a John Wayne movie. It didn't take long for the rec officer to call in the cavalry to break it up and take us into custody.

Shannon fared a little better this time, and I had picked up a new shiner, but by now his head was looking like Sloth from the movie *The Goonies*, so they took him to medical first. I was sitting outside, waiting my turn, just seething at the fact I was now going to the SHU. Everything my wife and I worked for and had planned for so long was going to be blown away like smoke in a breeze. I was so angry with Shannon and with myself for allowing him to do this to me and my wife, this second go-round so plainly designed to ensure that I went to lock-up also. I almost wished that I had taken a knife out there and punched a bunch of holes in him for the anguish it was going to cause Jenna when she found out.

The whole time I was sitting there cuffed, thinking about this. The officers standing there with me, escorting me first to see the doc, then to jail, were asking me why the fight occurred. I could give no reply. All I could do is sit there and growl in frustration and anger at the whole situation.

Though I may have had a good, even justifiable, reason for taking Shannon on, as far as I was concerned "the man" would never know the whys of this. Prison Law: no matter what, you never talk. I could not tell staff what Shannon had done to drive me to the point of taking this self-sacrificing action against him, no matter the cost to myself. That's just the price of the path I've chosen, but I would be lying if I said that it was not a hard price to pay sometimes.

Anyway, after the medical process of being looked over and cleared of any internal injuries, the officers took Shannon off to one wing of the SHU and me to another. They threw me into a cell by myself, which made contemplating my misfortune all the more miserable. I finally fell asleep with the thoughts of my impending visit with my wife the next day, our first visit since she'd moved. I knew this would crush her.

I woke up the next morning to the Captain and Lieutenant at my cell door yelling at me. Apparently there were a couple hundred white boys piled up on the yard. They were all the members of one family or another from the other states backing my Brothers, as they braced all the independent Caucasoid from every state. The Captain and the prison staff didn't know what was going on, and I certainly didn't either. I couldn't even see out of the window because of the metal shutters that were bolted to the outside wall in order to keep inmates in the SHU as clueless as possible. Nevertheless, it didn't stop them from demanding I stop whatever was going on.

"We've went to lockdown and I need this yard moving. We have a steel factory to run here, damn it!" the Captain griped at me. I replied that I didn't know anything. I was obviously unaware of what was going on, and had no way of stopping it if I did.

"I don't care! I know this shit is stemming from you and Fry's fight yesterday," he finished.

"Look, Cap, I'm not going to tell you what we were fighting about," I said. "But, maybe, you should just open the yard back up and let the *rest* of the trash be taken out." They walked off muttering to themselves about them taking the trash out and me not liking the trash that they collected. I went and sat down praying my visit wouldn't be affected by this, but also dreading the betrayed look I would see on my wife's face when she saw I was in lock-up.

Right on time, 9 AM, they came to get me for the visit. My heart pushed the blood through my veins with increasing urgency as it always did in anticipation of seeing Jenna. My feet were trying to hold me back, like I was walking through concrete, trying to keep me from the impending scene that I was fixing to endure.

I stepped through the door of the visiting room and looked over to the normal seats Jenna usually chose to sit us at. As I walked in, I watched the bright, excited smile fall from her face in shocked despair at seeing me led through the doors in handcuffs, wearing an orange detention jump suit.

"What did you do?" she yelled at me, and then erupted into tears. She knew what this meant. It wasn't the first time, but, after having her move away from everything she knew, with just her animals, to be with me when I got out, she felt betrayed. Jenna was bawling by the time she got moved from her normal spot to where the officer had me sit, which was right out in front of the desk where all SHU visits had to take place. She was hitting me even before the guard made it around into his cubical.

At 5'3" and 120 pounds, with long brown hair that hangs all the way down past her thin waist to her shapely ass, my wife can be the prettiest thing in the world. Along with the store-bought big C-cup boobs I'd bought her when I was in the State Penitentiary at McAlester, she could make my heart skip a beat with just a smile. However, it tortured my soul when she was sad or hurt. Now she wouldn't even look at me. I tried to get through her wall of tears, asking her to hear me out, that I had no choice, what had happened had caused me to momentarily lose control. I held her hands in mine, partly so she wouldn't hit me anymore, and quietly relayed the story to her as she sobbed.

Originally published
August 2013

by Steve Gerkin

WATTS AND CLARY

The odd couple of civil rights reconciliation

Johnny Lee Clary with Lynn Watts

Dressed only in his boxers, Wade Watts, a black civil rights activist reclined on the sofa. He read the morning paper while bacon, eggs, and pork sausage sizzled in the kitchen. The cook leaned into the living room doorway.

"Do you think your friend Martin Luther King, who dreamt that one day blacks and whites could come together, ever imagined it might include us?"

Johnny Lee Clary, former Imperial Wizard of the White Knights of the Ku Klux Klan, returned to the stove.

From the other room, Watts, an evangelist and longtime leader of the NAACP, shouted his answer.

"No," he said, "I don't believe the dream would have gone that far. But don't burn this couch after I leave, honky!"

A few years earlier, that may have been a possibility. While Johnny Lee was the Grand Dragon of the Oklahoma Klan, the Klan set fire to Watts' church, nearly burning it to the ground.

As the Grand Dragon of Oklahoma, Clary launched an all-out campaign of retribution against the disciple of love, the Reverend Watts. During a late-1970s radio debate in Oklahoma City, Watts tormented Clary, citing scripture and sprinkling his rebuttals with "Jesus loves you." Embarrassed Klan protégées listened to the destruction of Johnny Lee.

Wade Watts was born in the hills of Kiamichi, southeast Oklahoma, in 1919. Indoctrinated into the teachings of the Baptist church at a young age, he committed his life to Christian ideals. At 17, Watts joined the NAACP. The organization elected him the state president in 1968, a position he held for 16 years. His respect within the civil rights community escalated as he fought for desegregation of public facilities and institutions during the 1940s and 1950s. His work with Justice Thurgood Marshall paved the way for a Supreme Court decision to allow admittance of a black woman, Ada Lois Sipuel, to the University of Oklahoma law school in 1949. Even then, she was required to sit alone in class in a chair marked "colored." She ate in a section of the cafeteria cordoned off by a chain so she could not mix with white students.

Watts fought hard within Oklahoma to ensure that blacks received equal educational opportunities

Johnny Lee Clary in 1980 as the Grand Wizard of the Ku Klux Klan.

through segregation in the public school system. His efforts benefited his nephew Julius Caesar Watts, who was educated in the newly integrated schools in Eufaula. J. C., as he was known, became a national-class quarterback for the University of Oklahoma, and he was free to saunter the campus unencumbered by racial boundaries.

In 1965, Wade Watts marched with his good friend Martin Luther King Jr. in Selma, Alabama, to demonstrate for racial freedom, justice, and equality. President Lyndon Johnson appointed Watts to the Civil Rights Commission. Within his home state, he served on the Human Rights Commission while maintaining his day job as labor inspector for the Oklahoma State Labor Commission. His passion for racial acceptance started at an early age—after his first exposure to hate.

As a young boy, Wade played with a white companion who invited him home for lunch. He was not allowed to sit at the table; instead, he was led to the back porch, where the mother handed him a bowl of food. The family dog became incensed with Wade, barking and trying to bite him. His friend explained that the dog was mad because Wade was eating out of his dish. This would not be the last time a plate of food reminded him of racial discrimination.

In the late 1950s, Watts and his good friend, the powerful Oklahoma State Senator Gene Stipe, entered an Ada cafe for lunch. The waitress stopped them, saying, "We don't serve Negroes." Watts responded, "I don't eat Negroes. I just came to get some ham and eggs." Leaving the establishment, Stipes asked Watts: If God would grant you one wish, what would it be? The senator anticipated his companion might answer no more hate in the world. Without hesitation, Watts said he wanted to meet the leader of the Ku Klux Klan.

· · ·

In a small San Francisco suburb, during this time, Johnny Lee Clary was born into a hate-mongering environment. Soon after his birth, the Clary family returned to their small, central Oklahoma hometown of Del City—a predominately white city. His bigoted daddy continued his hard-working ways, while his alcoholic mother strayed with multiple lovers. Johnny Lee's dad, also, taught him those were not "chocolate-covered" men but "niggers." Clary's uncle, Harold, bragged he shot a black man for crossing his yard and only got fined for firing a gun within the city limits.

At age 11, Johnny walked into the house and witnessed his father's suicide. Just as Johnny screamed, "Don't do it," Dad put a .45-caliber slug into his head. Mom quickly moved in with her boyfriend, who beat the traumatized youngster, which prompted Johnny to complain to the police. After law enforcement threatened the couple with jail, the boyfriend delivered an ultimatum: Johnny or him. His mother kicked young Clary out of the house. The tough kid ended up with an older sister in gang-laden Los Angeles, where the beatings continued at the hand of her lover. A despondent Johnny Lee Clary desperately wanted a family that wanted him.

Watching TV one afternoon, Clary found it. The interviewer was questioning David Duke, the Imperial Wizard of the Ku Klux Klan. Recalling Uncle Harold's story, Clary contacted the Klan. An emissary of Duke knocked on his door several weeks later.

The KKK recruiter told him the Klan was a family with a spiritual basis and took him to weekly meetings where people who wanted to hear what he had to say surrounded the teenager. He diligently studied the Klan. He trembled with excitement the day he was officially inducted. Clary was 14. With his new support system's guidance, he had learned how to hate.

Clary ascended the Klan ranks quickly. He went from David Duke's bodyguard to an overly ambitious Kleagle (or recruiter) in Del City to the leader of the Oklahoma Klan as the Grand Dragon at the not-so-tender age of 21. Clary was on the career path he desired—to become Imperial Wizard of the KKK. His physicality would bring him other successes.[1]

In 1979, an Oklahoma City radio host invited Clary to participate in an on-air debate with a black man. Licking his chops at "a chance to put a black man in his place," Grand Dragon Clary jumped at the chance to spread the gospel of hate. Clary told all his buddies to tune in. His debate opponent was the Reverend Wade Watts, veteran pastor of the Jerusalem Baptist Church in McAlester, Oklahoma.

As the two approached each other for the 1979 broadcast, Clary was shocked.

"He caught me off guard," Clary told an Australian TV host. "I'm expecting this black militant to come in with a great big afro this big (gestures), and an African dashiki on, with bones around and a button on that says 'I hate honkies' and 'Death to crackers.'" But, what he saw was a well-groomed man in a suit and tie, carrying a Bible.

Watts put out his hand and the confused Clary took it, only to withdraw it quickly after the first touch. He had just broken a cardinal Klan rule. The Reverend saw Clary looking at his hand and reassured him, "Don't worry, Johnny. It won't come off."

Clary started calling him a string of epithets.

"I just want to tell you I love you and Jesus loves you," Watts replied.

The on-air back and forth featured Clary spouting off about how the races should not interact, while the reverend calmly quoted scripture. Clary was reduced to mumbling generic Klan slogans.

"I'm not listening to any more," Clary snarled, storming out.

Holding a baby in his arms, the Reverend approached the Grand Dragon, who was hurriedly gathering up his belongings in the lobby. Wade introduced his 14th child, an adopted baby girl, born to a young white girl and black teenage boy.

"Mr. Clary, this is my daughter, Tia." As he held out the little girl with shining black eyes and skin, showering Johnny Lee with a sweet smile, Watts said, "You say you hate all black people. Just tell me, how can you hate this child?"

The Dragon nearly ran for the door. Watt's final words rang out like church bells: "God bless you, Johnny. You can't do enough to me to make me hate you. I'm gonna love you and I'm gonna pray for you, whether you like it or not."

The embarrassment caused Clary to turn up the heat on Watts. But intimidating phone calls, crosses burning at his home, and garbage strewn in his front yard failed to curb Watts' public quest for equality.

---

1 While he was the Grand Dragon of Oklahoma, Clary became a professional wrestler. He called himself "Johnny Angel" and won the Arkansas Heavyweight title several times in the late 1980s. His final pro match was a win in Grove, Oklahoma, during a 10-Man Battle Royal in 1988. Still, the Klan was his oyster.

The Reverend joined up with politicians to outlaw the Klan's racist telemarketing hotlines that recruited for the Klan: "Save the land, join the Klan." Johnny Lee was incensed.

Sporting KKK t-shirts, 30 Klansmen, led by Clary, followed Watts into a McAlester lunch spot. Surrounding him and his plate of fried chicken, Clary chortled, "Hey, boy, I'm gonna make you a promise. We are going to do the same thing to you that you do to that chicken."

Watts surveyed the Klan before picking up a piece of chicken and kissing it. The room erupted with laughter, but Clary was livid.

Clary's robed friends set fire to the Jerusalem Baptist Church. The fire was extinguished before building was destroyed, but Clary felt like gloating, so he called Wade, using a disguised voice. Watts greeted him cordially, saying, "Well, hello, Johnny." He continued,

"A man like you takes the time to call me. Let me do something for you." He begins to pray, "Dear Lord, please, forgive Johnny for being so stupid." Then he invited all of them to dinner at Pete's Place in Krebs.

The Klan decided to leave him alone.

For more than a decade, Clary lived in Tulsa near 71st and Lewis. He was a drinker, a fighter, and a womanizer; yet, he never forgot the image of little Tia, and he never forgot the impact of his grandma in Del City praying constantly for him to quit the Klan and find the Lord. He admired Jimmy Swaggart and would smoke cigarettes while listening to Brother Swaggart go on and on about forgiveness. And Tia, who was the illegitimate daughter of a teenage J.C. Watts, sneaked into his consciousness regularly.

In 1989, Johnny Lee had reached his Klan goal. He became the Imperial Wizard of the White Knights of the Ku Klux Klan—the hate and white supremacy leaders of the world. Yet, there were serious divisions with the Klan. The feds trailed his every move. His girlfriend was unveiled as an FBI informant and the Klan pulled guns on Clary claiming he was untrustworthy. Clary pointed his gun at them and backed out of the room.

The Klan was not the family he thought it might be; rather, it was full of internal hate and mistrust. Like his father before him, Clary picked up his gun, intending to end his life. A ray of sun shone through the blinds and onto his Bible. Setting his gun down, he opened the holy book and read for hours.

Imperial Wizard Johnny Lee Clary quit the Klan after six months of failure. His effort to unite all the hate groups—skinheads, neo-Nazis, Aryan Nation—as a common entity ended in FBI phone tapping, arrests, and brothers of hate turning on each other. He burned his robe in the backyard, feeling that "1,000 pounds" had been removed from his shoulders. He joined Billy Joe Daugherty's Victory Christian Church across from Oral Roberts University and steadfastly immersed himself in Christian education. After two years, he called Reverend Watts.

Clary told him that he had a calling to preach, and Watts invited him to give his first sermon at his rebuilt church. Half of the congregation boycotted his service. When Johnny Lee made the altar call for anyone wanting to turn their life over to Jesus, a 14-year-old black girl came running down the aisle. More followed. As Johnny and the young girl passed Reverend Watts, there were tears staining the elder's face.

"Johnny, you are leading Tia to the Lord," Wade whispered. Three other Watts children joined them at the altar. The former Imperial Wizard brought the last of Watt's 14 children into the house of the Lord.

Watts and Clary became evangelical preachers that drove across the country together. Driving through Arkansas, Clary turned to Watts and asked if he ever thought the two of them would be driving in the same car on their way to save some souls. Wade looked at him, and quipped quickly, "I figured if we were ever in the same car together, you would have me in the trunk." But their relationship was on borrowed time.

Reverend Wade Watts passed in 1998. He is buried in McIntosh County, Oklahoma, beneath his tombstone that reads, "I'd give up silver and gold to have it said that I helped someone."

The Reverend Johnny Lee Clary is with the World Evangelism Fellowship and preaches for Jimmy Swaggart Ministries in Baton Rouge, Louisiana, where he often reminds his international TV audience that Wade Watts preached, "If you want to make beautiful music, you got to use those black and white keys together."

In the end, they enjoyed seven good years of harmony.

Ralph Ellison
Col-1   69

Originally published
April 2014

by Michael Mason

FATHER OF FIGHT CLUB

**The enduring influence of
Ralph Ellison's *Invisible Man***

In 1945, an unassuming black man from Oklahoma City began constructing an intricate book inside a barn in Vermont. Owing to its complexity and sophistication, the book took more than six years to assemble. When Ralph Ellison's *Invisible Man* exploded onto the scene in 1952, it caught countless minds on fire. Critics hailed it as one of the most important books of the times, a masterpiece that confronted America's race problem through a series of blistering allegories. What critics couldn't predict, however, was how prescient and influential the book would become.

The naked woman gyrates sensuously before the group of young black men, conjuring up as much awkwardness as arousal. Moments later, the young men are blindfolded, corralled into a boxing ring, and told to start fighting—a "battle royal." They pummel each other in a chaotic frenzy until one of them is declared victor. Following the fight, the sweaty and bruised contestants all clamor onto a pile of prize money that's rigged with an electrical current, shocking the young men into convulsions. It's all fun and games for the rich white men watching. The finale comes when one of the fighters, "the smartest boy we got out there in Greenwood," stands to deliver a speech. Blood spews from his mouth as he argues for the social responsibility of Negroes.

The opening chapter of Ralph Ellison's *Invisible Man* hooked America in the eye when it first appeared in 1952. It wasn't a friendly book then, and it's grown even more ferocious through the years. In those days, America's civil rights discussions had long been dominated by decades of polite, deferential rhetoric from black leaders like Booker T. Washington. America

RALPH ELLISON

UOMO INVISIBILE

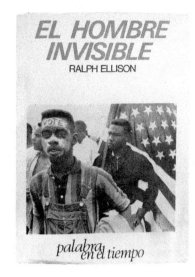

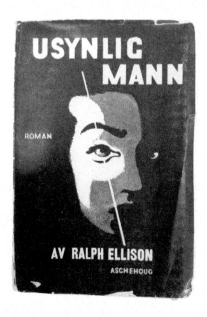

had never heard from a black man who dared scream in its face, at least not in the way that Ellison did. *Invisible Man* earned him a National Book Award and a reputation.

Ellison was a terror. Young black writers raged because he wasn't helpful to them and sometimes even hurt budding careers; he used his literary status to enjoy privileged (mainly white) company; he was "potentially violent, very violent" according to a friend; he unapologetically fucked women he wasn't supposed to, while married to a woman he loved and tormented. We owe him our thanks for not being a nice guy and instead choosing a life of passion and freedom. True to his sense of artistic integrity, Ellison eventually committed the ultimate crime of modern American literature: He refused to let filmmakers turn his book into a movie.

It only took Hollywood 47 years to figure out how to get around Ellison's disapproval. In 1999, it released a cinematic homage: *Fight Club,* based on the 1996 book by Chuck Palahniuk. Both works have nameless narrators. Both narrators live off the grid in desolate urban settings. Both become leaders of anti-establishment organizations (in *Fight Club* it's Project Mayhem, in *Invisible Man,* it's The Brotherhood). Both wrestle with madness vis-à-vis lobotomies, one by shock, the other by bullet. The two books tackle class warfare and culminate in scenes of social upheaval, with *Invisible Man*'s Harlem erupting into a race riot while *Fight Club* ends with exploding buildings.

In one direct parallel, Ellison's narrator gives the elegy for a fallen Brotherhood comrade, during which he repeats the phrase "His name was Tod Clifton" to drum in a sense of individuality. When a Project Mayhem comrade dies in *Fight Club*, the narrator repeats "His name is Robert Paulson" and the phrase echoes among the group. And then there are instances where *Fight Club*'s narrator argues with *Invisible Man*:

"Be your own father, young man," a man advises Ellison's narrator.

"Maybe we didn't need a father to complete ourselves," says *Fight Club*.

Nobody can accuse Palahniuk of plagiarizing *Invisible Man*. Palahniuk's book is one continuous monologue, a voice that epitomizes the barbaric yelp of today's disenfranchised cubicle workers. *Fight Club*'s young man tries to reclaim his masculinity while embracing the madness of a world. He's confused, irreverent, caustic, and earnest. Ellison's narrator is older, tougher, and more soulful than Palahniuk's speaker. Readers of *Invisible Man* aren't talked at.

Instead, they're led on an allegorical journey through America's racial divide.

While the congruence between *Invisible Man* and *Fight Club* seems uncanny, Chuck Palahniuk claimed that he was actually writing "*The Great Gatsby*, just updated a little." Ellison, on the other hand, credited the modernist poet T.S. Eliot as one of his major inspirations, and Ellison used the influence to let his subconscious flower. *Invisible Man* contains sudden turns into jazz song and poetry, interruptions that confound and entice. Ellison's narrator grapples with his plural identities of student, worker, leader, lover, and citizen, fragmenting his sense of self. *Invisible Man* isn't just a novel, but Ellison's own experience of individuation—the process whereby a person integrates his subconscious into his consciousness and emerges as a more authentic and fully-realized human.[1] As a human experience catalogued, *Invisible Man* is a thank-you note to the monsters who've betrayed you, a fist in the face of power, a triumphant reckoning with the mess in the mirror. Where *Fight Club* peaks as a manifesto against corporatism, *Invisible Man* is a transcendent bildungsroman for modern man.

Sixty some years after its publication, *Invisible Man* still feels dangerous and alive. Eyeballs pop out of heads, rape fantasies are entertained, boilers explode. You can practically feel the book ticking in your hands as you turn the pages. *Invisible Man* has a thrilling narrative, but it's also buttressed by existential meditations that now seem prescient. Ellison's notion of invisibility is no longer exclusive to the experience of black Americans, it's become a fundamental trait of the American anti-hero.

When *Fight Club* premiered as a movie, it achieved modest success and, like the book, missed out on major awards. Nevertheless, it became pop-culture shorthand for anything having to do with alienation and social rebellion. Though *Invisible Man* was a critically acclaimed, it has never been made into a movie. There are, however, indications that the Ellison estate is softening its no-film stance. In 2013, the estate allowed a stage production of *Invisible Man*, on the condition that the producer kept a strict adherence to the text. The play was well-received but short lived.

At some point, the book will become public domain and a film will be made, Ellison be damned. Whether or not it's a good idea to turn the book into a film is beside the point. *Fight Club* makes its clear that *Invisible Man* has, like any good rebel, already outgrown the control of its creator.

---

1 Decades before *Invisible Man*, the psychologist who came up with the theory of individuation wrote the book *Liber Novus*. Carl Jung claimed The Red Book (as it's commonly called) formed the basis for all of his future work on the collective unconscious, synchronicity, and individuation. It remained relatively unknown until it was published in 2009. Illustrated and calligraphed by Jung himself, the book looks like an ancient medieval text, decorated by mythic drawings. The prose reads like a dense sacred text, at times dreamlike and profound and at others inaccessible and unsettling.

Originally published
February 2012

by Collin Hinds

SERVING KAGAME

Paul Kagame

Genocide on trial in
Oklahoma federal court

On April 30, 2010, a team of lawyers and process servers arrived at the campus of Oklahoma Christian University (OCU) in Edmond to serve notice of a civil lawsuit that had been filed the day before in federal court in Oklahoma City. The defendant being served was His Excellency Paul Kagame, president of the long-troubled African Republic of Rwanda, a country famously drenched in the blood of genocide. While lawyers pleaded with American Secret Service agents and Kagame's body guards to allow them to deliver summons and the hundred-plus page long petition, Kagame was giving the commencement speech to OCU's graduating class, 10 of whom were Rwandan citizens.

The lawsuit was filed, in part, on behalf of Madame Agathe Habyarimana, the widow of Juvénal Habyarimana, the former President of Rwanda. It alleged that in 1994, Kagame, a Tutsi, assassinated former president Habyarimana, a Hutu, by ordering his jet shot down as it approached the runway in Kigali, Rwanda's capital. The suit claimed it was Kagame's intention to spark an outbreak of widespread violence, which ultimately resulted in genocide, by ordering the shooting of the Falcon 50 that carried Habyarimana and the president of Burundi, Cyprien Ntaryamira, whose widow is also a plaintiff in the suit.

The two presidents were flying back to Kigali from neighboring Tanzania after signing a peace accord between exiled Tutsi forces and the Hutu led government of Rwanda. The jet was struck by two surface-to-air missiles fired from close range. All aboard were killed. In retaliation, Rwandan Hutu extremists unleashed one of the deadliest acts of genocide the world has ever seen, systematically killing Tutsis and anyone sympathetic to them.

The lawsuit states, "General Paul Kagame deliberately chose a *modus operandi* that, in the context of the particular tension pervading both in Rwanda and Burundi between the Hutu and Tutsi communities, could only bring about bloody reprisals against the Tutsi community, and which offered [Kagame] a veneer of legitimacy for his renewal of hostilities and his seizing of State power in Rwanda by criminally violent means." In the lawsuit, the widows of the dead presidents accused Kagame of wrongful death and murder, crimes against humanity, violations of the rights of life, liberty, and security, and torture, among other things, and requested damages against him in the total amount of $350 million.

· · ·

The plaintiffs had to clear two procedural hurdles before the lawsuit could even begin in earnest. The most daunting issue was the question of service and notice to Kagame. Before a judge can make any order affecting the rights of a particular defendant, a defendant must be given notice. It is usually accomplished by a process server physically handing a copy of a filed lawsuit and other legal documents to the person being sued.

The other hurdle was jurisdictional. American law dictates that there must be a substantial connection between the person being sued and the place they are sued. In the case of Habyarimana v. Kagame, attorneys for Habyarimana would have to show that Kagame had substantial connections and contacts with the federal jurisdiction of the Western District of Oklahoma in order to maintain the suit there. It was the OCU-Kagame connection that the lawyers were counting on to fulfill the jurisdictional requirement.

In accordance with the Rwandan Presidential Scholars Program, scholarships funded by the Rwandan government are awarded to 10 Rwandans each year to attend OCU. Upon graduation with either bachelor's or master's degrees, the graduates are required to return to Rwanda to "help develop their country," according to OCU's website.

While lawyers negotiated with the Secret Service and Kagame's entourage, Kagame addressed the assembled graduates: "I am sure you know that among the distinguished [graduates] today are the first cohort of Rwandan scholars at OCU. Their graduation marks an important milestone in the partnership, and indeed, friendship between OCU and Rwanda." Extolling the necessity of an educated citizenry, Kagame said, "You need no reminding that in Rwanda, one of the long-lasting consequences of genocide was the decimation of the educated class."

Of the "decimation" of 1994, Philip Gourevitch, author of the book *We Wish to Inform You That Tomorrow We Will Be Killed With Our Families*, wrote:

> Decimation means the killing of every tenth person in a population, and in the spring and early summer of 1994 a program of massacres decimated the Republic of Rwanda. Although the killing was low-tech—performed largely by machete—it was carried out at dazzling speed: of an original population of about seven and a half million, at least eight hundred thousand people were killed in just a hundred days. Rwandans often speak of a million deaths, and they may be right. The dead of Rwanda accumulated at nearly three times the rate of Jewish dead during the Holocaust. It was the most efficient mass killing since the atomic bombings of Hiroshima and Nagasaki.

Ron Frost, Vice President of Communications at OCU, said that some of the first Rwandese students to attend the university were orphaned by the genocide. Some were old enough in '94 to have visible memories of family, friends and neighbors being murdered by machete.

• • •

Rwanda's intertribal animosities began with their colonial occupiers, the Belgians, as early as 1919. Through a mixture of biblical myth and Nazi-style eugenics, the Belgians decreed the Tutsis to be one of the lost tribes of Israel, and inherently superior to their countrymen, the Hutus. Tutsis took the flattery to heart. The Belgians placed Tutsis in middle-management roles overseeing and directing the hard and forced labors of their designated inferiors, the Hutus. The Belgians even went so far as to issue identification cards labeling a person either Hutu or Tutsi. Though there exists so much intermarriage between Hutus and Tutsis to blur any genealogical difference between the two, it was considered a high distinction and prize to have the word "Tutsi" printed on your identification card.

Rwandan history after the withdrawal of Belgium is pocked by a series of uprisings and clashes between the two tribes. In 1961, when Paul Kagame was three, he and his family fled for Uganda during a revolt that left as many as 150,000 Rwandans dead, with Tutsis taking the largest number of casualties. Kagame was raised and schooled in exile. As a young man, he became involved in military operations as a guerilla fighter in the Ugandan National Resistance Army that eventually overthrew the Ugandan government in 1985.

Shortly thereafter, Kagame helped to form the Rwandese Patriotic Front (RPF), which was comprised of both exiled Hutus and Tutsis in Uganda. From the start, their aim was to seek re-entry to Rwanda for its exiled population and to gain involvement in Rwandese governance.

In 1990, Kagame was the second in command of the RPF while he was undergoing special military training at Fort Leavenworth, Kansas, in the U.S. Army Command and Staff College. The training was offered to Kagame by the President of Uganda who had the backing of the U.S. Government after having overthrown the brutal regime of Milton Obote. Kagame quit his training early to return to Uganda when news reached him that the leader of the RPF had been killed in combat by Rwandese forces.

At about the same time, peace talks began between the RPF, with Kagame at the helm, and the Rwandan government, headed by then President Habyarimana. By all accounts, Habyarimana was less than enthusiastic about the proposals being generated in the peace talks. The talks revolved around proposals that would substantially diminish Habyarimana's influence as head of state.

Peace talks notwithstanding, a vicious propaganda machine was busy cranking up Hutu hostility towards Tutsis within Rwanda, with the apparent blessings of Habyarimana and his wife. A widely read newspaper called *Kangura*, founded in part by Agathe Habyarimana in reaction to a moderate periodical critical of her husband, became the daily digest for the "Hutu Power" movement that was picking up steam. One edition ran with an article entitled "The Hutu Ten Commandments." The eighth commandment stated, "Hutus must stop taking pity on the Tutsis."

The commentators at radio station RTLM, based in Kigali, and whose signal reached across Rwanda, began to refer to Tutsis as "cockroaches," and warned them to watch their backs.

The dreaded *interahamwe* was formed. *Interahamwe* means "those who fight/attack together" in the Rwandese African tongue. The *interahamwe* consisted of groups of young machete-wielding Hutu men who would be responsible for most of the 800,000 Tutsi dead by the end of the summer of 1994.

Interahamwe groups would regularly have rallies "where alcohol usually flow red freely, giant banners splashed with hagiographic portraits of Habyarimana flapped in the breeze, and paramilitary drills were conducted like the latest hot dance moves," writes Philip Gourevitch. "The president and his wife often turned out to be cheered at these spectacles, while in private the members of the *interahamwe* were organized into small neighborhood bands, drew up lists of Tutsis, and went on retreats to practice burning houses, tossing grenades, and hacking dummies up with machetes."

• • •

"Hutu Power" Radio RTLM reported to Rwanda that Juvénal Habyarimana was dead. Its commentators encouraged that "the tall trees be chopped down," code for "kill the Tutsis," and began almost exclusively referring to Tutsis as "cockroaches." According to multiple sources, commentators at RTLM would read out names of Tutsis and Hutus sympathetic to Tutsis, and give directions as to how to find them. In turn, RTLM would announce the news after someone on their list had been killed by the Hutu *interahamwe*.

At the outset of the genocide, Agathe Habyarimana flew to Paris, where she lives in exile to this day.

Some have speculated that Hutu extremists were responsible for shooting down Habyarimana's plane in retaliation for signing the peace accord with the RPF, and as a pretext for sparking the genocide that resulted. Others believe that the orders to shoot down the plane were given by the RPF, and specifically by Kagame himself, also as a pretext to spark the genocide and justify an invasion into Rwanda from the northeast in Uganda, which is exactly what happened. Kagame steadfastly denies the accusation that the

RPF, and he, had anything to do with the shooting down of Habyarimana's jet.

Lt. Col. Charles Vuckovic, a U.S. defense attaché for the Defense Intelligence Agency, was in Kigali when the president's plane was shot down. He told reporters for PBS' *Frontline*, "There are many theories as to who shot down the plane. I don't know if anybody has the answer to that. Was it Hutu extremists or was it Tutsi extremists? Was it done by the Tutsis as an excuse to begin the movement south by the RPF and take control of the country? Hard to say. Or was it used by the Hutu extremists to begin the genocide that took place? I don't know the answer to that."

After the RPF took over Rwanda and quashed the Hutu-led genocide, the French Government produced a report that concluded the genocide was intentionally sparked by the RPF and Kagame. The plaintiffs' case in the Oklahoma lawsuit relies heavily on that investigation conducted by French authorities.

An investigation was also undertaken by the Kagame-led Rwandan government. Not surprisingly, the report concluded that President Habyarimana was assassinated by members of his own inner circle. Kagame's report concluded, "The attack was a deliberate attempt by Hutu extremists close to the president to scupper an imminent peace agreement with the Tutsi-led Rwandan Patriotic Front (RPF) rebels."

A new investigation by the French corroborates Kagame's version of what happened, and directly contradicts the previous French investigation championed by the plaintiffs in the Oklahoma case. On January 11, 2012 two French judges announced that based on their investigation into the matter it is their belief that the missiles were fired from a Hutu military base by Habyarimana's own soldiers. For the foreseeable future that is the narrative the French government and Kagame's Rwanda have settled on, thereby thawing what had been a contentious relationship between the two countries.

In the commencement speech given by Kagame at OCU, he also said, "The ills that have characterized our country... such as conflict, poverty, disease, and corruption are in many ways a result of lack of value-based leadership. In Rwanda, we learnt that lesson the hard way..." He ended his speech by saying, "Congratulations again to you all, and may God bless you." Kagame left the OCU campus, surrounded by his bodyguards, without papers being served on him. University officials escorted the lawyers for Agathe Habyarimana off campus grounds.

Peter Erlinder, one of the lawyers for the plaintiffs in the case and an international law professor at the William Mitchell College of Law in Saint Paul, Minnesota, said, obviously disgruntled, "Rather than accept service, members of [Kagame's] staff refused to accept documents and the university ordered process servers and lawyers to leave campus... which is interference with service of process, a misdemeanor under Oklahoma law. ...[B]ecause the university has now involved itself in the conspiracy to cover up Kagame's crimes, they have exposed themselves to liability."

According to university officials, there has been no legal retaliation on the part of the plaintiffs in the Oklahoma City case to date, and there is none expected.

Ron Frost of OCU said with a chuckle, "There was no way [process servers] were going to get within 20 feet of President Kagame." According to Frost, Kagame's bodyguards numbered close to 30 and were armed with automatic weapons.

• • •

After months of legal wrangling between the plaintiffs' lawyers and Kagame's over the procedural issues of whether Kagame was properly given notice of the law suit, and whether the Western District of Oklahoma was the proper court to hear the case, the U.S. government stepped into the fight.

The Department of Justice (DOJ), at the behest of the Obama administration, filed a "Suggestion of Immunity" in September 2011. The DOJ's Suggestion of Immunity urged the court to dismiss the suit against Kagame citing international law, foreign policy and precedent. In the history of American jurisprudence a suggestion of immunity filed by the DOJ on behalf of a sitting head of state has never been rejected.

The Oklahoma City federal judge, Lee West, dismissed the suit against Kagame on October 28 of last year. The lawyers for the widows are appealing the Oklahoma judge's ruling.

In September, a French court rejected a case filed by the Rwandan government against Habyarimana to have her extradited to Rwanda to stand trial for the planning and execution of the genocide, an accusation she has always denied. A Rwandan official said that the French ruling would be respected "for whatever it is worth."

Rwandan students enrolled at OCU declined to be interviewed for this article. When asked why, Ron Frost said, "We asked a few of our Rwandan students if they would like to be interviewed. They would just rather not talk about it."

Maybe their silence is rooted in a pragmatic wisdom. That the blame for the genocide that occurred over a decade ago in Rwanda, leaving close to one million men, women, and children dead, can finally and legally be assigned to one person or another, to the satisfaction of all, seems as improbable and as unhelpful as the case against Kagame moving forward in Oklahoma federal court.

Originally published
July 2013

by Michael Berglund

MR. RAY FITS A SUIT

A Tulsa tailor recalls escaping
European genocide

When I walk into Ray's Tailor Shop, I immediately notice the ordered disorder of the two-room store. Directly in front of me, too near the front door, sits a table stacked with files and mail and a small radio propped up on a box. Towards the back of the room, I see a fabric-draped Singer sewing machine, circa 1950—the first sewing machine, I later learn, that Sherman Ray purchased when he arrived in Oklahoma City from Germany. Next to the changing room, a small step stool is positioned between three large mirrors. The last table I see is loaded with scraps of tweed, herringbone, and different varieties of worsted wools. And sitting on the table, in the middle of the material, is Ray, who when I enter is negotiating a thimble and needle to add a scrap of cashmere to a blazer.

He runs the thimbled hand over impeccably slicked back hair and looks me over through large-framed glasses that magnify his eyes, which knowingly search for details that often go unnoticed in casual conversation: Does one shoulder hang slightly lower than the other? Does my neck crane forward to make my spine curve? Does a 30-year habit of standing into my left hip make the left leg slightly shorter? All of this occurs instantaneously as I introduce myself. He's not sizing me up for a *mano a mano* fistfight. He's measuring me.

I tell him that I'd like to have a suit tailor-made, and that I was interested in gray tweed or a suit with a similar texture. He tells me that he stopped building suits because of the amount of energy it takes, but he'd be happy to alter a suit for me. He chuckles and riffles through a manila folder full of photos, newspaper articles, letters, and trinkets. Ray pulls out artifacts that show me the man he has become: champion weightlifter, avid rower, accomplished tailor.

"I'll tailor the suit so good for you, it'll fit you like a glove," Ray says in a thick Polish accent.

I ask him what kind of suit I should get and he sets down his folder and takes his measuring tape from around his neck and guides me so that my back is facing him.

"Drop your arms," he says. He measures me with lightning speed. "42 is too tight, and 43 they don't make. You'll have to go to a 44. 44 might be a little bit too large but it'll have to be tailored."

He grabs my hand and energetically guides me to

the stepstool in front of the mirrors. He checks my inseam and then whips the tape around my waist. "You need about a 35½ or 36 pant. Don't get 34, 36 on the pants. Go to Woodland. Then tell them, 'I will buy it but I will take to my tailor for approval.' See, when you cut it up then you cannot take it back. Then just come over. I'm always open."

Before I leave, Ray shows me one remaining photograph. It's a picture of director Steven Spielberg with his arm draped affectionately over Ray's shoulders.

"See," says Ray, "I was in the concentration camps. Not just a tailor."

A week later, I return to Ray's Tailor Shop with a gray wool suit bought from a department store at Woodland, as he instructed, and I made sure to get a suit that met the size specifications he recommended.

Ray says, "Let me see it."

I pull it out of the bag. Before he even looks at the tag he tells me he can't work on it. He goes over and grabs a suit jacket he's been tailoring.

"You think anybody in this town can do this?" he says, holding up the jacket front. "This is a hand-sewn buttonhole. See? Everything now is made by machine. From China."

Ray takes the newly bought suit from my hands, looks at the tag, and laughs. "China." He takes the jacket off the hanger and hands it to me to try on. We walk over in front of the mirror and shows me how it needs to be adjusted.

"The shoulders are too tight. I have to let out the shoulders but look—" He shows me the inside of the jacket. "Not enough material here. How'm I gonna let out the jacket with no material? Suits like this don't give me anything to work with."

He has me try on the pants. He points to the front pockets, and I see that the outside seams pucker out as I walk. The crotch sits too low. When I raise my arms, the jacket sleeves are too short. Suddenly, a suit that looked slick, modern, and slim-fitting on the rack looks dollar-store cheap. Ray works the material of the suit adroitly, sliding material through his fingers and stopping at all the imperfections: not enough material to let out the sleeve; frayed material on the pants leg; lapels that, because of mass manufacturing, sit unevenly on my chest. He's the doctor and I'm the patient. I ask him how he learned to become a tailor.

"I was trained in Europe," he says. "My grandfather was a tailor. My father was a tailor."

In 1938, when Ray was 12, Russia occupied Poland. Ray lived in a small village near Bialystok, and because of the widespread poverty in Poland, his family survived through bartering rather than money. At 13, Ray began to apprentice under his father after showing that he had mastered a hand-sewn buttonhole. His skills ultimately saved his life.

"When I went to Auschwitz, what would I do?" he asks.

Before I can respond, before I can ask, he tells me to take off the suit and take it back. He helps me out of the jacket, but when he hands it to me, doesn't let go. He looks at the cuff of the sleeve and begins to finger it, turning the sleeve inside out to reveal what seems to me now poorly sewn stitching. The stitches tack back and forth sloppily, string ends hang haphazardly, exposing precariousness where one thread, pulled the wrong way, leads to disintegration and ripped seams. Not the arrow-straight line that suggests good workmanship.

"You see?" he speaks softly, hanging onto the arm. "Before Hitler came we were under the Russians for 18 months. Russia took over half of Poland and Germany took the other half. The Russians told my father he had to do hard labor and I said, 'Dad, you stay home because you got to provide and make a living. I will go.' I used to come home with my hand bleeding. I was not used to the work they made us do: shovel mountains to make a road. During wintertime we would go to the forest to cut wood they sent to Russia. But that was not so bad. When the Germans came—that was impossible. They hardly gave you anything to eat. I never dreamed I would come out alive."

That, according to Ray, was in 1939, and was the beginning of the end. Hitler and Stalin agreed to share Poland but, without warning, Hitler forced the Russians out in three days. It happened with lightning speed.

Ray manipulates the jacket sleeve as he talks, exposing its inferior construction. He lets loose the sleeve.

"Well, you take this suit back and get a new suit. A Hickey-Freeman. Or Jos. A. Bank," he says.

I return the following week with a gray pin-striped suit from Joseph A. Banks: a Signature 2-Button Wool Pinstripe suit with plain front trousers. When I remove the garment bag, Ray's eyes light up. He shows me the strength and intricacy of the stitching. He sets it down on his material table and shows me the extra material, left for the express purpose of tailoring.

"This I can work with," he says.

I go into the changing room and put on the suit. It swallows me. The jacket fits more like a cloak, and I feel like a young boy playing dress-up with his father's clothes. The pant legs puddle at my feet and if I don't cinch the waist, the pants fall straight to the floor. Ray has his work cut out for him. He has me stand in front of the mirror on the stepstool and sizes me up.

He braces himself to bend down—a wide stance, then bending at the knee while resting both hands on the other knee. He lowers himself slowly until the

Sherman Ray in Ray's Tailor Shop, 2013

first bent knee rests on the floor, will-you-marry-me style. He works at the cuff using pins and chalk, marking at the material. I ask him how he was taken to Auschwitz and he stops.

Ray's shop is in the center of a strip mall, and when nobody's talking and the radio's not on, it's pin-drop silent. He looks at the ground without really looking at it. He drops his hands to his side and he's thinking, thinking. It's him and me and the crackly buzz of fluorescent lights that burn color away into dull monochrome. Under this stark whiteness, he schools me in history.

Ray had lived under the forced labor of the Russians, but the Germans were not so accommodating.

"The Germans put me and my family on a train to Auschwitz," he says. "I was 15 or 16 so that was '41 or '42." Ray had heard rumors that Auschwitz was a death camp, but his family refused to believe him. He begged his family to jump with him from the train.

"They said no," he tells me. "All the time I begged them. They thought they were going to the resort. Every time I think about it I wanna kill myself."

Ray stops talking. He raises his arm. He moves to the other leg and the chalk draws a trail of slash marks on the material to be eliminated. He pauses, hanging onto a piece of loose pant leg.

The Germans, Ray says, left the boxcar unattended because most Poles thought the train led to an internment camp where they would be kept for the duration of the war. They accepted their fate as prisoners of war. No one imagined the human capacity needed to carry out Hitler's *die Endlösung*: the Final Solution.

Ray and four other boys on his boxcar suspected the worst, and they wanted off.

"There was a little window on top of the boxcar of the train," Ray recalls. He had tried to squeeze through it, but his heavy fur jacket wouldn't allow it. He crawled back down, then tried again, this time making it out. A friend threw his coat out after him. Ray and four other boys escaped the boxcar and ran into the wilderness. He didn't realize then that it would be his home for the next year.

"You know, in Poland it gets cold like it's Canada," he says.

He takes pins and begins stabbing at the chalk marks. Purely. Precisely. He pulls the material close to his face. *Stab.* Instinct kicks in while his mind traces outlines of the past he'd rather not recall. *Stab.* He tells me it's a lot to talk about: the farmer who saved his life by providing a single spade but refused any other assistance for fear of retribution. *Stab.* I resist the instinct to flinch as he pulls needles from the pincushion. *Stab*. I trust in his experience as he sticks the pins and tells me more about the year in the forest.

"We took the spade and dug into the ground—about two feet down and then two feet horizontal into the ground," he says. "We make a little place in the earth where we can lay down but we can't sit up. At night, you know, we could get out. But in daytime it was us, staying underground. When the snow comes, we thought it was bad. But then later the rain came and we wish we could have the snow."

He stops stabbing and examines the material closely, running his fingers along the metal dashes that force the pant leg to conform. The pinpoints that poke and scratch stay safely concealed just beneath the surface of the material.

"One of the boys couldn't walk because his leg was frozen," he says. Ray begged him to walk to find food, but the boy's leg had turned gangrenous. Ray and the others eventually took the boy to the ghetto at Bialystok, where the boy's leg was amputated.

"There was no medication. No penicillin. Nothing. Not even aspirin. For Jews, they say let 'em die."

Ray stands back up. First the hands braced on the knee, then the push that shoots the upper body up. He's righted himself and he concentrates his chalk and pins on my shoulders.

"They shot him."

According to Ray, all of this occurred around the beginning of 1943. The Bialystok ghetto was close to his uncle's hometown, and when he and Ray found each other in the ghetto, he convinced Ray to remain there rather than attempting to escape back into the forest. Ray had lost his immediate family and his uncle's presence comforted him, briefly.

The Bialystok ghetto housed around 50,000 Polish Jews laboring under the Germans. In Bialystok, Ray began to realize the extent of the Nazi cruelty. Even physically challenged Germans wound up in the camps and then, not long thereafter, disappeared.

"The trains, the boxcars, was carrying the people to the gas chambers day and night," he says. "Women, young girls — they shaved off their hair and they was wearing wooden shoes. They put potato sacks on them to wear. They looked like monkeys. Killed them all."

It was during this time that Ray was separated from his uncle and shipped to the concentration camp at Auschwitz. It was 1943, when Ray was just 17.

Ray maneuvers himself behind me and I feel the weight of his hands on my shoulders. He pinches the shoulder material and lifts up. He holds the material from each shoulder between his thumbs and forefingers.

"Too much space, you see?"

I see my reflection in the mirror. He's lifted the shoulders of the jacket so that my head sinks.

The second train to Auschwitz was a different story. "Before, I was from a smaller town so it was easy to escape from the train. This time the Germans was starting to lose the war, so it was worse. You couldn't jump because on every boxcar was the SS with a machine gun.

"At Auschwitz they brought you in ... to vanish," he says. At 15 square miles, Auschwitz was the largest concentration camp, and the Nazis divided it into three sub-camps: Auschwitz I acted as the base camp, Auschwitz-Birkenau was the main extermination camp, and Auschwitz-Monowitz enforced hard labor. In all, Auschwitz housed a total of 1.1 million Jews, 960,000 of whom were killed. Ray was one of the few who survived the second camp, Auschwitz Birkenau.

"OK. Now you can step down."

I step off the chair. Ray grabs the back of the jacket at my lower spine and pulls the jacket tight against me. I fall back because I'm not ready for the force of the pull, the firmness with which he holds the coat. In the mirror I see him hunched over, marking the coat with his chalk. Lines and Xs, from the base of my neck to the small of my back.

"When I got there, in Auschwitz, they asked for tailors, shoemakers, bricklayers," Ray says. "I was making uniforms for the SS—you know, the riding breeches. Everything had to be tailor-made. Everything had to be done perfect. You had to do it right or boy, watch out. And when we got through with the uniforms we were making civilian clothes. I was 16 or 17 by then. If I wouldn't have been a tailor they would've killed me, too."

The lump in my throat prevents me from swallowing. I look at him in the mirror, bent over, measuring, marking barbed-wire Xs down my back with the hands the Germans forced him to use 67 years ago on the back of an SS officer. One who killed the elderly, who gassed the women and children and gypsies. His meticulous hands make the same Xs on me now as they did back then and I wonder at the weight of his hands, at how much they endured, and I wonder if the SS officer really believed in the solution to the *Judenfrage*—Hitler's "Jewish question"—or if he defied the illogic and appreciated the precision of the hands making Xs on his back, and I imagine each X marks another day of life for Ray in a place where a wasted day is another day of gained breath.

"Auschwitz was big," he recalls. "It was an old Polish cavalry camp. And the barracks they changed for the prisoners. Put some beds in that we lived in. Three-story beds. Everybody engraved their names and their town in the wood of the bed. On every bed you saw it. Everybody would take a little knife and engrave or they'd do it with little pencils. And every time I get up in the morning I wake up praying, and when I go to bed, too, if I'm still alive. I never dreamed I would make it 90 years."

It's the carved name that recalls his identity, and the commitment to prayer to a God against whom he can measure himself, that kept Ray going. His main drive, his mantra even today is, "Never give up." When others succumbed to their despair, Ray encouraged them to reject the anguish that paved the way for death. Hunger propelled the despair, and Ray never gave up finding various sources for food. In the middle of the night he'd risk certain execution and creep out of his bunk and sidle alongside the barracks until he reached the kitchen, hoping to see the window cracked with food on the sill or nearby counter. Numerous times, he'd filch a potato or two and make his way back to his barracks. Hunger pervaded each breath, and Ray says during the day and all night everyone dreamed about food, which meant that food was the goal, that hunger trumped risk, that life without food couldn't be living.

"You have no idea what hunger means," he says. "The biggest punishment if you want to punish somebody: Don't feed 'em."

He grabs the pants at either side of my waist and tugs. More chalk stitch marks moving down my hips. More pinning.

"Auschwitz was nothing but killing. When people went in, the music was playing because people was screaming. You know, in the barracks the walls was thin and you could hear the screaming. So the music was playing so you couldn't hear the voices. You saw in the chimneys not smoke, but flame—like they were shooting fire. And a lot of times they was making—from the flesh of humans—soap. The called it *reden Juden* fat: RJF. From human flesh. When you went to take a shower they gave you something that looked like a rock. But it was made from humans. They'd shave off the hair to make mattresses."

The pincushion he wears around his wrist has moved its way up his arm. As he moves to take another pin out to stick into the suit, I see, perched on the elastic band that inches up, on the soft inside of his forearm, a bird that looks like Tweety crossed with a macaw.

"Everybody used to ask me about the numbers," he says. "I got sick and tired of it, so I covered it. It didn't matter what in the hell it was because it wasn't doing me any good."

When he tells me B2526, he lets me look close to try to see it, but the tattoo artist executed his job perfectly. No trace of the number.

When the Germans began losing ground in Poland because of the advancing Russian troops, the SS implemented a plan to move healthy prisoners to Dachau, a concentration camp located in Bavaria,

Germany. In order to keep the prisoners from escaping during the transportation, the Germans told the Jewish prisoners they were exchanging them for German prisoners held by the Russians. It was a lie, of course. The ruse worked.

Some of the railroads to Dachau had been bombed into disrepair, which forced the Germans to take longer routes.

"It was three or four days on those goddamn boxcars," Ray recalls. "You have a bucket if you want to take a leak. You cannot describe it. Ninety, a hundred in a boxcar like sardines. It was packed. Had to stand you know? You cannot forget. Never. Never. You talk about punishment. In an American jail it's a pleasure. They got a television, they got a bed. They're treated like a human. But over there? They didn't give a damn. They wanted you to die."

Eventually, Ray made it to Dachau, where he was assigned a new number: 19465. They put him to work making parts for the Luftwaffe. He was assigned an impossible work shift of heavy manual labor: 12 hours for the day shift, and 12 hours for the night shift.

"In case you run away they looked right away on your arm," he says. "But we didn't have civilian clothes. Everybody was in blue and white stripes so that nobody could run. They had electric wires, and outside the wire was ditches with water. Nobody could escape. If you would escape they would catch you."

In Dachau, the slightest physical ailment meant certain death. On a regular basis, the SS inspected the prisoners' bodies by calling them out of bed in the morning and forcing them to assemble, naked, and stand motionless for 30 minutes. The winters proved most detrimental because those who exhibited any symptoms of a cold or flu were dealt with severely. After the liberation of Dachau, Ray asked his doctor how he survived, and the only explanation the doctor could provide was, "You was young."

In the mirror, I'm all white-dashed stitches held together with pins. The tailor gives me one more going-over, carefully examining how he's refigured and put the suit together. He steps back, satisfied with his work.

"I never dreamed I would come out alive," he says. "I weighed 75 pounds. Skin and bones."

May 2, 1945 changed everything for Ray.

"That's when there were white flags in the villages, hanging from the rooftops," Ray recalls. "It was snowing in Bavaria in the forest. They was marching us through the forest. They were trying to get rid of us. Russians and Jews in the thousands. And all of a sudden we look, and nobody's there. The SS is gone. The Russians were running to the dead horses along side of the road and cutting the meat and eating it. You have no idea what hunger means."

I take the jacket off. First one arm, then the other, carefully slipping the material off my body to avoid the potential pinpricks while at the same time maintaining the newer, more form-fitting shape of the jacket crafted by Ray. He takes the coat and carefully hangs it, then the pants.

"You know, when the war started, I had a family. They went to Treblinka in the beginning. But young and old, they got killed. When it was over, I was all alone. I was hoping maybe I will find somebody. After the war I went in the German museum and looked at the booth for Poland. The walls in the room were covered with lists of who was left alive and who is gone. I never could see anybody from my family. All of them gone."

He takes the hung suit and places it on a rack next to a row of similarly pinned and white-dashed cloth-ing, all standing at attention and waiting for Ray to reshape them permanently. He tells me to come back next week for the finished suit.

When I thank him, he replies, "Who shall ask, shall receive. Whatever you need, I will give it to you."

Originally published
May 2013

by Marcos Barbery

FROM ONE FIRE

The epic struggle between the
Cherokee Nation and its Freedmen

On an oppressively hot evening last May, David Cornsilk addressed a room of so-called "black Indians" at Gilcrease Hills Baptist Church in northwest Tulsa. He wore a leather-braided bolo tie clasped by an emerald quartz. Though Cornsilk never formally studied law, his voice bellowed with the rhetorical ire of a white-shoed seasoned litigator.

"By a show of hands, how many folks here tonight are Freedmen?" Cornsilk asked into the microphone. Each raised an arm. Visibly dismayed, Cornsilk shook his head. It was a trick question.

"No," Cornsilk said. "The Freedmen died a long time ago. You are not Freedmen. You are Cherokee, and it is time that you begin to recognize who you are."

Cornsilk is Cherokee, and a self-taught civil rights advocate and genealogist. He traces his slave-owning ancestors back to their aboriginal lands of Georgia and Tennessee—to a period before the Trail of Tears. Cornsilk is not a Cherokee Freedmen descendant. For nearly two decades, however, Cornsilk fought for the citizenship rights of Freedmen descendants—blacks who descend from slaves once owned by Cherokee and other tribes.

While working full-time as a clerk at Petsmart, Cornsilk took on America's second-largest Indian tribe, the Cherokee Nation, in what led to a landmark tribal decision. Cornsilk served as a lay advocate, which permits non-lawyers to try cases before the Cherokee Nation's highest court. When Cornsilk was not unloading dog food from truck beds and stocking shelves under the sounds of chirping parakeets, he composed legal briefs on the rights of Freedmen descendants, made oral arguments in court, and responded to a flurry of technical motions submitted by his opponents.

The legal advocacy would come at a personal cost for Cornsilk. Not long after his talk at Gilcrease Hills, he was unable to maintain two full-time jobs. So he sacrificed one. No sooner, Cornsilk failed to make rent on his one-bedroom apartment in Tulsa. He broke the lease and moved into his Honda Civic while seeking new employment. He began showering at the YMCA.

Outmatched and outspent by a team of Cherokee Nation lawyers, few considered Cornsilk a threat, and certainly not someone who could ignite debate on race and tribal power—but he did, and that debate would end up costing the Cherokee Nation millions of dollars in attorney's fees, lobbyists, and public relations campaigns.

The ongoing battle for tribal equal rights for Freedmen descendants has grown increasingly urgent. With other American Indian tribes across Oklahoma closely watching the impending U.S. court cases to signal the fate of their own Freedmen descendants and the extent of their sovereignty, Cornsilk believes that the present stakes could not be higher.

Not surprisingly, Cornsilk has grown more polemical. At the Baptist church Cornsilk said that if you do not think these folks in this room "have Cherokee ancestry and you have not done the research to find out, then you're a racist." Part of what helps make him so compelling is that on the surface—like Cherokee Principal Chief Bill John Baker and members of the Cherokee Nation Tribal Council—Cornsilk looks white.

Oppressed by the Oppressed

Headquartered in Tahlequah, Oklahoma, the Cherokee Nation and its wholly owned business arm earned over a billion dollars last year through a myriad of businesses such as gaming, U.S. Department of Defense contracts, and federally funded programs. Today, taxpayers help support the Cherokee Nation through federal grants.

The brutality committed by whites against American Indians—especially the Trail of Tears—has become a part of our national conscience. Yet it is hard to imagine that during this period an even more poorly documented atrocity was being perpetrated: The Cherokee were slave owners long before their forced removal from the southern states.

By the time gold was discovered in Georgia at the dawn of the 19th century, Cherokee slave codes were indistinguishable from those enacted by the rest of the South. Soon after, when the U.S. Indian Removal Act forced Cherokee and other Indians to relinquish their native land and move west, countless blacks enslaved by Cherokees crossed into the frontier bound and shackled. These black slaves suffered a far more violent experience than their Indian masters.

Nearly a third of the Cherokee Nation's citizens lost their lives during the Trail of Tears; the number of their slaves killed remains unknown. Once the Cherokee Nation arrived in what later became Oklahoma, they prospered in part due to their agrarian roots, large-scale plantations, and practice of slavery.

Three decades later, when the Lincoln administration threatened slaveholders, the Cherokee Nation signed allegiance with the Confederacy. Finding themselves on the losing side of the Civil War, and

their shrinking territory under threat once again, the Cherokee Nation sought to re-establish government-to-government relations with the US.

In the summer of 1866, just months after U.S. lawmakers amended the Constitution to bar slavery, the Cherokee Nation entered into a treaty with the federal government. Among a long list of terms, the treaty granted perpetual freedom and full tribal membership to Cherokee slaves and their descendants. The Treaty of 1866 named these black, newly minted Cherokee members "Freedmen."

Freedmen and Tribal Benefits

From the last row of Gilcrease Hills Baptist Church's recreation hall, Kenneth Payton listened to David Cornsilk's voice rise and fall. Payton looks like a professional basketball player. He is six foot five, wears a tracksuit, and drives a pick-up. Payton lives in Broken Arrow with his wife and three of his four boys. His young sons append the word "sir" to their responses, hinting at their father's service in the United States Army. When we first met, Payton's hand enveloped mine.

Payton and other Freedmen descendants are represented in the pending U.S. court case by Jon Velie, who is a licensed attorney based in Norman. Velie describes Payton as a "Cherokee of African descent." The unfolding lawsuit led by Velie challenges the Cherokee Nation's dismissal of its former black citizens. "It's not a damages case," Velie said. "The Freedmen citizens simply want to be reinstated as full members of the tribe."

The ongoing litigation demands that the federal government enforce the 147-year-old treaty between the United States and Cherokee Nation, and restore tribal citizenship to Payton, his children, and potentially, tens of thousands of others who share similar ancestry. "I tell my kids all the time, 'You are Cherokee,'" Payton said. "And they say, 'Oh Dad, he is crazy,' but it is true. We are Cherokee."

Payton is not alone. During the year I spent reporting this story, nearly everyone I met in Oklahoma claimed Indian heritage. To many, the notion that Indian blood pumps through them, irrespective of quantum or degree, is a birthright. It suggests a dual identity. And it insinuates indigenous roots—a deeper, more authentic tie to land and country that predates statehood and union. But unlike most, Payton possesses the documents to back his claims.

After a rare public debate between Jon Velie and the Cherokee Nation's Attorney General Todd Hembree, a young man stood to ask a question. Until this moment, the debate on Freedmen held at the University of Oklahoma School of Law had been pointed, though relatively cordial. An event

Kenneth Payton, a descendant of Cherokee Freedmen, searches his ancestry with Gene Norris, senior genealogist at the Cherokee Heritage Center.

Images by Sam Russell

Kenneth Payton

organizer rushed to furnish the young Indian a wireless microphone. "What I do not understand is, what is it that these people want?" the young man demanded, directing his questions about the Freedmen at Velie. His voice did not require amplification. "What do they actually want? Or as my parents and grandparents would say, *Gado usdi unaduli?*"

I later learned that the young man's name is Corey Still. He was a senior at the University of Oklahoma, and a full-blood Cherokee. Addressing Velie and the audience in his native Cherokee tongue was laced in subtext. If anyone else in the auditorium spoke Cherokee, including Freedmen descendants, it was not apparent. Cherokee Nation Attorney General Hembree has long argued that because his tribe is an independent sovereign with a distinct culture, it has an absolute right to self-determine its criteria for citizenship. Corey Still struck at the heart of a different, more veiled, but no less present sentiment.

To Payton and other Freedmen descendants, their ongoing lawsuit is about acceptance. Payton seeks on behalf of his family, living and dead, recognition of his tribal identity. But implicit in the enforcement of a century-old treaty—and this is what Corey Still was alluding to—are the present-day benefits that come with tribal citizenship: free health care, educational scholarships, and housing assistance, to name a few. In Indian country, the idea that black "non-Indians" are unjustly suing tribes solely for economic benefits has been the source of much racially charged vitriol.

Several months after the debate, clutching his birth certificate and grandparents' death certificates, Payton drove his pick-up from Broken Arrow to Tahlequah. Dense woods conceal the Cherokee Heritage Center's genealogy center, which offers free services to would-be Cherokee. Gene Norris, the center's senior genealogist, told Payton that Cherokee citizenship is determined by linking an ancestor to the federal Dawes Rolls, which were completed in 1907. Norris inspected the authenticity of Payton's paperwork, led Payton to a computer, and searched for Payton's relatives on a digitized version of the rolls.

"Here's Emma," Norris said. Norris discovered Emma Mackee, Payton's great-grandmother, listed on the rolls. He then attempted to explain that there are subsections to the rolls. They include "By Blood" and "Freedmen," among others. The nuance left Payton scratching his shaved head. Your great-grandmother is on the Freedmen subsection, Norris explained, adding that until the litigation is resolved, the Cherokee Nation is not accepting any Freedmen applications for citizenship.

"You can go ahead and apply but they probably won't process it," Norris said.

INDIAN BLOOD

For hundreds of years, the question of who is an Indian has vexed the federal government and tribes alike. By the end of the 19th century, being an Indian usually came with one of two things: benefit or despair. More often, it came with both at once. Tribal economic benefits encouraged fraudulent citizenship claims by white, non-Indian imposters. Despair drove many true Indians away from federal officials.

Up until 1893, the dozens of tribes residing in Indian Territory owned millions of acres communally. The Cherokee Nation was the largest and most powerful tribe among them. Cloaked under efforts to assimilate Indians into American society and usher greater economic opportunity, in 1887, the federal government passed a law that began negotiations to chop up tribal lands. A federal commission was later organized and tasked with persuading the Cherokee Nation and other major tribes—known as the Five Civilized Tribes—to carve their land into allotments that could be bought and sold. The man appointed to lead the commission was a former abolitionist, Massachusetts Senator Henry Dawes.

On November 28, 1893, U.S. Secretary of the Interior Hoke Smith[1] issued instructions to Dawes and other commission members. The contents of that letter, according to Kent Carter, author of *The Dawes Commission and the Allotment of the Five Civilized Tribes*, were not made public at the time.

"Success in your negotiations will mean the total abolition of the tribal autonomy of the Five Civilized Tribes and the wiping out the quasi-independent governments within our territorial limits," Smith

---

1. After U.S. Secretary of the Interior Hoke Smith wrote the letter to the Dawes Commission demanding the abolition of tribal governments, he moved from Washington, D.C., to Georgia. In 1906, Hoke Smith ran successfully for governor—an event that sparked race riots across Georgia's capital. Hoke Smith ran on a platform promising to pass a state constitutional amendment striping the voting rights of blacks. The Civil War had ended nearly half a century earlier, freeing slaves and outlawing its practice across the country. Yet under Hoke Smith's administration, Georgia passed some of the most virulent Jim Crow laws. Over the next six decades, they assured the dominance of white political and economic power at the expense of blacks.

wrote to Dawes. The feds were making way for the 46th state: Oklahoma, which derives from Choctaw words, "okla" and "huma," or "red" and "people."

Tribes "absolutely decided to take a united front and oppose the allotment of their land and the termination of tribal governments," Dr. Brad Agnew, a history professor at Northeastern State University in Tahlequah, said. After multiple attempts, Dawes failed to convince leaders of the Cherokee Nation to split and relinquish their lands. Congress responded by passing another law. In 1898—just a a year after the region's first commercial oil well was drilled[2]—a new federal law effectively forced the Cherokee Nation and other tribes into submission. The plan: Each Indian citizen or head of household would be granted over a hundred acres. Before the land could be divided, Dawes and his commission had to answer: Who is an Indian?

The challenge was further complicated by internal tribal factions, which were a consequence of removal. Over time, many white colonialists had married into the tribe, and their light-skinned descendants often ascended to positions of power. "If you look at pictures of the leaders of the Cherokee Nation, most of them, they dressed white, they looked white," Professor Agnew said. "They were white for all intents and purposes." Principal Chief John Ross, for instance, who led the Cherokee Nation from 1828 until his death in 1866, was seven-eighths Scottish.[3]

While the Dawes Rolls were finalized, a succession of new oil wells sprouted across the region. Railroad systems linking east and west coasts that had once been obstructed by Indian reservations were either fully connected or on the way to becoming so. During his final years, Senator Dawes, who had once been viewed as a friend to American Indians, was plagued by sickness. He died in 1903. His colleagues helped finish what historians agree was a herculean task.

The federal Dawes Rolls of the Five Civilized Tribes closed on March 5, 1907, superseding all previous Indian citizenship rolls. Seven months later, tribal jurisdictions crumbled. Borders of what had been Oklahoma Territory were expanded and redrawn. Oklahoma became a state on November 16, 1907. At its birth, Oklahoma was the leading oil-producing state in U.S. It would maintain that distinction until 1921—the same year, it turns out, Oklahoma's Adair County would earn two distinctions of its own: highest concentration of Cherokee full-blood residents, and poorest county in the nation.

STATE OF THE NATION

During Labor Day weekend of 2012, as most Americans relished the final days of summer, the Cherokee Nation erupted in celebration. The festivities marked the commemoration of the signing of the Cherokee Tribal Constitution. On Friday night, a powwow commenced the weekend's events. Beads of sweat streamed down faces masked in paint. Full-blood Cherokees cloaked in tribal regalia—brightly colored feathered headdresses, leather leggings, and beaded dresses—howled and chanted and struck communal drums. Hundreds danced to the throbbing beats. Cherokee folklore says that the pounding of drums embody the tribe's pulsing heart and enduring fire.

For three days, over the course of dozens of dizzying events, despite a dogged heat, potent displays of tribal nationalism did not subside. "Once that fire dies down, then that's when all the tribes will die down," a young Cherokee said, "and it is our job to pass it from generation to generation." If the federal government had attempted to wipe out the Cherokee Nation, they had done so in vain. Bill John Baker, Principal Chief of the Cherokee Nation, who has a shock of white hair, spent the long weekend promoting a message of tribal unification. He seemed to emerge magically at each event, serving as master of ceremonies. "We all come from one fire," Chief Baker said.

To Rodslen Brown-King, a Freedmen descendant, Chief Baker's message stood in contrast to his actions—or lack there of—upon entering office. Cherokee people, she says, derive from "one fire," but it is the inclusion of the Freedmen in that metaphor where her interpretation diverges from the chief's. The morning after the powwow, Brown-King, her three brothers, eight sisters, two sons, two daughters, and ten grandchildren, displayed their own message

---

2. The Nellie Johnstone Number One was the first commercial oil well drilled in what was then Indian Territory. After obtaining a lease from the Cherokee Nation, George Keeler, William Johnstone, and Frank Overlees, working with the Cudahy Oil Company, drilled the well on April 15, 1897. According to Frank F. Finny, in *Chronicles of Oklahoma*, until the "Cudahy well came in the evidence that oil could be found in important quantities in Indian Territory was inconclusive . . ."

3. Subsections of the Dawes Rolls served to distinguish the tribe's primary factions: mixed-bloods, full-bloods, adopted Indians, and Freedmen. Historians argue that the distinctions were designed not because one group listed on the Dawes Rolls was considered more or less Indian than the other, but rather to protect the economic interests of full-bloods, who were still rooted in their own language and culture. Many full-bloods were so distrustful of the federal government that they hid out from Dawes commissioners. "The tragedy is, those who are the most Indian are not considered Indian today," Professor Agnew said. Many Freedmen, meanwhile, descended not just from slaves but African mothers and Cherokee fathers. "Masters frequently made use of female slaves, and those slaves produced children," Agnew explained. "John Ross was an eighth Indian. And I suspect that many of the Freedmen have more Indian blood than that."

2012 Cherokee Nation Holiday Parade

of tribal unification—not in a courtroom but in the Cherokee Holiday Parade. Just after dawn on Saturday, Brown-King and her family applied final touches to their Freedmen parade float, which included an eight-foot working waterfall. Before the parade began, sidewalks lining Tahlequah's Muskogee Avenue were littered with lawn chairs and young families eager to secure good views.

Between floats, sirens wailed as local fireman crammed in buzzing go-carts spun in circles. A college marching band honked freshly polished golden horns. As the army of floats drifted down the street, it grew increasingly apparent that nearly everyone—both parade participants and bystanders packing the streets—looked the same: white. The fullblood Cherokee who had starred at the powwow the night before had all but vanished. Save for Rodslen Brown-King and her family, no other blacks were in sight. So when they were finally directed by tribal officials to pull their oversized pick-up truck into the parade line, it was not just the extravagance of their float that drew attention.

Rodslen, who is in her late 40s, fit, and has long, locked hair, jogged alongside the Freedmen float. She waved and tossed candies to the small children dotting the street. As the Freedmen float rolled by, an elderly white woman seated in a canvas chair rocked her head back and forth in apparent disgust. The overwhelming majority of those in attendance, however, cheered Rodslen and her family along. Most agreed that the Freedmen float was impressive. Willoman Brown, Jr., Rodslen's son, gazed at onlookers as he steered the pick-up pulling the float with one hand on the wheel and an elbow fixed on the window ledge. "They welcomed us. It was quite unusual," he said. "The way they looked at us and clapped, it was like, 'Glad y'all here. You made it.'"

Several hours after the parade, on the other side of town, Chief Baker delivered his State of the Nation address to a large, air-conditioned auditorium. More than once, he was overcome by emotion. While discussing his efforts to bridge a divided Cherokee Nation, Chief Baker choked up. He was forced to pause until the threat of his own tears subsided. U.S. Congressman Tom Cole and Baker's cabinet, including Attorney General Todd Hemebree, along with members of the Cherokee Nation Tribal Council, crowded the first rows. Baker's predecessor, Chief Chad Smith, who led the Cherokee Nation for 12 years—and oversaw a tribal constitutional amendment that removed Freedmen descendants—did not attend. During last year's highly contested tribal election, Smith lost to Baker by a sliver of votes.

Chief Baker did not mention the Freedmen descendants, or how their ongoing litigation bled into the election he ultimately won. Baker did not bring up or explain why, just a year earlier, the federal government turned off a faucet flowing millions of dollars to the Cherokee Nation. And he did not mention the costs—both to the Cherokee Nation's coffers and reputation—of maintaining the fight to keep Kenneth Payton, Rodslen Brown-King, and thousands more Freedmen descendants out of the tribe.

The exclusion of the Freedmen in Chief Baker's State of the Nation speech reflects the chasm between how the tribe perceives itself internally and how outsiders perceive it. For a tribe that has fallen victim to unspeakable crimes historically, it is difficult to accept its own original sin. "We never held slaves," an elderly full-blood Cherokee told me after the speech.[4] Perhaps the reason Chief Baker passed over the Freedmen is because so few members of the tribe acknowledge their own stained history, let alone recent events that shaped the Freedmen dissension. Advocates say that much of what occurred in the Freedmen case took place in secret, or as a tribal judge put it, "through silence."

The 2007 constitutional amendment that permanently removed the Freedmen descendants, even Attorney General Hembree concedes, was done in haste. In that special election, which clenched the disenfranchisement of Freedmen descendants, less than seven percent of the tribe cast votes. The Freedmen descendants are easy to ignore. They make up a minority of the tribe. But like African Americans in state and national elections, Freedmen descendants might constitute a powerful block. After more than a century maintaining tribal voting rights, it was this threat—the fear that the Freedmen descendants may band together to unseat an incumbent chief—that

---

4. Many Cherokee slaves were branded like cattle, stripped of their identity, and bestowed with the surnames of their Cherokee masters. According to Rudi Halliburton, Jr., author of *Red Over Black:* *Black Slavery Among the Cherokee Indians,* slaves who attempted to escape—and there were many—were hunted with dogs. Cherokee militias were often formed to track and capture runaway slaves, who were promptly returned to their masters or publicly executed, serving as a warning to others.

first led to their ouster. The extent of their unwillingness to go quietly was impossible to foresee. So too was the resolve of their advocates.

THE RISE OF DAVID CORNSILK

The two men met while standing beside each other under a blistering sun. The line to vote for the next Cherokee Principal Chief snaked around the courthouse. The man who would later reach the voter registration table first was elderly, smallish, and appeared black. The man who stood directly behind him was young, tall, and appeared white. It was 1983—a century after the Dawes Commission was established. As the line inched forward, the two men struck up a conversation on tribal politics and Oklahoma's relentless heat. The black man introduced himself as Roger Nero. The white man introduced himself as David Cornsilk.

When Nero reached the registration table, a light-skinned Cherokee woman requested to see Nero's tribal identification card. "'We don't let you people vote anymore,'" Cornsilk recalled the tribal official saying to Nero. The official instructed Nero to vacate the building. "When I handed her my card, she smiled and said no problem and handed me a ballot," Cornsilk said. Cornsilk did not discover until after the election that Nero was a Freedmen descendant. At

the time, Nero was 82. He was an infant during Oklahoma statehood; Nero's name appears on the original Dawes Rolls.

Nero filed a lawsuit against the tribe in U.S. courts. The court dismissed the suit and ruled that Nero's case was a tribal matter. "He was old and didn't have any money and pretty much let it go," Cornsilk said. Nero's failure to gather traction and his subsequent death haunted Cornsilk, who later landed a position within the Cherokee Nation's department of tribal registration. "Part of my job was to deal with Freedmen applicants," Cornsilk said. "I started reading their histories, and I came to the realization that we really screwed these people."

During the two decades that followed, Cornsilk advocated for the rights of Freedmen descendants with mixed results. In 1988, while still a tribal employee, he wrote a letter of protest on behalf of Freedmen—garnering the support of six additional tribal employees who signed in solidarity—and sent it to then-Principal Chief Wilma Mankiller. Cornsilk told me that his letter resulted in threats by senior tribal officials. "I never heard from the chief, but I got a call from the chief's aide who said, 'We do not talk about the Freedmen, and anyone who does, does not work for the tribe.'" Tribal officials deny these claims.

After a decade of advocating for the Freedmen while still a tribal employee, Cornsilk grew disenchanted by tribal leadership. He quit working for the tribe, and after a quick stint working for the Bureau of Indian Affairs in Washington, D.C., Cornsilk returned to Tahlequah to begin his work as an official "lay advocate." After an elderly black woman named Bernice Riggs was denied Cherokee citizenship by the tribe, Cornsilk obtained permission from the Cherokee tribal court to petition an appeal on her behalf. Cornsilk said that Cherokee tribal members told him that Riggs lived on "Nigger Hill," a neighborhood outside Tahlequah where many Freedmen descendants reside. The Riggs case was not successful, yet it solidified Cornsilk as an unwavering Freedmen advocate.

With a receding hairline and newly separated from his full-blood Cherokee wife, Cornsilk moved to Tulsa in 2000 and accepted a full-time clerk position at Petsmart. While working there in the summer of 2003, Cornsilk received a phone call from Marilyn Vann, an engineer by trade and leader of the Freedmen Descendants of the Five Civilized Tribes. Jon Velie, the Norman-based attorney, represents Vann.

After helping to bring legal action against the Seminole Nation several years earlier, Velie earned a reputation as a civil rights attorney.[5] In 2000, the Seminole Nation, which is smaller than the Cherokee Nation and based in Wewoka, stripped their Freedmen descendants of citizenship rights with a tribal constitutional amendment. Velie was part of the legal team that secured a federal court decision in favor of Seminole Freedmen. Now, with Velie on the Cherokee Freedmen case pro bono, he and Vann were preparing a legal offensive against the Cherokee Nation.

Vann called Cornsilk and invited him to address a Freedmen descendants' meeting in north Tulsa. Vann believed that Cornsilk understood the Freedmen plight as well as anyone. "He knew a great deal about Cherokee law and history and genealogy," Vann said.

To Vann and other Freedmen advocates, the summer of 2003 brought with it a great sense of urgency. Principal Chief Chad Smith, who was first elected to the tribe's highest office in 1999, had just clinched his second term. According to Cornsilk, designating Cherokee Freedmen as "non-Indians" was a priority throughout Smith's first term. That May, Cherokee Freedmen descendants were excluded from the general election that secured Smith's second term.

But there was something else at stake during the 2003 general tribal election to which the Freedmen were not a party. Smith had run in part on a platform to remove federal oversight of the Cherokee Nation. At the time, the Cherokee Constitution required approval of new tribal amendments by the Secretary of the Interior—the head of the same federal agency that attempted to wipe out the Cherokee Nation's government. The 2003 general election included a tribal constitutional referendum. Smith's administration presented Cherokee citizens with an opportunity to vote to approve a tribal amendment removing federal approval of *future* amendments. To fellow Cherokees, it was an easy sell. If American Indian tribes are truly sovereign, what business is it of the U.S. government to approve their constitutional amendments?

But Smith still needed federal approval for such an amendment. That May, in addition to voting for Chief Smith, the majority of Cherokee citizens—excluding the Freedmen—had just voted in favor of the constitutional amendment. This was not enough to win over Department of Interior officials. Senior members within that federal agency realized the implications of approving such a measure—one that would forever forfeit their veto power over changes to the Cherokee tribal constitution. That same summer, the Department of Interior received alarming letters from Jon Velie; he warned of legal action should the Department of Interior fail to "honor its treaty obligations" and enforce the voting and citizenship rights of Cherokee Freedmen descendants.

The feds were now apprehensive. They worried that approving the amendment to remove oversight of future amendments would equip the Cherokee Nation—much like the Seminole Nation had a few years earlier—with the legal framework to turn around and remove their Freedmen by constitutional amendment.[6] Still, there were deeper tensions at play. After centuries of federal encroachment over tribal affairs, the Department of Interior labored to implement a policy that provided greater sovereign power to tribes, not less. The feds sought to strike a balance between providing more autonomy to Indian Nations

---

5. Indeed, Jon Velie's pro bono civil rights career launched when the lawsuit he and is team filed on behalf of Seminole Freedmen in the U.S. courts was ruled in their favor. To Velie and other advocates, it was a win. But today, 13 years later, it is also perceived as a loss. "Does racism exist? Of course it does," Jon Velie said. "But this is legal racism." And to Velie, the implications of the ongoing Cherokee Nation litigation extend from Tahlequah to Wewoka and across Indian country.

6. These sentiments emerged in the exchange of letters written by officials from the Department of Interior to Chief Smith and the Cherokee Nation.

and protecting the civil rights of Freedmen descendants. It was a tenuous balance at best.

In a letter to Chief Smith, Neal McCaleb, assistant secretary of the Department of Interior at the time, expressed the federal government's willingness to approve the amendment under the following conditions:

> All members of the Cherokee Nation, including the Freedman descendants who are otherwise qualified, must be provided an equal opportunity to vote in the election. Second, under current law, no amendment to the Nation's Constitution can eliminate the Freedmen from membership in the Nation absent Congressional authorization.

While serving as Cherokee Nation Principal Chief, and after he was defeated in 2011 by challenger Bill John Baker, Chad Smith refused multiple requests to be interviewed for this story.[7] An examination of the letters he wrote over the last decade, court documents, and his speeches illustrate that Smith's stance toward Cherokee Freedmen descendants is unambiguous. In response to the Department of Interior's letter, Smith assured the federal government that citizenship rights would not be affected by the tribal constitutional amendment. Smith responded to Department of Interior:

> Nothing in the pending Constitutional Amendment will substantively alter in any manner whatsoever existing rules under the 1976 Constitution governing citizenship in the Cherokee Nation.

Smith was not being disingenuous, but he was not being forthcoming either. Though he did not say so at the time, Smith had always held the position that it was the original intention of 1976 Tribal Constitution—the most recently ratified Cherokee constitution at the time—to remove Freedmen citizenship. Smith, who was a trained lawyer and had recently spent a semester teaching Indian law at Dartmouth College, kept quiet on the issue. The Cherokee Nation's highest court would later disagree with Smith's interpretation.

In May 2003, the Cherokee Nation held its tribal elections. The tribal constitutional amendment to remove federal approval of future tribal amendments was placed on the ballot. The majority of the Cherokee Nation's citizens voted in favor of the amendment. Also, Chief Smith was elected to his second term in office. The Cherokee Freedmen, however, were not permitted to vote in this election.

That summer, the Department of Interior, Jon Velie, and Chief Smith exchanged a flurry of letters. To Smith, the controversy over the tribal citizenship rights for Freedmen descendants was an internal tribal issue. At stake was the Cherokee Nation's right to self-determination. When the Department of Interior officials directly questioned Smith's interpretation of the tribal constitution, and expressed reluctance to approve the tribal amendment removing its federal veto powers, Smith's tone grew more antagonistic. Smith wrote back to the Department of Interior:

> In the age of self-determination and self-governance, I am shocked to find the contents and tone of your letter to be both patronizing and very paternalistic. It appears that some officials in your department desire to return to the era of "bureaucratic imperialism."... It is a fact that the Cherokee people have decided their leadership and approved a constitutional amendment on May 24, 2003, by a democratic process in accordance with Cherokee Law.

Velie saw it differently.[8] However, the Department of Interior ultimately caved. Near summer's end in 2003, the Department of Interior formally recognized Smith as Chief of the Cherokee Nation for his second term—despite the Freedmen's exclusion at the polls. They did not, however, approve the tribal amendment removing federal approval of future tribal amendments. Nevertheless, on August 11, 2003, on behalf of Marilyn Vann, Kenneth Payton, Rodslen Brown-King, and other Freedmen descendants, Jon Velie filed a lawsuit in district court against the Secretary of Interior, claiming that Smith was elected as chief without the Freedmen vote, in violation of the 1866 treaty.

Cornsilk, paradoxically, was not pleased to learn

---

7. When Smith was still chief he said through a spokesperson that he could not comment on the case because it was currently being litigated. I later approached him personally, he refused to answer my questions regarding the case. After he lost the tribal election, I called his private law office and left multiple messages with his secretary requesting an interview. He did not return my calls.

8. Velie felt that all elections that took place in 2003 were illegal because the Freedmen were not permitted to vote. Velie wanted the elections invalidated.

about the lawsuit. Make no mistake, Cornsilk was vehemently opposed to the Cherokee Nation's exclusion of their Freedmen. But it is difficult to overstate just how deeply Cornsilk's Cherokee nationalistic sentiments run. Cornsilk was—and generally remains—against involving the federal government in tribal affairs. Velie's maneuvering, meanwhile, was strategic. Velie did not file suit directly against the Cherokee Nation. Such an approach, as the Nero case illustrated, risked early dismissal. Instead, Velie filed suit against the Department of Interior in an attempt to compel the federal agency to enforce treaty obligations over the Cherokee Nation. But to Cornsilk, the Cherokee Nation had been betrayed by federal government too many times to justify their present-day involvement.

When Cornsilk received the call and invitation from Vann to address the Freedmen descendants, he appeared after a day's work at Petsmart. The meeting took place at the Rudisill Regional Library, located in a predominately black neighborhood in north Tulsa, though within Cherokee Nation boundaries. "This woman stands up and talks about how she was mistreated by the Cherokee Nation," Cornsilk said. She said that Cherokee Nation officials had abused her because she appears black. The woman speaking was clad in formal dress and an old-fashioned hat. Her name is Lucy Allen. Cornsilk then stood up and addressed the room. He spoke of Roger Nero and Bernice Riggs. He also expressed his contempt for Chief Smith and his removal of the Freedmen. After the meeting, Lucy Allen pulled Cornsilk aside. Allen asked Cornsilk what could be done to combat Chief Smith.

"Let's sue," Cornsilk told Allen. Of course, he was talking about tribal court.

"I don't know what came over me. I was overcome with emotion, and concern for her, the Freedmen, and the future of my tribe," Cornsilk said.

It took nearly a year for his Petsmart colleagues to realize that Cornsilk was actively litigating on behalf of Lucy Allen and Cherokee Freedmen descendants outside of work hours.

"Whenever I had free time, I worked on the Freedmen case," Cornsilk said. At first, Cornsilk did not own a computer. He ended up purchasing one after securing a line of credit with Dell. He named his personal computer "Cherokee War Machine."

Early attempts by Cornsilk's opponents to dismiss the tribal case on various technicalities were unsuccessful. At least two out of the three tribal judges did not wish to see a tribal constitutional case dismissed on anything but the case's merits. "I would say that I didn't have a personal life," Cornsilk said. "My life was the case."

Cornsilk was a registered tribal lay advocate, working on behalf of Lucy Allen, so the majority of the court awarded Cornsilk a wide breadth of latitude—similar to one who represents oneself in court.

"I didn't try to twist anything or dazzle anyone with fancy words," Cornsilk said.

As Cornsilk pushed through early stages of the case, the Department of Interior took notice, as did the Justice Department. Cornsilk's tribal court case threatened Velie's ongoing litigation in the U.S. court system. The two cases more or less concerned the same issue. Through the lens of outsiders, Cornsilk's lawsuit supplied credence and legitimacy to Cherokee Nation tribal courts.[9]

Velie realized that Cornsilk's tribal suit supplied new ammunition for Smith's response to the feds. Smith had always argued that the Cherokee Nation had its own court system intact. In letters and briefs filed by the Cherokee Nation seeking early dismissal of Velie's suit, Smith often cited the older Nero case. Smith and his administration argued that the proper venue for the Freedmen grievances was indeed in tribal court. And no sooner did Cornsilk bring the Lucy Allen petition forward did Velie urge Cornsilk to drop the case. There was too much at stake. Also, as Cornsilk began litigating in tribal court, more obvious risks emerged. Cornsilk worked at Petsmart. What could he possibly know about tribal law? If Cornsilk lost—and most experts expected him to do so—it could thwart success of future litigation. What's more, Chief Smith had appointed the majority of tribal judges to the Cherokee Nation's highest court. Few expected Cornsilk to prevail.

And then there was the issue of Cornsilk's opponents. Cornsilk's preliminary research led him to believe that his best tactic was to file the Lucy Allen lawsuit against the Cherokee Nation Tribal Council, which functions as the tribe's legislative body. Cornsilk argued that the new Cherokee Nation

---

9. Like the federal government and states, federally recognized tribes normally enjoy general immunity from lawsuits. For petitioners like the Freedmen, this often leaves no other option but to sue in tribal courts. In Roger Nero's case, which was in essence, a civil rights case, Nero attempted to sue in US Courts over his right to vote in a tribal election. But his petition was too narrow and focused on the particulars of tribal registration policy. As a consequence, a judge held that permitting the case to be decided in US Courts would curb the tribe's capacity to "maintain itself as a culturally and politically distinct entity." It ruled that the proper jurisdiction for Nero's suit was in tribal court.

requirement that determined tribal citizenship link to the "by blood" subsection of the Dawes Rolls was extra-constitutional, and therefore unconstitutional. At the time, one of the tribal council's longtime members—with greater political ambitions—was Bill John Baker. The tribal council selected their attorney to defend Cornsilk's petition: a young rising Cherokee Nation tribal lawyer, Todd Hembree.

Velie was correct to worry about Cornsilk's tribal court filing. It would emerge later in a congressional investigation that the feds perceived the Cherokee Freedmen differently than the Seminole Freedmen case. In the Seminole case, Jon Velie's legal team had already convinced the federal government to force the Seminole Nation to reinstate citizenship rights to its Freedmen descendants, or forfeit federal funding, and with it, a license to operate lucrative casinos. The Department of Interior later told members of Congress that they involved themselves in the Seminole Freedmen case because, unlike the Cherokee Nation, the Seminole Nation did not have an adequate tribal court system in place. The Cherokee Nation did, and as the tribal case dragged on, Cornsilk helped prove it.

As Cornsilk's case reached its final stages, Hembree and Cornsilk filed motions almost daily.

"I threw everything in except the kitchen sink," Cornsilk said.

On March 7, 2006, nine months after Cornsilk's closing arguments, a tribal court clerk placed a call to Petsmart. One of Cornsilk's colleagues paged him over the loudspeaker. Cornsilk was unloading dog food from a truck bed out back and missed the page. The colleague tracked down Cornsilk and informed him that he had a call. When Cornsilk lifted the phone, Lisa Fields, the court clerk asked Cornsilk if he was sitting down.

"No," Cornsilk replied. "Should I be?'"

"You won," she told him. "You won the Freedmen lawsuit."

"My knees got weak and I felt myself get faint," he recalled.

Cornsilk asked Fields to fax over the decision. Petsmart staff packed around the office watching the fax machine spit out pages.

"They were like, 'There's another one,'" he said. "Everything I had done: writing the letter to Wilma Mankiller, standing there with Nero, everything flashed before my eyes."

Petsmart later promoted Cornsilk to assistant manager.

Bending the Will of a People

The day after David Cornsilk defeated Hembree in tribal court, he received a congratulatory call from an official at the U.S. Justice Department. Two weeks later, Chief Smith issued a memorandum to the Cherokee Nation registrar: "With no requirement for proof of Cherokee blood, certain Registration procedures must necessarily be adjusted accordingly," Smith wrote. "Applications from prospective citizens without Cherokee blood are to be processed on the same basis as all other applications for citizenship."

In light of the Lucy Allen decision, Smith instructed senior tribal leaders to revise forms and brochures and to inform other staff of the implications of the tribal court's decision. "I thought it was over," Cornsilk said, "but I underestimated the racism of Chad Smith." In a letter Smith would later write to members of Congress, he denied that the following events were motivated by racial prejudice.

Cornsilk's victory, however, was accompanied by a curious opinion. Stacy Leeds, then a Cherokee tribal court justice, wrote the majority decision, the precise wording of which armed Smith's administration and their supporters with new leverage. Leeds

narrowly wrote that there is no "clear language in the 1976 Cherokee Constitution to exclude the Freedman from citizenship." However, Leeds also noted that the Cherokee citizenry has the ultimate authority to define tribal citizenship, but they "must do so expressly":

> If the Cherokee people wish to limit tribal citizenship, and such limitation would terminate the pre-existing citizenship of even one Cherokee citizen, then it must be done in the open. It cannot be accomplished through silence.

It was around these few sentences that Smith and his supporters would stage a new strategy. Smith proposed passing a tribal constitutional amendment on Freedmen citizenship through public referendum. This presented a chance, Smith claimed, for Cherokee citizens to vote—in the open—to overturn the result of the tribal court's decision.

"The issue at hand is what classes[10] of people should be citizens of the Cherokee Nation, and who should make that decision—the courts or the Cherokee people themselves," Smith said during his 2006 State of the Nation address, after the Allen decision.

"The process to decide the issue of Freedmen citizenship is a constitutional amendment at the polls."

With another election for Principal Chief looming, Smith faced an important year. Smith's third-term as Principal Chief was at stake, and he and his supporters acted swiftly. Almost immediately after the tribal court decision, Smiths' supporters and anti-Freedmen advocates advanced a tribal petition. Their goal was to garner enough signatures to bring forth a referendum at the polls. Cornsilk countered by launching an aggressive campaign to register new Freedmen. As a result of Cornsilk's tribal court win, Cherokee citizenship rights had been restored to Freedmen descendants. Cornsilk and Vann's efforts helped secure Cherokee citizenship to about 2,800 Freedmen descendants. Though they didn't know it at the time, the window for Freedmen descendants to apply for tribal citizenship was closing.

Velie contends that after the Allen decision, Smith and his administration set out to increase the size of the Cherokee Nation's then-highest court. The Allen case had been decided by three judges in a 2-to-1 decision, with Stacy Leeds writing for the majority. After the Allen decision, Smith appointed two new members to the court and renamed it: The Cherokee Supreme Court. During a rare public debate, Velie said that Smith intentionally "dismantled the court" to exert tighter control over its decisions. Smith interrupted Velie's allotted time to say, "That's not true." Stacy Leeds contends that court expansion plans were set in motion before Smith became chief. Leeds said that the court's expansion had no correlation to the Freedmen issue. Nevertheless, the court's expansion would play a critical role in a lawsuit Cornsilk would file next.

In late 2006, David Cornsilk, Marilyn Vann, and other volunteers began inspecting various signatures gathered by petition leaders. Cornsilk and Vann discovered inconsistencies, and what they believed were fraudulent signatories. Cornsilk once more filed suit in tribal court challenging the authenticity of the various petitions. The recently expanded tribal court invalidated some signatures, but overall ruled against Cornsilk. Stacy Leeds, in this case, wrote a lone dissenting opinion calling the petition glaringly fraudulent.

That December, Stacy Leeds's term as tribal justice expired. Chief Smith did not appoint her to an additional term. In January 2007, Leeds launched a campaign to run for chief of the Cherokee Nation against Chad Smith in the forthcoming general election. Leeds, who had supported Smith in a prior campaign, said that that Smith lost all objectivity and was not listening to or considering different perspectives. "There were subtle abuses of power occurring at many levels in the government," Leeds wrote in an email. "But the idea that a sitting Principal Chief would orchestrate a popular vote to overturn a ruling of the Nation's highest court and thereby strip a group of Cherokee citizens of their legal rights is a good example of why new leadership was necessary."

With the petition's 2,100 signatures now authenticated by the Cherokee Nation's highest court and the tribal council, the date for the special constitutional amendment was set for March 3, 2007—just several months before an already scheduled general election. On this day, out of the 8,000 Cherokee citizens who cast votes, over three-quarters voted in favor of permanently excluding Cherokee Freedman descendants from tribal citizenship.[11] The nearly 2,800 Freedmen who were permitted to vote during the special election fell short of a victory. Nearly one year later to the day, Cornsilk's victory was overturned.

Three weeks later, the Cherokee Nation tribal registrar issued letters to Freedmen descendants: "We regret to inform you that you are not eligible for citizenship in the Cherokee Nation." Six days later, another letter was issued to each enrolled Cherokee Freedmen descendant. "This letter is to inform you that because of the Constitutional Amendment, you are no longer eligible to receive health services through Cherokee Nation," the Cherokee Nation's clinic administrator wrote. Two months later, Stacy Leeds lost in the general election to incumbent Chief Smith. She is now dean of the law school at the University of Arkansas.

"With only four months to put a campaign together with zero dollars in an initial campaign fund, we came very close to unseating a two-term incumbent," Leeds said. Nearly twice as many Cherokee voted in the general election compared to the special election.

---

10. Here, Chief Smith's choice of word ("classes") is laced in racial undertones. It is precisely this kind of tone and choice of wording that caused many Freedmen to feel offended by Chief Smith's political rhetoric.

11. During an interview with Todd Hembree, I asked if the 2007 Cherokee constitutional amendment that overturned Cornsilk's

landmark tribal ruling and removed the Cherokee Freedmen was political. Hembree said that he is a realist. "It wasn't a mere coincidence that we had a special election in March of 2007 when there was a general election a few months later." But then he revealed that after years fighting against Cornsilk in tribal court and losing, during the 2007 special election he personally voted

against the constitutional amendment that removed the Freedmen. "I did not vote for that petition, but that is my right as an individual," Hembree said. "Now, when the Cherokee people speak in overwhelming percentages, that's who I represent

Later that summer, in Washington, D.C., Representative Diane Watson, D-Los Angeles, caught wind of the Cherokee Freedmen's disenrollment. At the time, Representative Watson served on the Congressional Black Caucus. After studying the case, meeting with Freedmen and their advocates, and checking the veracity of their statements with officials at Bureau of Indian Affairs, Watson drafted legislation.

From the moment Watson began seeking co-sponsors to the bill, the Cherokee Nation unleashed a comprehensive response. The bill's scope and substance was sweeping and unequivocal. Its purpose was to "sever the United States relations with the Cherokee Nation of Oklahoma until the Cherokee Nation restored the rights of the Freedman." Congressman Mel Watt, D-North Carolina, who like Watson is black, co-sponsored the bill. "Once I reviewed the facts and the background information and history," Congressman Watt said, "you don't turn and look the other way."

With hundreds of millions of federal dollars on the line, and millions more at stake related to its gaming license,[12] the Cherokee Nation applied extensive resources to its defense. Jack Abramoff, the Cherokee Nation's former lobbyist—who was hired by Chief Smith to lobby on behalf of "sovereignty issues," and who personally contributed to Smith's campaign for Cherokee Principal Chief—was serving time in federal prison on unrelated convictions. The Cherokee Nation's hired external lobbyists, Tony Podesta of the Podesta Group and brother of John Podesta, who was White House Chief of Staff in the Clinton Administration, and Lanny Davis, special counsel to President Clinton during his impeachment proceedings and now a D.C.-based lobbyist. The Cherokee Nation's D.C. team applied primary pressure against Congress.

Officially, Podesta concentrated on battling against the proposed bill while Davis focused most of his energy on the ongoing Vann case. In practice, Davis also helped the Cherokee Nation lobby Congress to kill Watson's proposed bill. As a former attorney to President Clinton, Davis is well connected in Washington—connected to a degree his fees reflect. "The Cherokee Nation put on a full court press," explained Bert Hammond, principal advisor to Representative Watson. "I'm sure that their law firm got paid millions and millions of dollars to lobby on their behalf."[13] As part of its policy, the Podesta Group does not discuss its relationships with current or former clients, and Lanny Davis did not respond to interview requests.

Watson, and other members of the Black Caucus introduced the bill, which was submitted in 2008 to the House Natural Resources and House Judiciary committees. The National NAACP supported the bill, framing the Cherokee Nation's 2007 constitutional amendment as racist. Smith rejected the "inflammatory misrepresentations" against the tribe. "The 2007 vote to amend its constitution was a crucial vote for the future of the Cherokee Nation and its own sense of identity," Smith wrote to members of Congress. "This vote has been falsely characterized as racist, while, in fact, the vote was for an explicit clarification of who is a documented Indian in regards to citizenship in the Cherokee Nation."

Podesta and Davis, along with Paula Ragsdale,[14] the Cherokee Nation's in-house D.C.-based lobbyist at the time, argued that the bill's central issue was currently under judicial review by U.S. Appeals Court and District Court of Washington, D.C. Cherokee lobbyists now felt that U.S. courts were best positioned to rule on the issue. Nearly five years after filing, the Vann case had not yet reached the merits stage.

Watson eventually changed the bill's language so that it would be referred to the judiciary committee. The change was strategic because John Conyers, another member of the Black Caucus, chaired the committee at the time. It was expected that as a representative known for his leadership on civil rights issues, Conyers would lend his support to the Freedmen. But the bill failed to gather steam. Asked why the bill was eventually killed, Hammond replied, "my clinical reaction is that the Cherokee chief had been around here spreading money around," he said. "And they have money to spread around."[15]

Members of Congress, including Barney Frank, a Massachusetts representative at the time known for backing civil rights issues, lobbied the U.S. Justice

---

12. Cherokee Nation's chief concern, according to interviews, was that the bill threatened the tribe's license to operate casinos. At the time, gaming made up the majority of the tribe's business arm's $520 million in annual revenue. Curiously, members of Congress who ultimately co-supported the bill were unaware that the Cherokee Nation's business arm, then known as Cherokee Industries, was engaged in manufacturing contracts with the Department of Defense. Also, according to a senior official within the Cherokee's business arm, had the Watson bill become law, the tribe's defense contracts would have remained intact, though this seems unlikely.

13. According to public filings, the Podesta Group, a registered lobbying group, earned $60,000 per year for their directly lobbying efforts and certainly much more for "counsel" and "advice". However, because Lanny Davis was hired as an attorney, as opposed to a lobbyist, his fee remains unknown. He has been rumored to charge $600 per hour.

14. Findings also suggest that relationships—which in this case extended even beyond the incestuous nature known for fueling D.C. politics—played a significant role in killing the proposed legislation. Pat Ragsdale, the then number three at the Bureau of Indian Affairs within the Department of Interior, is married to Paula Ragsdale, the Cherokee Nation's internal D.C. lobbyist.

Freedman Lane is located in the area known as "Four Mile" outside of Tahlequah. Some of the Cherokee Nation's former slaves are buried nearby in unmarked graves.

Department to take action against the Cherokee Nation. The Podesta Group made similar appeals, this time before the Obama administration. On April 30, 2009, Representative Watson submitted a letter to U.S. Attorney General Eric Holder requesting that the Justice Department's Civil Rights Division open an investigation into the "plight of the Freedman" and Smith's "illegal elections." Holder did not respond until nearly four months later—that is, after President Obama appointed Kimberly Teehee, a Cherokee, as his Senior Policy Advisor for Native American Affairs. On August 12, 2009, Holder notified members of Congress of his unwillingness to open a civil rights investigation on Smith. Holder cited the pending Vann case in U.S. courts.

THE JURY WITHIN

To ascend to the main floor of the National Lincoln Memorial in Washington, D.C., Marilyn Vann, who suffers from health problems, required the assistance of an elevator. To reach it on a cool night this past October, Vann shuffled uneasily through a corridor beneath the memorial. The corridor doubles as a museum illustrating critical events that shaped the civil rights movement. Walls are etched in black and white portraits of Dr. Martin Luther King Jr., whose "I Have a Dream" speech crackled over loud speakers. Vann's attorney, Jon Velie, joined her. The next morning, nearly a decade after they first filed their lawsuit, the two were once again due in federal

15. During a 2011 public event in Tulsa marking the commemoration of the Tulsa Race Riot, then-Chief Smith responded to accusations of tribal racism targeting blacks by showing the audience a video recording of a speech John Conyers delivered at the tribe's headquarters in 2009. The substance of Conyers' speech focused on the Trail of Tears; he did not mention the Freedmen. It is presumed that Smith hoped Conyers' presence at the Cherokee Nation alone was vindication.

court. But tonight, Vann wished to set her eyes on the memorial depicting the former president. Once at the top, the elevator's doors drew open like stage curtains. When Lincoln's statue revealed itself drenched in light, Vann, who had been chatting with Velie, fell silent.

From the outside, it is difficult to understand why the Vann case has yet to be argued on its merits. It is helpful to think about the case not as two parties on the same playing field seeking to right a wrong, but rather one party demanding that one country apply its laws or treaties over another. The case continues to unravel at a glacial pace because to the Cherokee Nation, its supreme authority to self-determination is at stake. Perhaps nobody understands this better than David Cornsilk. In spite of his staunch role advocating on behalf of the Freedmen, Cornsilk believes that each time the Cherokee Nation is dragged into a U.S. court, the tribe's sovereignty is diminished.[16] Cornsilk blames the Cherokee Nation for exposing the tribe—and potentially establishing a dangerous precedent for all American Indian nations—over what he calls an unequivocal repression of the Cherokee Freedmen descendants' tribal rights. Cornsilk says that there is simply no other option than to pursue justice in U.S. courts. To Cornsilk, the only hope for the Freedmen's chance of regaining their tribal citizenship hinges on the work of Vann and Velie.

At the U.S. Federal Court of Appeals hearing the morning after Vann and Velie visited the Lincoln Memorial, those anticipating a resolution were sorely disappointed. As Jon Velie's and Todd Hembree's legal teams argued before three white federal appellate judges, there was a sense that something historical was unfolding. But nobody—not even the local law students who crowded near the front of the courtroom—seemed to have a firm grasp of what was occurring. "To me, that was all legal mumbo jumbo," a Freedmen descendant who lives in Washington, D.C., told me after the hearing. The lawyers argued over whether the chief of the Cherokee Nation could be named as a defendant—or in legal jargon, if *Ex parte Young* applies to the Cherokee Nation. Two months later, in December, the court ruled in favor of the Freedmen, delivering a blow to the Cherokee Nation and a victorious jolt to Vann, Velie, and Freedmen advocates.

The Vann case may now proceed, but in spite of the latest Freedmen victory, the case could drag on for years to come. In one instance, the Cherokee Nation could appeal this latest decision—a legal procedural decision—to the U.S. Supreme Court. It's an attractive option. So far, the Cherokee Nation's legal maneuvering has succeeded in stalling the Vann case. "The Cherokee Nation says that it wants this case to be settled, but what they're really doing is delaying," Velie said, "while over 90 percent of the Freedmen are denied citizenship." And at least in one glaringly obvious way, even if Velie's team were to ultimately win the case, they have already lost. The Cherokee Freedmen descendants remain disenfranchised. It is no surprise then that nearly two years into his tenure, Freedmen descendants have grown increasingly disillusioned by Smith's successor: Principal Chief Bill John Baker.

While Baker was still running for Chief of the Cherokee Nation and serving as a member of the Cherokee Nation Tribal Council, he agreed to sit down with me at his campaign headquarters. Baker's campaign occupied a front office within Baker Furniture—a sprawling warehouse store he owns along Tahlequah's main drag. Outside, a red, white, and blue two-story banner depicting Baker's image fluttered against a breeze. I said to Baker that the majority of Cherokee Nation leadership positions appear to be filled by white-appearing Cherokee citizens. "Well, we've never been a tribe of full-bloods," Baker said. When I mentioned that historians suggest that Freedmen descendants may have more Cherokee blood running through them than white-appearing "by-blood" Cherokee, Baker conceded that it wasn't fair.

"Why don't you and the tribal council change policy?" I asked.

"It is not fair," Baker said. "But it is our way."[17]

Advocates say, however, that during his campaign, Baker positioned himself politically as an ally to the Freedmen cause only to later betray them after he won. Indeed, his rise to the tribe's highest office was a consequence of the Freedmen vote, they say. Today, under federal agreement, only a small fraction of potential Cherokee Freedmen are permitted to vote in tribal elections. These are the 2,800 Freedmen

---

16. Though they share similarities, Native American tribes are not states. They are semi-autonomous nations with inherent sovereign rights. "Without sovereignty, we're nothing more than a Kiwanis club or a Rotary club," Todd Hembree said.

17. Since last year's election, Chief Baker has turned down requests to be interviewed.

descendants who successfully registered during the year-long window following Cornsilk's tribal court victory and the tribal constitutional referendum that stripped it away. This highly limited number of Freedmen descendants are permitted to vote in tribal elections under an agreement between U.S. Congress, the Department of Interior, and the Cherokee Nation—while the Vann case plays out in U.S. courts.

In the June 2011 general tribal election, in which incumbent Chief Smith campaigned for his fourth term, it was first reported that Baker beat Smith by a handful of votes. Given Smith's 12-year posture toward Freedmen descendants, advocates say that the fraction of potential Freedmen descendants who were permitted to vote supported Baker as a block—handing Baker an edge. The Cherokee Nation's highest court later ruled that the June 2011 tribal election results were too close to call. Another general election was scheduled for that September. Then, in August, just three weeks before the newly scheduled special election, the same tribal court ruled to strip the voting rights of the marginal 2,800 Cherokee Freedmen descendants—in apparent violation of the federal agreement. Baker, joining the side of Freedmen advocates, was outraged. After all, without the fractional Freedmen vote, the election would have no doubt once again swung in Smith's favor.

After Representative Frank and his colleagues protested, the federal government froze tens of millions of dollars in U.S. taxpayer funds scheduled for distribution to the Cherokee Nation that fall. An emergency U.S. court hearing took place in Washington, D.C., days before the September election. The ruling—another Velie victory—led to the reinstatement of voting rights to the limited 2,800 Freedmen. The public relations damage to Smith and his administration surged. Smith never recovered. Baker ended up winning the special general election by an even wider margin.[18] Now, thrust into his second year as chief, as the Vann case drags on,[19] the hopes held among Freedmen descendants that Baker would drop the U.S. court case and support their cause have all but evaporated.

Many of those sentiments have served to only strengthen the case against the Cherokee Nation within the court of public opinion. It is here that the Cherokee Nation may be fighting a losing battle. Each time the Vann case twists and turns, the tribe is forced into the public relations quagmire that comes with defending against a decade-long lawsuit in which race—apparently—plays a critical role. For years, Freedmen advocacy journalists and bloggers have vilified the tribe and its leaders with little balance, framing the Cherokee leaders and citizens as racists. In cases where race is the central question of law, this court tends to favor the plaintiffs.[20]

On the ground in Tahlequah, there are signs emerging that the entrenched division surrounding the Freedmen controversy that once so heavily blanketed the Cherokee Nation is slowly receding. Cherokee citizens have grown undoubtedly more docile, and in many cases, supportive of the Freedmen. "I think they have a right to claim citizenship," a teenage full-blood Cherokee told me after a powwow. Perhaps unfairly, fear of appearing racist—even if

18. "Let's hope that the new chief has a better attitude," Congressman Watt said. "And if he doesn't, we'll fight the new chief just like we did Chief Smith." Freedmen advocates, particularly David Cornsilk, have been disappointed in the apparent reluctance of members of Congress to take action to support the Freedmen cause.

19. Today, the Cherokee Nation argues that the 1866 Treaty guaranteed membership rights to Freedmen and their descendants. In 1867, the Cherokee Nation amended their tribal constitution to include the word "citizenship" rights to their Freedmen. Now, the tribe says that it had a sovereign right to do so, just as it had an equal right to amend their constitution nearly 150 years later to remove their Freedmen descendants by tribal constitutional amendment. The tribe supports the 1866 Treaty, but believes there is a distinction between membership rights and citizenship rights.

20. Where Baker has largely fallen silent on the Freedmen controversy since taking office, Todd Hembree has spoken openly about the case. In doing so, Hembree is leading the official shift in tone toward the Cherokee Freedmen—from the top down. It is an important front in the tribe's new public relations strategy. Gone is the combative tone toward Cherokee Freedmen that helped define the Smith administration. Hembree has helped replace it with a sense of transparency and civility, while still doggedly litigating against Velie and the Freedmen's claims. The night before the Cherokee Nation Tribal parade—as Rodslen Brown-King and her family wheeled the Freedmen float into place for the next morning's festivities—Hembree dined with the owners of one of Tahlequah's finer dining establishments. Comfortable in a dark suit, seemingly earnest, and at ease rubbing shoulders with Tahlequah's elite, it's hard not to see Hembree for his own political ambitions. He looks like a lot like a chief waiting in the wings.

As it turns out, tribal politics are in Hembree's blood; he is the great-great grandson of Cherokee Nation Principal Chief John Ross, who was seven-eighths Scottish. This helps explain why Hembree also looks white. The color of Hembree's skin makes him no less Cherokee, he says. "If someone thinks that just because we're light-skinned we don't live a Cherokee life or believe in the Cherokee ways," Hembree said, "I'm just going to sadly disagree with them." David Cornsilk finds this double standard prevalent throughout the Cherokee Nation. Cornsilk says that one who looks Caucasian and calls oneself Cherokee isn't questioned, but if one who appears black claims Cherokee citizenship, he or she is discriminated against.

Hembree, like his former boss, Chief Smith, is adamant that the Freedmen case has never been about race. What matters to Todd Hembree now, however, is that the people of the Cherokee Nation have spoken; the referendum that led to the Cherokee's tribal constitution amendment was legal, and his job is clear: to defend Cherokee law and the tribe's sovereign rights. "Without sovereignty, we're nothing more than a Rotary club," Hembree said. American Indian tribes are sovereign, but to what extent? Stacy Leeds, the former tribal justice—whose crucial tribal court decision ruled in favor of Cornsilk's legal argument over Hembree's—said that there is no doubt that a tribe has a sovereign right to define its citizenship. "There is also no doubt that sovereignty cannot be a reason for casting legality and morality aside," she said.

David Cornsilk in his Honda Civic

race is not, in fact, a factor—has taken a stronger hold. This may help explain why Corey Still, the University of Oklahoma full-blood Cherokee, had a change of heart. After the public debate in Norman, when the floor opened for questions, Still aggressively cross-examined Jon Velie from the audience. When I approached Still afterwards and introduced myself as a journalist and filmmaker, he agreed to share his personal feelings about the Freedmen during a formal interview. Months later, Still changed his mind.

Cornsilk attributes any changing tide, however slight, not to the tribe's public relations woes or new strategy, but to education. He says that the case has helped reveal the truth about the Cherokee Freedmen to the rest of the tribe. Many Cherokee who did vote against the Freedmen in 2007 are regretful of doing so now, he said. "Overcoming racism is a long process," Cornsilk said. He believes that if another constitutional referendum took place today, while close, the Freedmen would be welcomed back into the tribe. What Cornsilk and Velie have achieved through their legal advocacy—from within and outside the tribe, respectively—has given voice to Freedmen descendants like Lucy Allen and Marilyn Vann. And if part of their goal is to force more Cherokee to confront their own stained history with slavery, and move closer toward tribal reconciliation, then no matter the outcome of the Vann case, they are winning.

Velie is less optimistic, not about the potential of the Cherokee people to support the Freedmen, but of their tribal political leaders to abstain from leveraging race for political gains. Velie says that, at present, the vast majority of the Cherokee Freedmen still cannot vote or run for tribal office. He is charging on. If Velie is ultimately successful in the U.S. courts, one person now poised to help process Freedmen descendants—like Kenneth Payton[21] and Rodslen Brown-King and their children—as newly minted Cherokee citizens is none other than David Cornsilk. This January, Chief Bill John Baker hired David Cornsilk to return to work within the Cherokee Nation Registration Office. There was one condition. Cornsilk would have to cease from publically criticizing the tribe's position toward its Freedmen descendants. When the job was first offered, Cornsilk was still living in his car. Regardless, Cornsilk refused to sign the gag order. In need of a talented genealogist—or perhaps in the execution of the long-tested political strategy of keeping friends close, enemies closer—the Cherokee Nation hired Cornsilk anyway. Cornsilk has since moved into a new apartment.

---

21. On an overcast afternoon last spring at Kenneth Payton's home in Broken Arrow, he flipped through a series of family photographs. "To be included and to feel included would change the whole dynamic," he said. As Payton's sons horsed around upstairs, I asked Payton if his children understood their heritage. "The younger ones, if somebody came up to them they would say, 'Yeah, I'm Indian," he said. On the surface, Payton appears black, and Hembree white, but draw in closer and gradations emerge. For all of their divisiveness, Freedmen and Cherokee officials share one common purpose: closing the gap between how they perceive themselves from the within, and how they are perceived from the outside.

Originally published
April 2015

by Rilla Askew

TRAIL

For David Rain

On Tahlequah and the difference
between a place of memory and a
place of dreams, a place longed for
and the place of the present

Long after I left Tahlequah I dreamed of the place. Not just the town but the earth and waters that surround it. The Tahlequah of my dreams looks nothing like the real landscape. In my dreams the images are primitive, iconic: a dark symbol land. Still, I always know where I am. Usually it's the small cabin above the Illinois River where I once lived. Sometimes it's the steep, stone-filled path leading down to the cabin. Except, in reality, there was no such trail. That treacherous footpath above the Illinois belongs to Goats Bluff, miles upriver from where the cabin stood. But the mind will blend. The mind grabs hold of symbols. It tells you what matters. What you long for. What you fear.

There's the Tahlequah of my memory, a place crystallized in the seventh decade of the last century when I lived there with hippies and rock musicians and Indians and actors and the first gay community I ever knew anything about. I went to school at Northeastern, studied special ed and theater, danced at the Trail of Tears Outdoor Drama south of town. I picked up trash in the little park below Seminary Hall where Town Branch trickles lively over bright green watercress in springtime, creeps slow and debris-cluttered over quarried stones in high summer. I didn't pick up litter because of any acute environmental consciousness—it was just my work-study job, strolling around campus with a shoulder satchel and a long stick barbed with a nail on the end, stabbing up gum wrappers, red paper Coca-Cola cups, and pale golden Coors cans.

There is also the Tahlequah of now, of course, with its bypass roads and corporate fast-food corridor, its tourists and traffic and burgeoning Cherokee tribal complex: a vital place, growing, active—very much changed from the sleepy town I remember. I go there sometimes, to see friends. To search for something. But the Tahlequah of now isn't the place I long for.

When I first moved there I was told the town's name means *Two Will Do* in Cherokee. The Cherokees had lost a quarter of their people to suffering, starvation, and disease on the Trail of Tears. When they arrived on that terrible journey, the story goes, three scouts were sent out to discover the best place to set up their new headquarters, their "capital." Two men returned, saying this place here, nestled at the edge of rolling hills near a clear river and running streams, was the best location. The third scout never showed up. Tribal leaders decided that the word of the two who returned was enough, and they set their capital here, calling it *Ta'ligwu: Two Will Do. Two Is Enough.* I heard this story many times, from many sources, or versions of it. Sometimes the men are called "braves" or "elders." Sometimes they're meeting for council, not going out to search. I believed the story then. I doubt it now. It sounds to me like a white man's story, like the jokey stories I was told as a kid about how Nowata got its name, or Eufaula.

In the Tahlequah of my memory, it is always summer. Say the name, and I see the old Cherokee courthouse on the green lawn of the square, the bustling Shack Café and Morgan's Bakery down the street, the busy Safeway store with the tree-shrouded park rising above it and the street called Choctaw dividing at the cement wall. I see the deep, still waters of Lake Tenkiller miles away, where we used to swim late at night after rehearsals, leaping off the rocks into the black water at Wildcat Point, leaving behind the litter of our own pale golden cans when we piled into our vehicles at dawn. I see the rippling, stone-bedded waters of Baron Fork Creek east of town, remember the blond girl who floated away from our party on an inner tube one summer day stoned on pot and beer and was found later, drowned.

I see the winding green snake of the Illinois River, the dense woods pressing in on all sides, thick with vines and clotted undergrowth. I feel the humid air on my skin. My ears buzz with the din of cicadas in the hot afternoons, the relentless *scritch-scritch-scritch* of tree frogs at night. I see an army of black specks marching up my leg from where I've stepped in a nest of newly hatched seed ticks, hear the slaps of paddles on water, the shouts of drunken canoeists coming down the Illinois. "Do you work here?" they ask as I collect their empty beer cans and drop them in a pile on the gravel bar below the cabin. The river is a drinking game to them, a Disney ride, an exotic adventure.

"I *live* here," I say.

How long was it before I came to understand that my life was only superimposed on the land? That I was not *of* it, merely *on* it. I don't know. Years maybe. But I do know when my awakening started—in summer, in the 1970s, when I hung out day and night with the dancers and actors and Cherokee villagers I worked with at Trail.

The full title of the pageant was *The Trail of Tears Outdoor Drama at Tsa La Gi*, but most of us just called it "Trail," or sometimes "Tsalagi" (the initial sound pronounced halfway between *dja* and *cha*), which I was told meant "Cherokee" in Cherokee, implying it was their own name for themselves, though in fact their name in their native language is *Ani-yun-wiya*,

or the "Real People." Not that anyone explained that to me then.

Tsa La Gi was also the name of a place—not designated so by the Cherokee people but by an organization called the Cherokee National Historical Society, unaffiliated with the tribe, formed in 1962 by a white retired army colonel, Martin Hagerstrand, who was married to a mixed-blood Cherokee woman, the kind and lovely Marion Brown. The site near Park Hill had been the original home of the first school for women west of the Mississippi, the Cherokee National Female Seminary, built in 1851 at the height of Cherokee flourishing after the Trail of Tears, and destroyed by fire in 1887, the same year Congress passed the Dawes Act forcing allotment of tribal lands. Forty-four wooded acres of tall oaks and thick-leaved hickories, the compound featured a museum, a replica of an early day Cherokee village, and the Tsa La Gi Amphitheater where the Trail of Tears drama was performed. Excavated out of the earth itself, the theater had steeply raked seating so that audiences might look directly down on the action, a lushly wooded mountain, crisscrossed with stone walkways, rising in back of the performance space, and, on either side of the stage, giant turntables on wooden platforms to facilitate scene changes. Not far from the entrance, three enormous columns from the burned seminary stood like haunting memento mori amidst the trees.

Some local Cherokee women and their offspring would work all day in the Ancient Village, weaving baskets, demonstrating how to make blowgun darts or play stickball, and then walk across the shaded park to the amphitheater at dusk to perform in the drama as villagers—extras, essentially, who had no speaking parts and were paid less than the actors and dancers, but if they were Indian they did get to go onstage in their own hair and skin. Most of the white female dancers had to sweat under the stage lights in bulky black braided wigs, their skins smeared rust red with a theatrical compound known as Texas Dirt. I was only an understudy dancer, and not a very good one, as I will tell you now and would have told you then, but I tried very hard. My own hair was long and thick and dark enough that I was allowed to go wigless, though I still had to dab my damp sponge in the ruddy powder and smear my face and arms and legs before donning my costume—at least until midsummer, when my tan got dark enough that I could go onstage in my own skin. Halfway between dark and light, that's how I saw myself. The program listed me as part Cherokee because that's what I thought I was. That's what I'd always been told.

Each evening at 8:00 the stage lights came on, the music roared to life, and we all shuffled onto the stage in rags and tattered blankets, reenacting the forced march of the Cherokees from their homelands to this

Dewey Dailey, 1974, Tahlequah
Photo by Rilla Askew

territory in the west. The full cast drudged slowly through ominously lit space to the accompaniment of dirge-like music while the white actors who played Cherokee leaders began to orate. We stumbled and collapsed, some of us dying dramatically and being carried off—a bit of staged business we'd negotiate ahead of time, because it was our only chance to grab the audience's attention. Offstage, we'd sit on the concrete ramps leading to the turntables, our skirts hiked to our thighs or our shirts open, the scratchy blankets thrown aside as we sweated in the sultry evening heat, smoking cigarettes, flirting, fooling around. I didn't then think it an insult to make an entertainment of that brutal American act of ethnic cleansing, that homegrown death march known as the Trail of Tears. It was my understanding that the tribe approved of the drama, and none of the villagers seemed bothered by our lack of reverence. And anyway, the history in the play was true. More or less.

The script in those years, and for most of the amphitheater's history, was an epic melodrama by a white professor named Kermit Hunter, who'd also penned the script for a twin pageant in North Carolina about the Cherokees in the years before Removal. It was a white man's version of Indian history, told simplistically, if sympathetically, with spectacular special effects—dance! music! costumes! flash pots in the Civil War scenes!—but none of that bothered me. It was, after all, a pageant: by definition "an elaborate public spectacle illustrative of the history of a place." I did object to the fact there was only one significant female character, a sappy love interest named Sarah who spends most of the play acting like as big a ninny as any white female character in an old Western. I also didn't much care for how the Green Corn Dance had us all stooping over and whooping like bad imitations of Hiawatha and Pocahontas to a pounding Russian composition by Shostakovich. Overall, though, I loved working at Trail.

My nights were filled with excitement and performances and partying and learning people's ways I'd never known before. The choreographer was a wonderfully flamboyant Jewish man from New York City named Marvin who taught me words like *schmatta* and *mensch*. I felt ushered into a secret world with my gay friends, a kind of parallel hidden society that had been around from time immemorial, though I'd never known it. The dancers, both gay and straight, accepted me. They were kind to me, actually. Sometimes I wondered at how these performers who'd been training all their lives could be so tolerant of a clumsy girl who couldn't tell step-ball-change from chassez, or execute either very well. But they plopped their dance bags next to mine on the gym floor at rehearsals, showed me how to stretch my muscles without pulling a hamstring, how to wrap my ankles, avoid

shin splints. I felt at once inside and outside, a part of and apart from.

I can't say at what point I began to be uncomfortable with how the tragedy was told, the message the audiences left with. In the play, after much fighting and killing between Cherokee factions and a great deal of flashy spectacle, the story ends with the Cherokee people and the white citizens of Oklahoma uniting joyfully on the first day of statehood in 1907. The Cherokees are relieved and happy; they dress up in straw boaters and bustles, and dance a celebratory ragtime dance. The music swells, and Sarah's voice, cracked with age, weighted with wisdom, comes over the loudspeakers to tell the audience, in an astonishing mixing of metaphors, that the Cherokee people did not die in 1907 but were reborn, like the ancient phoenix: "The red man is like a crimson thread running through the texture of this new state... like red flowers growing on the green bosom of Oklahoma." And the largely white audiences shake themselves loose from the dream, climb the steep stairs to return to their tour buses and cars believing this is all to the good: no more sorrow, no more deadly divisions between the Cherokees, no more white folks taking away Indian homelands. A blessedly unified, peaceable world on the shining green breast of Oklahoma.

Except, I grew up here. I knew it wasn't so.

I couldn't then have named for you the kinds of troubles that lay ahead for Indian people in Oklahoma after 1907—the Osage Reign of Terror in the 1920s, for instance, when scores of Osages would be murdered for their oil headrights; or the federal relocation policies of the 1950s and '60s, when Indian families would be relocated from their allotted lands to distant urban areas, as Wilma Mankiller's family was moved to San Francisco in 1956; or the chillingly named "termination" policies that would continue to steal Indian children by systemically adopting them away from their tribes into "civilized" white homes; not to mention pervasive poverty, lack of self-determination, the relentless leaching away of Indian lands. But I knew intuitively, and by witness, the power of racial bias in this state. I'd seen it growing up in Bartlesville, living in Shawnee, Tulsa, Tahlequah—more subtle for Indian people than for black people, true, but it was surely there, a wordless color hierarchy within the dominant culture that said the darker your natural skin color, the lower your status.

It may be hard for some contemporary readers to recognize the racist underpinnings of a state that today proudly proclaims itself to be "Native America" and uses a sanitized version of Indian history to draw tourists, a place where half the white population claims the ubiquitous "Cherokee" great-grandmother. I don't know why *Cherokee* became the proprietary eponym for *Indian*, but it happened long before my time, along with the obligatory "high cheekbones" proof of such ancestry, as my Papaw Allie always pointed to on his own face. His purportedly part-Cherokee mother was born in Texas and migrated to Indian Territory with her family as a young girl—and, yes, from her pictures I believe she could have been part Indian, and, yes, there were Cherokees in Texas in the mid-1800s, a few, but there were also Comanches and Wichitas and Caddos and Tonkawas and other tribes you don't hear white people claiming to be "part" of. Maybe it's because the word *Cherokee* sounds so nice in English—it's easy to pronounce, has that satisfying throat click in the middle, and white history has proclaimed the Cherokees to be a "civilized" nation, so somehow that led to the adoption, even in my grandfather's still very prejudiced era, of Cherokee as the only acceptable tribe to be from—if one were going to claim to be Indian at all.

The 1970s were a transitional period between the overt racism of my great-grandparents' day, when some families hid their Indian blood because they thought it not good or smart to be Indian, to the tremendous surge of Native American wannabes today. Even in the '70s it was acceptable, though not yet chichi, to be of Indian descent. But the bias against full-bloods remained. I could hear it in the racist "drunk Indian" jokes told by white friends, see it in the faces of certain dark-skinned kids who were bullied or ostracized at school. The progression from covert prejudice to it's-cool-to-be-Indian accelerated rapidly toward the end of the century, a cultural shift that was hard to miss. I've often remarked that when I left Oklahoma in 1980, nobody was Indian. When I came back in the 1990s, everybody was.

But in Tahlequah, and especially those summers at Trail, it seemed to me that traditional Cherokees and those of us from the dominant culture lived side by side, our worlds superimposed one on the other, as my life on the river was superimposed on the landscape, but our realities did not touch. Somehow either they, or we, were a hologram. Many of the performers were of Indian descent, proud of their heritage, but white in their way of being. Others looked as white as I did, or more so—pale skin, auburn hair—and yet had more kinship to Indian ways than others with greater blood quantum. There was an unfathomable difference, which I felt but could not name. The layers were beyond my ken: there was a social layer, how we all behaved with one another; a layer of ceremony and tradition, which I heard about but was not privy to; layers of politics, sentiment, romanticism, culture; a hidden spirit layer that was palpable to me but beyond my grasp. I felt it most acutely in the natural world around Tahlequah, the hills cradling the town, the rivers and streams that lace through there, the thick woods closing in on all sides. I sensed it in the shaded grounds of the complex itself, with its ghostly post oak trees, its charred brick columns from the old female seminary standing sentinel as the tourists filed back to their buses in the dark.

My first summer at Trail there were two star dancers, Eddie Burgess and Dewey Dailey. Both were Indian, both stunningly talented—gifted beyond the level of ability one might expect at an outdoor drama. Their dancing dominated each night's performance. They were point and counterpoint, darkness and light: Eddie, compact, muscular, was the Death Dancer who followed the Cherokees through all their dark days on the Trail, shaking his rattles, taunting them, leaping and tumbling about the stage in scenes of death and destruction. Dewey, long and lithe and graceful as a Balanchine, was the Phoenix who rises from the ashes at the end of the play. These days I can't imagine not knowing the tribes of any of my Indian friends, but in those days I didn't think about it. I never asked what tribe they were, whether either of them was Cherokee or not.

Eddie and I had grown up together in the same Oak Park neighborhood in Bartlesville; his house was just a few blocks from mine, his younger brother in the same class as my sister. I hadn't known him well then because he was a couple of years behind me in school, but I did know he was a fabulous gymnast. It was Eddie's gymnastic mastery, incorporated into the dance, that made his performances so breathtaking. He had an almost terrifying skill. He rolled and tumbled about the stage in a kind of controlled frenzy that seemed to me at once balletic and thrillingly wild. Eddie partied as hard as any of us (in that summer stock milieu drinking and carousing were just what we did), but he was also the hardest-working performer I'd ever seen in my life. The first to arrive at the theater, he'd be warmed up and ready to go, having practiced some uncountable amount of time by dusky evening when we all came sauntering and chattering in. His girlfriend, Cindy, is one of the dancers I especially remember as being kind to me that summer, and so was Eddie, in fact, though he was so much the star, and had the authority of dance captain besides, that I recall admiring him more from afar than being inside his circle.

Dewey was simply beautiful: sculpted face, arched brows, lush lips. The first time I saw the musician Prince I thought, God, he looks like Dewey Dailey. In fact, though, Dewey was even more beautiful than that. His performances as the Phoenix were exquisite: feathered, weightless, lighter than air, he seemed to soar beyond the reach of gravity, the symbolic creature who does battle with Death near the end of the travails, is vanquished, burned in the fire, but rises again from the ashes, transfigured to a small Indian boy on a shield, lifted above the heads of the danc-

Trail of Tears Historic Drama brochure, 1976

ers in a triumphant drum-pounding, brass-thrilling, heart-racing theatrical climax at play's end.

Night after night we dancers ran in circles around the leaping, pirouetting, half flying Phoenix, flapping our sheer red and orange and yellow flags—the *schmattas* of Marvin's designation—like flames of fire around the dying bird. Night after night, Dewey died in the flames, and night after night, was reborn as one of the little Cherokee villager boys raised up on a shield. Night after night, Sarah's aged voice came over the loudspeaker to declare that the Cherokees had always believed that the "Great Spirit" had destined them to do "one great thing," and to suggest it was perhaps this, the creation of this new state of Oklahoma, that fulfilled their destiny. And night after night, in bustle and gingham skirt, I kicked and strutted that two-step ragtime "1907" with a silent, inarticulate rebellion in my chest, an inchoate sense of wrongness: Surely the Cherokee people did not see it this way.

How could they? Statehood meant further destruction of the Nation, more land theft, the complete usurpation of self-determination. It meant this land they had suffered so terribly to reach was no longer Indian

Territory but, in a brutal transmogrification of two Choctaw words meaning *red people*, this place was now White Man's Land.

I don't mean to say I was outraged back then, or that I understood yet how my own family's migration into I.T. in the late 1800s was part of the relentless story of theft and displacement, or that I was attuned to how thoroughly white-biased and appropriated the script at Trail of Tears was. I mean only that I'd started seeing things in a new way. I mean that, deep inside me, an awakening had begun—an awakening that was as much artistic as it was social or political, because I loved what Eddie and Dewey did on the stage every night. The acting in the play was heavy handed, oratorical, overwrought. The choreography was a New Yorker's stereotyped vision of how to evoke Indian dances, even though, yes, we had shell-shakers in the Green Corn Dance—Cherokee women with heavy pebble-filled turtle shells strapped to their calves—and there was a dance called the "Ribbon Dance" which had the men and women in beribboned "tear" shirts and dresses, though the movements looked rather like a European maypole dance. But the sheer artistry of those two dancers, night after night, took my breath away. Death Dancer and Phoenix. Darkness and Light. Destruction and Survival. Their unending duel, vanquishment, and triumph epitomized the layers of spirit and story I could perceive but not name.

• • •

The last summer I danced at Trail was 1977. That was the summer Elvis died, and New York City went dark in a blackout that wrapped the city in violence and fear. The summer Florida voters heeded Anita Bryant's anti-gay crusade and repealed their gay-rights ordinance. The summer three little girls were brutally murdered near Locust Grove and a Cherokee man named Gene Leroy Hart hid out in the hills north of Tahlequah, evading capture for that horrific crime which many locals said he did not commit. I heard talk. The Little People hid him, they said. No, others countered: It was the old Cherokee full bloods living deep in the hills who kept the fugitive from being found. Some said Hart was *stigini*, a shapeshifter, a night-walker-about.

Hart's disappearance seemed, that summer, another part of the ineffable mystery, another layer of what I could not understand. There were haunting, persistent rumors. He would never be found, some said. He was a modern day Ned Christie, a Cherokee man unfairly declared outlaw by the white man's law, but not by his own. Others hated and feared him, had convicted him already in their minds because of the news stories. Details of the manhunt covered the news every day, along with veiled rehashings of the unspeakable crimes against three innocent little girls—a tragic, horrific outrage, an unendurable heartbreak for their families that I could hardly bear to think of it. How could someone, *anyone*, do such a thing?

We know the ending now, or part of it anyway, what eventually was told in the news: how Hart would elude the searchers well after summer's end, through the winter and into the following spring, when he would be captured and brought to trial. How he would be acquitted of the Girl Scout Murders for lack of evidence but sent to the McAlester State Penitentiary anyway to serve out time on a prior conviction. And how, three months after that, he would fall dead of a heart attack while running laps in the prison yard, which some said was inmate justice, covered up, and others said, no, it was Cherokee justice, because Hart really did do those terrible murders, and Cherokee medicine had taken care of him in that way.

I don't know the truth now any more than I knew it then, that last summer in Tahlequah, when Hart was a fugitive hiding in a landscape of clotted undergrowth and clear running streams—like the area where I lived with my boyfriend in an isolated cabin on the banks of the Illinois. I thought of him out there sometimes. If I happened to awaken on a moonless night, say, to lie in darkness as thick as a wall, listening to the night sounds all around me: the tree frogs' insistent chorus, rhythmic and relentless as torture; the scrabbling of tiny mousefeet in the pine rafters overhead. The low, repetitive hoot of an owl in the trees across the river. I don't remember being afraid. Only watchful. Only listening. I began to understand in a feeling way, a wordless gut- and dream-level way, that I was no more a part of the landscape than the weekend float-trippers. I was only passing through, my life merely superimposed there. I was the hologram. The night sounds could have been anything, I told myself. Animal creatures, human fugitive, or something more intangible and dangerous—a shapeshifter, perhaps. But if so, it didn't have to do with me. I wouldn't be vulnerable. I was too white.

• • •

In 1989 my first published story, "The Gift," about a mixed-blood Cherokee boy who descends a steep treacherous path to a cabin above a river, appeared in *Nimrod*'s spring "Oklahoma Indian Markings" issue. Those same pages are where I first read a Joy Harjo poem. It's where I met the work of Linda Hogan, Joe Dale Tate Nevaquaya, Louis Littlecoon Oliver, where I first saw the gripping photographs of Richard Ray Whitman, the drawings of Shan Goshorn. I had left Tahlequah, left Oklahoma, left acting for the life of a writer, and was then living and teaching in New York. In December that year, I attended the Modern Languages Association conference in Washington, D.C., because the brochure I'd received in my mailbox at Brooklyn College included a listing for a gathering of Indian writers: "Readings by Emerging American Indian Poets." That listing was the only reason I went.

I sat in the back of the conference room, shy and self-conscious, acutely aware of my separation. My aloneness. On the front rows the writers all sat together. I could see the backs of their heads as they leaned toward each other, their long hair fanned out on their shoulders as they laughed together. They were familiar to me in a way that I didn't know anyone else in that room, none of the other white teachers, academics, students. I couldn't hear what they were laughing about, but I knew the kind of laughter it was, could hear it in my mind, that dry, ironical *aaaayyy* Indian humor. The feeling I had as I watched them was like going home after a very long time away. Like being almost there.

Yuchi poet Joe Dale Tate Nevaquaya was one of the writers; his brother Richard Ray Whitman also read, and Elizabeth Woody, Carter Revard, many wonderful writers. When Joe read his poems, though, I had an experience, heart-catching, indefinable, that burned the poem in me, not with intellect but in silence, in fiery recognition. I can't explain it exactly, but it happened that night and every time I've heard him read his poems since. Afterwards, I loitered at the edge of the crowd angling forward to talk to the writers. I wasn't leaving but I also didn't know anyone to talk to, or what to say if I did. Joe Dale was standing off to one side near the front, leaning against a wall, quiet and watchful; his separation from the others made him seem as alone and shy as I felt. I went up and told him how much I'd enjoyed his reading. We started talking, I don't recall about what—it wouldn't have been poetry because I'm inarticulate on that score; very likely it was about where we're from, the Oklahoma we grew up in. Later, as the writers were all making plans to go out to a restaurant, his brother Richard Ray (I didn't know yet they were brothers) said to me, "You coming?" I said, "Um... yeah!"

For a few hours a bunch of us sat at pushed-together tables in a D.C. restaurant, talking hard and fast as we could talk, laughing and joking, and the feeling I had was one of familiarity and discovery, and also of coming home. When the place closed, we spilled out onto the sidewalk, where snow was beginning to fall. We all milled about in the snow-sifted light, still laughing, still joking, exchanging phone numbers and trying to recall directions to our various hotels. I had my car because I'd driven down from New York, but they'd all flown in from Oklahoma, St. Louis, Washington state, so it took a while for everyone to sort themselves into various cabs for the trips to their hotels. Moments later I stopped at a red light and glanced over at the vehicle idling next to me, a yellow taxi, where I saw Joe Dale and Richard and some others in the backseat waving at me; we all waved and laughed, rolled down our windows to holler at one another, till the light changed, and they went their way, and I went mine.

Long months later, on a summer night in his mother's backyard in Oklahoma City, during one of our long, late into the night, word-firing conversations that made my heart and the top of my head feel like they could explode, Joe Dale and I spoke about that evening, the final hours of the year, the very decade, and he said, "The universe shifted that night." I said, "Oh, yes."

Because, for me, it was true. Looking back, there are only a few things I know for sure about my journey to becoming a writer, and one is that the first most powerful influence on that journey was my husband, and the second most powerful was Joe Dale Tate Nevaquaya. In concentric, radiating circles the influences ripple out from there. I wouldn't be the writer I am or write what I do without those friendships that forged and shaped me, the ones that began that snowy

night in Washington, D.C. The first Oklahoma writers I knew were Indian writers. They were the first to make me see, through their words, friendship, books, poems, passionate discussions deep into the night, what this place is, what it has been, what we are all doing here, or trying to do. To this day they're the community I feel most... well, not a part of. Not apart from. They're where my heart is. Their imprint on me is unchangeable. They were the first pure artists I'd known, the first "makers," whose very way of seeing is art, and back before them, there were Eddie Burgess and Dewey Dailey and their exquisite artistry at the Trail of Tears Outdoor Drama at Tsa La Gi.

• • •

Eddie left Oklahoma, as I did, to pursue an artistic career. We met for drinks one night in New York in 1981. We talked about Trail, the people we'd known, how far it felt like we'd come. He was then dancing with a New York company, Jennifer Muller/The Works. Later he would travel the world as a dancer and teacher and eventually become the respected and much beloved chairman of the dance department at the University of Wisconsin-Milwaukee's Peck School of the Arts. A photograph of him at the barre with other dancers shows a warm, affable smile, sleek bald head, fringe of gray hair, and, still, that compact, ferocious dancer's body, even in middle age. It's strange to see him that way, so different from the dark long-haired young dancer he was when I last saw him, and yet the same. The photo is on his memorial page, along with testimonials from other dancers whose lives Eddie touched, because he's gone now. He died too young, in his sleep, at the age of 58. His bio on the website doesn't mention that he was full-blood Cherokee.

I don't have a middle-aged picture of Dewey Daily to contrast with my memories. He didn't make it that far. He was Otoe-Missouria and also Kaw and Muncie. He, too, died too young, much younger than Eddie, in Dallas, from complications related to HIV. In my mind I can't see him any way except as the soaring, unfettered, red-and-white-winged Phoenix. Like Tahlequah itself, Dewey is crystallized in my mind at the height of his young beauty.

• • •

When I return now I drive by the old haunts looking for what has changed and what hasn't. Some places have vanished, like Sixkiller's Barbecue and the tiny frame rent house on Allen Road where I once lived. Some have been transformed, like the old Quik-Trip on Goingsnake, which is now the continuing education office for NSU. Some remain the same. In the park below Seminary Hall, Town Branch still rushes or trickles over the stones, the watercress is still a bright springtime green, campus litter still catches in sluggish rotations in the slow eddies in summer. South of town, fast food joints are strung now like bright corporate Legos on the road to Muskogee.

Sometimes I turn east off that road toward Park Hill, winding my way along the two-lane blacktop to the Cherokee Historical Center. That's what they call Tsa La Gi now, and it very much lives up to its name: a beautiful native stone museum with a permanent exhibit about the Trail of Tears, a newly built village, where visitors can see the same kinds of flint napping, basket weaving, stickball demonstrations tourists saw in the Ancient Village, but with a difference— there is an atmosphere of pride and autonomy, an authenticity of ownership I didn't feel at the outdoor drama back in the day. The three giant columns from the Cherokee National Female Seminary stand where they've always stood, a place of honor, in front of the museum.

If you walk around back, through the tree shrouded parking lots and beyond, you can just see the mottled gray roof of the amphitheater rising barely above the earth. Bypass the yellow caution tape sealing the area off for safety, angle your way around to the west, where the tape has deteriorated and begun to sag, and you can enter the amphitheater at the end of the dim covered hallway where the audiences once went in. The wooden slats at the bottom of the housing are ragged, eaten away, black with damp and mold. Everywhere is the odor of mildew, rotting wood. Here the audiences would wind their way around the perimeter to their numbered rows, line up during intermission for popcorn and hotdogs and the colorful souvenir programs that told all about the Trail of Tears, stand in urgent lines snaking from the restroom doorways into the crowded hall. If you move through the shadowed space to the open archway, you can look down onto the stage, where small trees and sumac bushes are growing up through the asphalt. The giant overhead fans are broken, hanging loose from their moorings. The loudspeakers, where Sarah's voice came on to tell audiences about the Cherokees' destiny, have been torn out, wires dangling from the sound booth. The folded seats rim the stage like teeth, faded pink, mildew stained. And the little mountain behind the stage, where the Death Dancer once shook his rattles in the searing lights and leapt and tumbled in an orchestration of death-defying movement and sound, is overgrown as a jungle, chaotic, forbidding. All is rot and deterioration, the slow leaching away, through years of sun and cold, drought and rain, of what had been built here. In the distance you can hear the shouts of the stickball players inside the village— Cherokee players, men and boys, their cries of tri-umph, their joking laughter, just as it should be. As it should always have been.

I never go back to the river to see if the cabin is still there. I think I know it isn't—the place was decrepit, little more than a tarpaper shack even when I lived there decades ago. It lives on in my memory, though, that cramped, one room cabin and the treacherous path leading down to it—a trail that, in reality, doesn't exist. Except in my dreams. Except in my stories. The steep rock-strewn path where a young mixed-blood boy is carried down to the cabin under his father's arm in "The Gift." The home, in my novel *Harpsong*, of Calm Bledsoe, a mixed-blood Cherokee trapper who is murdered by white thieves. These places are seated deep within me; they're not the landscape of my heart but a dreamscape seared in my subconscious, my memory, everlasting, waiting to be dreamed awake.

Originally published
August 2014

by Russell Cobb

AMONG THE TRIBE OF THE WANNABES

How Iron Eyes Cody made a career
out of pretending to be an Indian,
and why white people continue
to fashion Native identities out
of thin air

Let's take a voyage to a not-so-distant land and visit a strange tribe. Or maybe not so strange. In fact, you may even belong to it. Before we begin our expedition, a trivia question: What do Bill Clinton, Miley Cyrus, Johnny Cash, and Elizabeth Warren all have in common?

Answer: All of them have claimed to be part Cherokee, but none have been able to prove it. Not that any of these celebrities are unique in this regard. Rare is the Oklahoma family that doesn't think it possesses at least one-sixteenth Cherokee blood.

But here's a fun fact: according to the Cherokee Nation, there are approximately 120,000 tribal members living in the state, which has a population of 3.8 million people. That's only about 3 percent of Oklahomans. The tribe we're going to visit, however, is bigger than the Cherokee Nation and perhaps even bigger than the entire state of Oklahoma—although that's difficult confirm, since the Census Bureau doesn't keep statistics on this subset of the population.

We are among the tribe of the Wannabes: non-Native Americans who insist on claiming Indian heritage. Why do Wannabes appropriate, fabricate, and invent a Native identity? Is it for pure financial gain? Is it part of a colonialist project to speak for the Other? College admissions? A highly subjective existential crisis? Examining the motives of the Wannabes is a fraught subject, one where good intentions rub up against old racist habits and where narrative embroidery easily morphs into self-delusion. It's where the personal is political and politics get personal.

. . .

Our voyage begins in earnest with the case of Iron Eyes Cody, a man better known to the world as "The Crying Indian."

If you watched TV at any time in the 1970s, you'll remember the Crying Indian. He debuted on television on Earth Day, 1971, in an event some people have called the birth of the modern environmental movement. The ad, produced by the pro-bono advertising group the Ad Council, is one of the most emotionally powerful one-minute spots ever produced.

It begins with a vague image of a man in a canoe barely visible through the leaves of a tree. He paddles gently down a river to a slow thud of drums. The fringe from his buckskin jacket, two braids of long hair, and a single feather in his headband come into

President Jimmy Carter
with Iron Eyes Cody, 1978

RACE READER

view. We briefly glimpse the idyllic image of unspoiled America: pine trees, a glistening lake, and a Noble Savage in a canoe. Here is the natural man as Jean-Jacques Rousseau once imagined him: the human being at one with nature and freed from the shackles of societal conventions.

Now we are face-to-face with our stoic warrior. He paddles with more vigor as the tempo of the music picks up. The camera zooms in on two pieces of garbage in the water. A brassy soundtrack starts to blare, and the camera sweeps out to reveal a factory belching smoke into the air and more litter in the lake. Our Noble Savage drags his canoe to a shoreline littered with plastic cups and aluminum cans, his head bowed in sorrow.

He walks to a road filled with traffic, his once-stoic face now showing signs of a profound sadness as he watches garbage being tossed out of passing cars.

An off-screen baritone narrator intones the following: "Some people have a deep, abiding respect for the natural beauty that was once this country. And some people don't." A plastic sack dropped by a motorist explodes at our Wise Elder's feet, his buckskin now soiled by fast food.

The narrator pauses a beat, allowing a sense of collective shame to wash over the audience. The narrator starts back in again. "People start pollution, and people can stop it." A single tear wells up and then rolls down the Indian's cheek as the screen fades to black.

Many people have wondered about this tragic figure, and in his 1982 memoir, *Iron Eyes: My Life as a Hollywood Indian*, Cody purported to give a full account of his life. He tells us he was born and raised on a ranch in Oklahoma to family of Cree and Cherokee farmers, only finding fame years later as a character actor and consultant on Indian dress and sign language to famous directors such as Cecil B. DeMille and John Ford.

Iron Eyes traced his ancestry all the way back to the Trail of Tears. During the Civil War, his Cherokee grandfather joined up with a bunch of Confederate outlaws known as Quantrill's Raiders. This mixed-race posse terrorized Missouri, Kansas, and Indian Territory, pillaging Union forces and riding off into the Ozarks with their loot. They were indomitable, submitting neither to the Confederate military brass nor to the victorious Union army. They were, in effect,

professional badasses—some wearing black sombreros with silver inlays and bullet bandoliers across their chests. Among their posse was a black man named Two Bits who acquired the name for his piano-playing in whorehouses. If this is starting to sound like a Sam Peckinpah or Quentin Tarantino Western, remember that Iron Eyes' memoir is subtitled: *My Life as a Hollywood Indian.*

But Iron Eyes, well, according to his memoir, was just a regular old "Injun" who "wandered off the reservation into fame and fortune." The fact there were no Indian reservations in Oklahoma and that the eastern portion of the state—which included the Cherokee area—was known not as Oklahoma Territory (as Iron Eyes calls it) but Indian Territory, and that statehood occurred when he was just two years old, might raise a red flag among literal-minded readers. But for the sake of our journey, let's give him a pass. We'll assume he is speaking metaphorically of "the reservation." In any case, the narrative quickly shifts from an undisclosed location on an Oklahoma ranch to Hollywood, as Iron Eyes recounts a lifetime of work during the Golden Age of the Hollywood Western, and it is here we see the formation of the iconic American Indian take shape.

Most of the first half of the book is devoted to celebrity yarn-spinning, recalling Gary Cooper's terrible horsemanship and incorrigible playboy vices. Or John Wayne's terrible alcoholism and fear that his real name—Marion Morrison—sounded like a "fairy." More importantly, however, the book reveals the solidification of the American imaginary regarding Native Americans. Iron Eyes recalls how he butted heads with the legendary Cecil B. DeMille, insisting that Indians be represented "authentically" in the filming of *The Plainsman*. On set, Cody assembled a cast of "Indians," some belonging to local tribes but mostly white actors dressed in headdresses and war paint:

Everybody stood at attention while he walked up and down the ranks. "Okay, take that off," he said, stopping at one end, pointing to a beaded vest. He stopped again, "Take that off, and that, and —" "Wait, *wait* a minute, C.B. You can't take those things off. He's gonna be a chief. Cheyenne chiefs wore vests like that. And he's a warrior,

1   Cody and Perry, 1982: 194-195.

they always wore leggings. That's a medicine pouch on him. It stays." "You've got too much clothes on them." "Not for these Indians, C.B. We either do an authentic picture or I'll walk off and the Indians will come with us." [1]

Iron Eyes also taught actors a few rudimentary Plains Indian sign language gestures. Cherokees are not Plains Indians, but somehow Iron Eyes established himself as an authority on the subject. Some tribes have different gestures, but Iron Eyes created a fusion, an Esperanto of hand talk. In 1970, he documented this language in a book called *Indian Talk: Hand Signals of the American Indians*. The book was reviewed positively by one of the most prestigious scholarly journals in anthropology, *American Anthropologist*, in 1972.

As Hollywood moved from the era of pure spectacle and illusion to a politicized and realistic aesthetic in the late 1960s, Iron Eyes followed suit. Working with the mercurial British actor Richard Harris on the 1970 *A Man Called Horse*, Cody began to insist on authentic portrayals of initiation rites and medicine rituals, often over the demands of the producer.

Although Iron Eyes played bit parts in dozens of Westerns over five decades, it is this film that may hold the clue to his transformation from a supporting actor into America's most recognizable Indian. *A Man Called Horse* tells the story of an English aristocrat, John Morgan, who is captured by the Sioux and enslaved by them until his cunning and dogged determination wins the Natives over and he becomes a Sioux warrior. Unlike previous Westerns, however, *A Man Called Horse* spared the Armenian bole (a reddish-brown chemical often sprayed on white actors to make them look Native) and convinced many moviegoers that they were finally catching a glimpse of authentic Plains Indian culture.

Some Native American activists, however, saw the film as inauthentic. Among them was Ward Churchill, who wrote that the movie "depicts a people whose language is Lakota, whose hairstyles range from Assiniboine through Nez Perce to Comanche, whose tipi design is Crow, and whose Sun Dance ceremony and lodge in which it is held are both typically Mandan."

Churchill's critique hinged on a strident defense that "authenticity" is something that can only be defined from within a given culture. Churchill, like Iron Eyes Cody, claimed part Cherokee ancestry, and set about defining the parameters of Indian authenticity in books like *Fantasies of the Master Race*. Churchill himself, however, turned out to be more parts Wannabe than Cherokee. [2]

· · ·

By the early 1970s, then, Iron Eyes Cody was not only simply a Native American character actor, but one of the most important figures in fashioning Americans' ideas about the "authentic Indian." The culmination of his long career was undoubtedly the "The Crying Indian." The Ad Council, a pro-bono conglomeration of companies that creates public service announcements, sponsored the commercial. Rosie the Riveter, Smokey Bear, "Just Say No": all public service announcements produced by the Ad Council. During the Cold War, the Ad Council turned to blatant U.S. propaganda, urging Americans to take an active role in promoting U.S. industry in the fight against communism. At the same time, the modern environmental movement was born and urged industry to promote recycling and reuse of materials. The Ad Council countered with its own "environmental" message, which stressed the responsibility of individuals—not corporations—to fight pollution.

One of the taglines of this Keep America Beautiful campaign was "People start pollution. People can stop it," which seemed benign enough, but turned out to be part of a political attack on more progressive environmental groups such as the Sierra Club. Keep America Beautiful was a non-profit group supported by bottle manufacturers to prevent bottle deposit laws, and encouraging more and more consumption, according to investigative journalist Ginger Strand. Bottle deposit laws—most enacted with the birth of the environmental movement—were driving down demand for new glass and aluminum. The Ad Council's "Crying Indian" spots tried to change the conversation, making the environmental movement a question of personal ethics, not corporate responsibility.

Iron Eyes initially declined the role as the Crying Indian. He didn't know how to swim and was afraid

---

2 Churchill continually cautioned readers that Wannabes or "Friends of the Indian" — such as the Richard Harris character — are almost always neocolonialist wolves in sheep's clothing. The best white people could do, in his opinion, was to sit back and listen deeply to real Indians such as himself. In 2005, Churchill began to be hoisted on his own petard. Following academic misconduct allegations, the Cherokee Nation retreated from Churchill, saying that he only possessed "associate membership" as an honor, and that all associated memberships were rescinded in the 1990s. Like Elizabeth Warren, Churchill refused to back down, and presented evidence that may identify him as one-sixteenth Cherokee.

to be out in a canoe in San Francisco Bay by himself. The director promised to have a helicopter hover over him in case he tipped over. When it came time for the money shot—the tear rolling down the cheek—Iron Eyes was ready. He knew how to cry on demand for the camera, but there was a problem: His real tears did not show up well enough on camera. The director used glycerin to created one large tear that rolled down Iron Eyes's cheek at the last minute.

In 1996, the journalist Angela Aleiss revealed that the man known to the world as "The Crying Indian" was born Espera Oscar de Corti in the small town of Kaplan, Louisana. Aleiss told me it was an open secret among Native American actors in Los Angeles that Iron Eyes wasn't Indian, but no one had thought to figure out who he really was.

Aleiss consulted records from a small Catholic church in the town and found that de Corti's father, Antonio, had been the victim of vicious anti-Italian sentiment in turn-of-the-century Louisiana. The decade before Oscar's father came over from Sicily, more than a dozen Italians in the state had been lynched. To make matters worse, an extortion racket commonly referred to as the Black Hand Society (an early version of the Mafia) had sprung up in southern Louisiana. Antonio de Corti had to give up his small shop and flee to Texas, where his three sons eventually joined him.

Somewhere along the way, young Oscar de Corti saw a Wild West show and became enamored with all things Native, always playing the Indian in Cowboys and Indians. Aleiss wrote that the de Corti family remade themselves in Texas; the father slightly Anglicized his name to Tony Corti. Oscar made his way to Los Angeles in the teens, becoming Oscar Codey and finally Iron Eyes Cody. By the time Aleiss interviewed him in 1996, he had been widowed by his Native wife and brought up the two sons they adopted. When he died in 1999, everything indicated that he convinced himself of his own lie.

• • •

Iron Eyes Cody may have been a Hollywood Indian, but there's more to the tribe than show business. There are many subcategories of Wannabes, but the most common member of the tribe we might call the Almost Native—the white person who claims one-sixteenth blood quantum, just enough to squeak by America's arbitrary racial standards that designate who is and is not a minority.

The most famous and most controversial Almost Native of the moment is Oklahoma City-born Elizabeth Warren, who is rumored to be a candidate for president in 2016. During her 2012 campaign for the U.S. Senate in Massachusetts against incumbent Sen-

ator Scott Brown, Warren frequently described "family lore" about her Cherokee forbearers as part of her hardscrabble, coming-of-age story. Conservatives mocked her for identifying herself as a "Native American" minority during two stints at law schools in the 1990s. While it appears that she never benefited from affirmative action for minorities and stopped listing herself as a minority lawyer by 1995, she has refused to back away from claims of Native ancestry.

When Warren's claims to Cherokee ancestry were scrutinized closely by genealogists, no one could find her ancestors among those named on the Dawes Roll, which the government intended to be a master list of Cherokee surnames and finalized in 1906. (Although they did find one ancestor during territorial days who had actually boasted of killing a Cherokee.) Like many dubious narratives of whites passing for Native, Warren's story takes many twists and turns, some of which receive a gloss in her new memoir, *A Fighting Chance*. In the book, Warren weaves her "Native American heritage" (specific references to the Cherokee have now disappeared) into a narrative of working-class struggle, with her "mamaw and papaw" handing down stories and recipes from their days in Indian Territory.

And then there's Aunt Bee, who told Liz Warren that her papaw had inherited high cheekbones from his Indian ancestors but did not passed them down to the little girl. It's all part of a home-spun narrative of authentic Americana: Daddy worked hard as a janitor, but had a heart attack and couldn't pay the medical bills. Mama was devoted to her family, but sometimes didn't have enough money to put food on the table for the four kids. Eventually, little Liz had to work, too, before she dropped out of college at age 19 to support her husband's professional goals. Then she picked herself up by her bootstraps and put herself through law school in the wake of a divorce. It's like a PG-rated Loretta Lynn or Tammy Wynette song with all the cheating and drinking purged from the storylines.

A lot of people scoffed at fair-skinned, blue-eyed Warren's claim of Native American heritage. But, as an Okie myself, I instantly recognized the narrative. It has an undeniable pull and a certain degree of truthiness, as Stephen Colbert would say. The mythic Native ancestor in the white settler family lends a folksy, feel-good element to a narrative of colonization, exploitation, and plunder.

• • •

We still are left with a nagging question for the Wannabes: Why do they do it? Why do so many white people—from Elizabeth Warren to Miley Cyrus to Iron Eyes Cody—fashion a Native identity out of thin air? I contacted Aleiss about her research to ask her

if there was anything that united this unruly tribe. The one common denominator she cited was "financial opportunity." Indeed, there are many instances of whites making a buck while trafficking in faux-Native identity, but I'm not totally convinced it all boils down to money. According to the 2010 census, more than a quarter of Native Americans live in poverty, contrasted to only 10 percent of whites. There's more money to be made in the white world than on the reservation.

I suspect that the claim of Native identity bestows upon a prospective author a sort of symbolic capital that works in inverse proportion to white privilege. Fake Indian personae have allowed otherwise un-publishable white authors to achieve notoriety. There are many examples, including Forrest Carter, the author of *The Education of Little Tree*. Carter turned out to not be Cherokee, as he claimed, but a former Ku Klux Klansman from Alabama named Asa Earl Carter. The case of Carter's memoir is laden with even more ironic twists and turns than that of Iron Eyes Cody, as Carter made a name for himself in the public sphere by becoming one of Alabama's most vocal white supremacists. He is reputed to have written Alabama Governor George Wallace's *cri de guerre*: "Segregation now, segregation tomorrow, and segregation forever." Carter disappeared from public life only to remake

himself years later as Forrest "Little Tree" Carter, an orphaned boy raised by his Cherokee grandparents, wise elders who taught the boy to live a simple, natural life until he confronts the racist system of an Indian residential school.

To this day, critics are divided about how to view *Little Tree*: Is the book an opportunistic play on white America's hunger for the "authentic" Indian, or is it Carter's secret confession of guilt for having been such a vocal racist for decades. The writer Sherman Alexie has summoned up this contradiction nicely: "*Little Tree* is a lovely little book, and I sometimes wonder if it is an act of romantic atonement by a guilt-ridden white supremacist, but ultimately I think it is the racial hypocrisy of a white supremacist."

Perhaps racial hypocrisy explains the extreme case of Asa Earl Carter, but there's undoubtedly something strange in the American psyche regarding the Wannabes, and I haven't been immune from their truth-y allure.

• • •

I owe my rather unusual middle name—St. Clair—to a notable Choctaw artist named St. Clair Homer, a man I once understood to be my maternal grandfather. As a boy, I hated my middle name. Who would name their boy St. Clair?

"Isn't that a girl's name?" I asked my mom one day.

My mom told me I should be proud of the name because St. Clair Homer was a famous artist and somehow (I wasn't quite sure how) a part of our family. Homer is known to the art world as Homma (the Choctaw work "homa" which means "red"—as in "Oklahoma").

Let's get this straight: Homma was no Wannabe. He traced a lineage back to Pushmataha, a general who fought the British in the War of 1812; his grandfather had been Secretary of the Choctaw Nation. The thing was, I wasn't quite sure if Homma was actually my grandfather because my grandmother started living with another man who wasn't Native at all. When I was three years old, though, Homma won first place in the Oklahoma Bicentennial Indian Art Exhibition at Gilcrease Museum for a bronze sculpture called "Spirit Horse." I was too young to remember the exhibit, but I saw it later during school field trips.

What struck me about Homma's work was its stark defiance of much of the art in Gilcrease. He engaged in a playful mocking of Western mythology. There was none of the rugged individualism of the American West: the white cowboy facing down the harsh environment and the Indian savages. In 1976, for the centennial of the Battle of Little Big Horn, Homma declared that he was going on "full war-path mode" and made a series satirical postcards "commemorating" the event.

In the meantime, I had learned the truth of my connection to Homma. My biological grandfather had died shortly after my mother was born during World War II. Homma and my grandmother lived together off and on for decades, and he practically raised my mom. Later, they drifted apart and my grandmother remarried.

His presence in my life was still there, however, especially every time anyone asked me about my middle name. My first year of college, I met a group of exchange students from Great Britain. I told them I was from Oklahoma, a place they only knew from the musical and Westerns.

"You must be part Indian or something," one of the Brits said. I thought about this for a minute. Yes, I must be part Indian. Not only am I named after one, I'm darker than most white people. The British exchange students really seemed interested. They clearly wanted to know an Indian.

"I think I'm part Choctaw," I said. "But only, like, one-sixteenth, so I'm not on any tribal roles or anything."

There, I'd done it. I felt good to be part Indian, as if I belonged to something big. Something noble, wise, and timeless. Now that I'd said it, it had to be true. After all, my mother's family came from rural east-ern Oklahoma, right on the dividing line between the Choctaw and Cherokee Nations. The family's cemetery plot in Checotah was right next to the Indian section. And, like Liz Warren's Papaw, we had high cheekbones.

So I would belong to the tribe of the Wannabes for a while, especially during my early 20s, when I actually didn't know what the hell I was. The tribe gave me a sense of identity and it carried some instant prestige when traveling abroad. Europeans love Indians, I discovered. I never fully bought in, however. I knew plenty of people who tried to cash-in on some supposed Indian great-grandfather to qualify for a tuition break or minority status. That wasn't me.

There was one small problem: The only Indians I knew in Tulsa were a lot like me. They grew up on the same '80s pop music and TV shows, followed the same sports teams (even the Oklahoma Sooners, who got their name illegally stealing Native land in the late 19th century). They didn't ride horses and they didn't even have cool names, like Iron Eyes. Most of them weren't any darker than I was. So I didn't want to be them. I wanted to be like that Indian in that commercial, stoically paddling his canoe through the American landscape, offering a rebuke to the crass commercialism of mainstream America. Oh, wait...

Originally published
October 2012

by Joe Medina

IKE'S WOUNDED KNEE

When Thorpe's Carlisle beat
Eisenhower's Army in 1912,
several debts were settled

Throughout history, American army generals have faced bitter defeats before achieving their greatest military triumphs. General George Washington lost the Battle of Long Island before leading the colonial army over the British during the Revolutionary War. General Douglas McArthur was commander of military forces on the Philippine Islands when the chain fell to the Japanese army in 1942. Three years later he fulfilled his "I shall return" promise and the invaders were expelled, changing the momentum of the war in the Pacific. General Dwight Eisenhower also faced a devastating loss before leading one of the greatest military operations of all time, the D-Day invasion of Europe. Unlike Washington and McArthur, this setback did not occur on the battlefields of a war but rather on a football field in West Point, New York, nearly 100 years ago.

At the end of the 19th century, expansion in the United States was creating tension across the states of the Dakotas and Wyoming. The ideology of Manifest Destiny, which implied that the United States had the God-given right to expand from the Atlantic Ocean to the Pacific, was driving out Native Americans from their tradition lands. The plains tribes, in particular the Sioux, tried to defend their territories and the federal government charged the United States Army to deal with the Indians by any means necessary to ensure the protection of industry and settlers. On December 29, 1890, the conflict came to a boiling point in what became known as the massacre at Wounded Knee. The 7th Calvary was ordered to the Lakota Indian Reservation to remove all weapons from the tribe. In a heated negotiation, a nervous soldier fired his weapon and chaos ensued. The soldiers responded with overwhelming force, including the use of Hotchkiss canons fired from a ridge above the reservation. Before the day was over, an estimated 180 Lakota men, women, and children lay dead on the frozen ground.

There were many, including some in the federal government, who felt that the "Indian problem" needed to be dealt with by the complete eradication of the tribes. The Indian was nothing more than an uneducated, non-Christian, inferior human being who was standing in the way of the nation's progress. Another proposed solution was to establish Indian schools as a means to indoctrinate Native Americans into Anglo culture by giving them a basic education and teaching them vocational skills that they could use to earn a living by working for the white man.

The Carlisle Indian Industrial School was started in 1879 in Pennsylvania by Army captain Henry Pratt. Pratt believed in "assimilation through total immersion" and the first order of business for Native Americans once they entered Carlisle was to be stripped of their heritage. Young boys had their hair cut, their buckskins exchanged for military uniforms, and were forbidden to speak their native language or practice their spiritual beliefs. Pratt professed that the goal of Carlisle was to "kill the Indian and save the man." The success of Pratt's experiment was marginal, as several students ran away, turned to alcohol, or committed suicide because of the restricted way of life they were forced to live. The only respite from this miserable existence was in the white man's recreational games they learned to play on the fields of Carlisle. It was here that the Native American boys regained some of their freedom by playing baseball, basketball, and the relatively new sport that was popular on the eastern seaboard, football.

Football at the turn of the 19th century was a brutal game played mostly by the Ivy League universities. Harvard, Yale, and Cornell were the top teams of the era in which the game was not much more than a glorified and violent scrum. Colleges loaded their teams with the biggest, strongest, and meanest people that they could find. The offensive strategy was simple. Go straight ahead, knock down anything that was in front of you, and push your player with the ball across the goal line. It was power football and its popularity was that it appealed to man's primal instincts. It was common in games to have several fights, broken bones, severe head injuries, and an occasional death.

Pop Warner, the most innovative football mind of the time, was hired to coach the Carlisle team in 1899. Warner was revolutionizing the game of football by introducing new formations such as the single wing, encouraging the forward pass, and using deception by running counters and reverses. He became intrigued by the Native American players after watching his mighty Cornell team barely defeat Carlisle in an 1898 contest. Warner was fascinated with their athleticism and how the smaller Native American players played a faster game than the traditional powers. They had speed, agility, and a tenacity that enabled them to compete with much larger teams on their schedule.

At the same time that Warner was building Carlisle into a contender, the United States Military Academy at West Point became enchanted with football. It was natural at West Point, the training ground for future military officers, to embrace the competitive and strategic nature of the game. The football field became another battleground for the Army to claim victory and soon the Cadets were in the upper echelon of college football.

In 1912, both teams were at the height of their football prowess and were led by two players that epitomized their respective programs. Carlisle's Jim Thorpe, the Oklahoma Sac and Fox fresh from winning the pentathlon and decathlon at the Olympics in Sweden, was the best runner, kicker, and passer on the field. His only weakness was that his level of effort

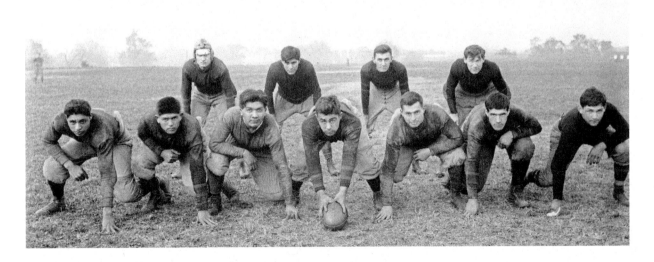

Carlisle Indian School 1912 football team
Photo by A. A. Line
Courtesy Cumberland County Historical
Society, Carlisle, Pennsylvania

Front row (L–R): Charles Williams, Peter Calac, Elmer Busch, Joe Bergie, William Garlow, Joe Guyon, Roy Large

Back row: Alex Arcasa, Stancil "Possum" Powell, Gus Welch, James Thorpe didn't match his talent. Warner was often frustrated by Thorpe's lack of motivation.

The antithesis of Thorpe was Army's Eisenhower. "Ike" came to West Point a scrawny but scrappy farm boy from Abilene, Kansas. His passion was football and he trained relentlessly to be the best player he could be. Not the fastest or the biggest on his team, Ike's tenacity made him the team's best runner and hardest hitting tackler. His effort and dedication endeared him to his coaches.

On November 9, a titanic collision of football powers occurred as Carlisle met Army at West Point. It was the most anticipated game of the season with national championship implications. Carlisle—the only blemish on its record a single tie—boasted the best offense in the nation. Army had only lost once and claimed the best defense. The contrasting styles of play also added to the intrigue. The Cadets still played traditional power football with larger players while Warner had his "dream team" of athletic players with which he built his game plan around speed and deception. Adding fuel to the fire was the massacre at Wounded Knee, still fresh in the minds of both sides, a point that Warner referenced in his pre-game speech to motivate his team.

The Cadets were also not lacking motivation, as they were envious of the headlines that Carlisle's circus style of football was generating. Ike was obsessed by the fact that he would compete against Thorpe. Winning wasn't enough: Ike wanted to create his legacy at West Point by hitting Thorpe so hard that it would knock him out of the game. The game became a battle within a battle as the over-achiever was looking to outshine the world's greatest athlete on the game's biggest stage.

Tensions were high on both sides from the opening kick. A first-half fight led to the ejection of players from each team. Army used its power running game to score first. Carlisle confused the Cadets with a new formation, the double wing, and took a 7–6 lead at halftime in a physical game. Ike managed a salvo of hard tackles on Thorpe—including one that dazed the Olympic champ—but the star never missed a play. At halftime, Ike was still driven to take Thorpe out of the game. He and a teammate planned that the next time they had the opportunity they were going and use a high-low tackle on the Indian. The move would prove to be a tactical blunder by the future General Eisenhower.

In the second half, Ike finally had his chance for the hit he had been planning. Thorpe broke through the middle of the line at full speed. His defining moment in hand, Ike lined him up in his cross-hairs. Ike aimed high while teammate Leland Hobbs went low. They launched their bodies at Thorpe with all they had. Anticipating the tackle, the athletic Thorpe instantaneously stopped his momentum causing the two

tacklers to fly by. Ike and Hobbs crashed into one another and lay semi-conscious on the cold, hard field. Undaunted, Thorpe gained 10 more yards before being pushed out of bounds. Hobbs would need a stretcher to take him off the field, dazed and confused. Ike struggled to stand and required assistance to reach the sidelines. His knee was completely destroyed by the collision, effectively ending his day, his playing career, and his chance for football immortality.

Carlisle and its deceptive double-wing formation ran roughshod after that, confusing the Cadets and claiming a decisive 27–6 victory.

The players knew that they had not only won a football game but also a triumph for all Native Americans. They proved they were not inferior to the white man by beating him at his own game.

The celebration was short lived. The following week, with the National Championship at stake, Carlisle fell to Penn. Pop Warner would eventually leave the school after the 1914 season and the football program would never be the same. The Carlisle Indian Industrial School would be closed down in 1918 by the War Department. The government believed that it was more important to use the campus to house the World War I wounded than continue the education of Native Americans.

Thorpe never returned to athletic greatness. He was stripped of his gold medals when it was found out that he had played minor league baseball prior to the Olympics. After Carlisle, he had limited success in Major League Baseball and the upstart National Football League. When he retired from athletics, Thorpe bounced from job to job, including acting, where he was often cast as an Indian chief. Thorpe died at age 64 of a heart attack.

Eisenhower struggled to get over the Carlisle outcome. A bout of depression made him consider leaving the Army and returning to Kansas to become a farmer. He held himself personally responsible for the loss. Ike knew that he had committed the cardinal sin that many players do when playing in a big game. His ego and obsession with knocking out Thorpe caused him to play out of his realm as a player.

Although he did not create his defining moment on the football field, Ike may have applied a lesson from the epic game that would aid him in his greatest military victory 32 years later. With Hitler's mighty German army entrenched in northern France, anticipating an Allied invasion force, General Eisenhower stole a play from Pop Warner's playbook. On June 6, 1944 he used deception and speed to land his troops further south on the beaches in Normandy catching the Germans by complete surprise. Ike had his D-Day victory and cemented his legacy as one of this nation's greatest generals.

Originally published
July 2013

by Hunter Howe Cates

YOUNGWOLFE ACCUSED

An Atticus Finch story
set in Tulsa County

Phyllis Jean Warren was missing for three weeks when she was found strangled in a brush pile 300 yards from her home. Wrenched around her swollen neck was her blue plastic belt and stuffed in her pocket were her own blood-stained panties. It was April 2, 1953. She was 11.

It was a short hunt before the police found their man in Warren's neighbor, a 21-year-old Cherokee Indian named Buster Youngwolfe. Childlike himself despite being a husband and father, Buster was always friendly with his gleeful neighbor, no doubt suspecting he was the object of her adolescent affections. Already on probation for a botched burglary committed in his teens, he'd twice lied about his alibi for March 12, the night Phyllis disappeared. First he told the police he was at the movies. Then he admitted he had been out drinking.

After five days and nights in a Tulsa County jailhouse, Youngwolfe broke. Re-enacting the crime, he confessed to taking Phyllis out to a field, crushing her jaw, then raping her. When she threatened to tell his wife, he covered her mouth until she stopped moving. Not sure if she was dead, he unfastened her belt and strangled what life she had left. He then dug a hole with his bare hands and buried her body in the brush.

Her daddy did always warn her to stay away from that Indian man.

The police made an announcement and all that remained was the formality of a trial. A penniless roofer, Buster was assigned a public defender named Elliott "Bill" Howe, only 33 and barely out of law school. Making $250 for 50 cases a month, he did this job part time without an office or secretary. But not much was needed for a case this cut and dried.

Attorney and client met the day Buster confessed. The case wasn't even discussed, as the two men shared a cigarette and not much else. But the next morning Buster called his lawyer and said it was urgent. Not sure what to expect, Bill arrived as soon as he could.

"You had something to tell me?" Bill asked.

"Yeah," Buster whispered, sticking his head through the bars. "I didn't do it."

But Buster had already confessed, which his lawyer pointed out.

"Sure I confessed," Buster said. "They worked on me for five days. I only had two meals. I only slept four hours." Besides, he was an ex-convict. Who'd believe him? The police told him the best he could hope for was a life sentence. Otherwise, he'd die in the chair.

Skeptical, Bill called in a reporter friend and the two grilled Buster for three hours. The more they talked, the more Bill found himself believing in Youngwolfe's story.

"If you're lying now," Bill warned, "you will get the chair."

Buster's eyes widened. "I *didn't* do it."

Bill believed him. Most of Tulsa County didn't—or couldn't. But Bill did. By defending Buster, he would be risking his reputation, something he valued as much as anything in the world. But Bill was convinced he had an innocent man.

The murder of Phyllis Warren and trial of Buster Youngwolfe was a huge story in its day, receiving national coverage ranging from *Inside Detective* to *Redbook* and *Newsweek*. Unfortunately, that is now about the only place you will find it—dusty, old magazines. And with each passing year, those who remember it are lost to time. I am lucky. I know this story because Bill Howe was my grandfather.

To know why my grandfather fought for this young man, you have to know the journey that brought him there. Four years old when his white father died, eight when his Creek mother followed, Bill was sent off to Chilocco Indian School on the Kansas border. The only reason he went was because his well-bred Virginia relatives would take him—with his blond hair and blue eyes—but not his brown-skinned, raven-haired little brother.

My grandfather wouldn't have it. Despite his quarter-Creek blood, he found himself the only fair-skinned kid in the school. According to him, he got his nose bloodied three times the first day. The combined weight of poverty, bullying, and loneliness made him bitter and rebellious. His headmaster told him, "Howe, you'll be in the penitentiary before you're 21."

He may have been right. My grandfather could've become a Buster Youngwolfe. Ironically, it was this frigid comment that inspired him to prove the headmaster wrong. He set himself straight and became a lawyer, one in whose hands Buster had now placed his life.

Bill recognized in Buster the natural reticence he'd seen growing up around American Indians. His life at Chilocco, and among his own flesh and blood, taught him that even the most jovial among them could close off around those outside their group. Buster was no different, which made defending him difficult. The police were convinced he was hiding something.

Bill had no proof that Buster was innocent, except his word. That, and a gut feeling.

• • •

If Buster was convicted in the court of public opinion, Bill now hung next to him. Gossipmongers said he was just juicing up publicity, all the while defending a monster who had murdered a child. But my grandfather couldn't worry about that. There was too much work to do.

Truth was, Buster *had* lied about his alibi. He didn't go to the movies on March 12, but had spent the day scouring bars with his father and brother to celebrate his 21st birthday. Because drinking would've violated his probation, he lied to keep himself out of jail for two years.

Even after learning these facts, the sheriff never bothered to check the bars. Bill did, and found several waitresses who remembered seeing Buster. Buster's father also remembered a traffic ticket they received that night, proving they were out driving as they claimed.

Bill also examined the crime scene, where Buster confessed to digging Warren's grave with his bare hands. Even for a healthy young man like Buster, that would've been nearly impossible, as tightly packed as the dirt was. Finally, Bill visited Warren and Buster's neighborhood, though to call it such is a stretch. A morbid collection of two-room tar paper shacks, this slum was home to at least six sex offenders. None were ever questioned.

My grandfather kept the facts close to his chest, even as public opinion grew vicious. By now strangers and friends alike would walk on the other side of the street simply to avoid him.

To ensure there were no doubts about Buster's innocence, my grandfather petitioned for a lie detector test. At that time, the test could only be admitted as evidence if both sides agreed to it. County Prosecutor Robert L. Wheeler went along with Bill's "crazy idea."

The region's best administer of lie detector tests was Kansas City Police Captain Phil Hoyt, who, it was said, had never been proved wrong in 6,052 tests. Buster, joined by the county attorney, a handful of deputies, and Bill, was driven 243 miles for the test. It was agreed the results would not be revealed until Hoyt took the stand as the last witness of the trial.

My grandfather was confident in Buster's innocence and in the case he'd prepared. But the enormity of his responsibility was taking its toll. "I had convinced [Buster's] family I would get him free," he told *Redbook*. "They were sleeping nights. I wasn't."

• • •

His fears were unfounded. The county's case against Youngwolfe unraveled from the start. Waitresses testified to Buster's whereabouts on the night of March 12. Neighbors reported seeing him drunk when friends brought him home. On the stand, the sheriff admitted to pressuring him during his five-day incarceration. A local reporter even testified that Buster had confessed to him his innocence—a bombshell that never made it to print.

The trial was going in my grandfather's favor. But then, in an instant, everything fell apart. Bill had placed great weight on the traffic fine as evidence that Buster and his family were out driving on March 12. However, the county attorney produced the document, showing it was dated March 13—the *day after* Phyllis disappeared. The one recorded piece of evidence supporting Buster's alibi crumbled.

The county's victory was short-lived. As the record book made its way through the jury, one juror pointed out that the dates had been changed. It *had* read "March 12," but had obviously been rewritten to "March 13." Buster's alibi stood.

Finally, Hoyt took the stand. He detailed his methods just shy of an hour, as silence and stifling heat swept the congested courtroom. Then he delivered his final statement. When he said he did not kill Phyllis Warren, Hoyt testified, "Buster Youngwolfe has been telling the truth."

. . .

The county attorney threw in the towel, telling the jury, "I cannot conscientiously ask you to convict this defendant."

"We knew you had it all the time!" friends told Bill, pretending they were on his side from the beginning. Politicians emerged, discussing this young defense attorney's prospects. Bill would have none of it.

"I'm no hero, and don't you forget it," he told *Redbook*. "I had an innocent man, and that's the most any attorney can ask."

This story was a natural sell for the national media—a heinous crime, a wrongfully accused man, a crusading attorney, all set in the wildcatting, cowboys-and-Indians landscape of Tulsa. Pulpy true detective magazines, which covered the story before the trial, treated it as a noir-ish tale of sordid crime, depicting with a flourish Youngwolfe as a cold-blooded savage. *Newsweek*, which ran the story after the trial, used the exotic title "Lie-Detector Indian," as if my grandfather possessed supernatural powers: half witch doctor, half defense attorney

. . .

Justice is allegedly blind, but the court of public opinion follows no rules, now or in 1953. And, when the case involves a former felon and a murdered girl, the truth can be buried deeper than Phyllis Jean Warren ever could be.

My grandfather knew better. While, like any man, Bill Howe had his flaws, his trademark characteristic was an almost stubborn fairness. Certainly he understood how much he was risking in taking Youngwolfe's case. Even so, I suspect it simply never occurred to him not to. He had an innocent man to defend and didn't give a damn about the consequences, personal or professional. That sounds just like him.

Youngwolfe's fate is unknown to me, and tragically Phyllis Jean Warren's killer was never found. As for my grandfather, he never pursued politics, nor was there another Buster Youngwolfe in his career. What followed for him were two of the things he wanted most—a respected practice and a devoted family, like the one he lost as a boy. It was the latter that was by his side the day he died on January 21, 2007.

I don't know why my grandfather trusted Youngwolfe, a man most of the city had condemned before even the trial. Maybe he saw in him what he easily could have become himself: a life left behind simply because no one believed in him. Buster Youngwolfe deserved justice. He deserved a defense. In my grandfather, he found it.

Originally published
July 2016

by Jezy J. Gray

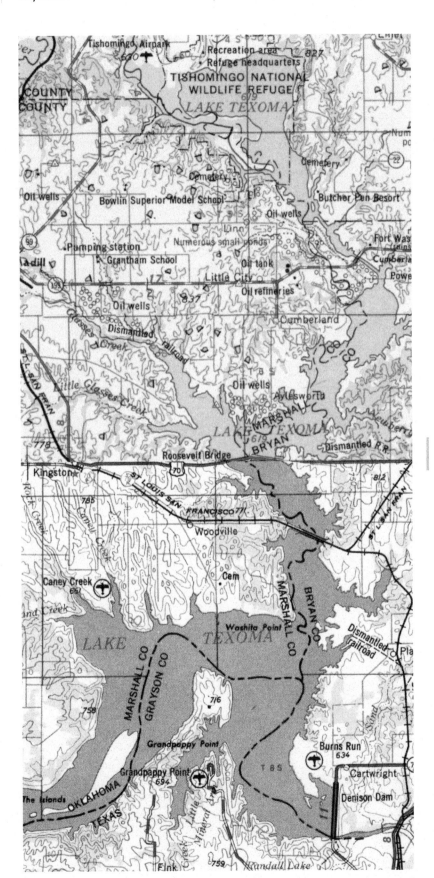

IN MY TRIBE

Anecdotes on water and
blood, race and family

A childhood summer afternoon is thrown into relief.

I'm 10 years old. My big sister Kat and I are spending the day at Lake Texoma, the man-made gulf between the Choctaw and Chickasaw Nations of south-central Oklahoma. I'm scratching my initials into the shore with a snapped twig, letting them wash gradually into the lake: a satisfying private ritual. Kat is further upshore, propped on her elbows across a terrycloth Garfield beach towel, reading *The Babysitters Club* and eating Bugles from a Ziploc bag.

A young boy walks between us, dripping wet, and calls out to her:

"*¿Qué pasa guapa? ¿Serás mi novia?*"

She thumbs her page and turns toward him, not bothering to look over the polka-dot Minnie Mouse sunglasses she's weeks away from outgrowing.

"No habla," she says in a bored Okie drawl, and returns to her book.

I watch this boy as he walks away, deflated, beads of lake water drying on his brown shoulders in the early August sun. I remember other kids assuming my sister was Latina. I never wondered why no one made a similar mistake about me.

I look back at her, wiping Bugle dust on Garfield's dispassionate smirk. I want to ask about the Spanish thing, but I'm afraid the answer might be embarrassing for one of us. I'm not sure for whom.

. . .

"Austin says we're not really brother and sister," I tell Kat one night from the bottom bunk in the bedroom we share. I don't know what I expect her to say to this. I know we're not related *by blood* (an enormously upsetting phrase) but I also know that she's my sister. The few years of my life before we became family are far-away and gauzy, like a dream, or the faint rhythm of a misremembered poem.

I need her to confirm our connection to each other.

"Austin's an idiot," she says. "Go to sleep."

. . .

I'm interviewing for a copywriting job at a public radio station in Dallas: a failed eleventh-hour effort to avoid going back to grad school. I tell my interviewer that I just published an article—my first!—about Ralph Ellison. I also casually mention, with the nonchalance of a seasoned humble-bragger, a recent talk I gave at a conference dedicated to the work of James Baldwin. ("In France. Ever heard of it?")

This prompts the question I'm somehow never prepared to answer:

"Why are *you* so interested in black people?"

He doesn't say it like this, but that's what I hear.

It's not the first time I've been asked this question. When some people encounter a white person who studies anything that sounds like "race," they demand an explanation. (This, I should say, only happens with other white people. No black person has ever asked me why I read black writers.)

"Well, my family is Choctaw," I stupidly begin.

Then it happens. His face changes. Suddenly, I see him see something else.

I mean to walk him through my braided family history, explain how the threads came together, and tell him how being seen differently from parts of my own family woke me to the social construction of racial categories. But I don't.

He's embarrassed. He's sorry.

"That," he concludes, "is what you get for making assumptions about people."

Here I could say the two words that will release him: *I'm white!* But I just sit there, letting my misread identity hang above us like mistletoe, waiting to be kissed.

. . .

"I come from a multiracial family," I could have said. But I've never said that.

Multiracial. It sounds so clinical, so cold: like *respiratory,* or *stepbrother.*

Kat has two kids: a boy and a girl. Her son, my nephew, has chocolate brown eyes and skin the color of burnt caramel. His mom styles his deep black hair in a fauxhawk that drives me up the wall, and he can count to 20 in Choctaw. ("That's it?" I tease him. "Not impressed.")

His little sister is a bowl of peaches and cream. I assume her auburn curls were passed down from her white dad—a Skoal-dipping deer hunter from Anadarko—but I've never seen him without a baseball cap, so I can't confirm this.

They have a cowdog named Sampa, a Choctaw word that means *dig.*

Side by side, these "blood" siblings look like they come from different families. Strangers must think so. I imagine the explaining they'll have to do as they move together in a world that will feel entitled to—will demand—that explanation.

I wonder what it means to satisfy that demand, and what it means to refuse.

Originally published
July 2016

by Molly Bullock

A NEW DAY

Relearning the difference
between history and legend

Last September in the town of Bartlesville, 15-year-old Blue Haase got a ride to his local school board meeting. During the time for public comments, Blue, an enrolled member of the Cherokee Nation, took the mic and identified himself as a student representative of Operation Eagle, Bartlesville Public Schools' district-funded Native education program. Reading from notes he had prepared, Blue asked why the district was still recognizing a holiday that honors Christopher Columbus, the Italian explorer whose colonization efforts included unspeakable atrocities. He asked the board to undertake a district-wide adoption of Indigenous Peoples' Day, a celebration of Native culture and contributions.

When the *Bartlesville Examiner-Enterprise* ran a story about Blue's remarks, a backlash followed. Blue had attended the meeting on a whim and hadn't cleared his statement with Operation Eagle. His words were received as a blow to the district, which has been working closely with Operation Eagle for decades to support Native kids. To complicate matters, his mother, Jessie Haase, is president of parent committees for the program.

"The district doesn't want to look bad," Jessie said. "And Blue didn't hold back."

Jessie ran interference, fielding calls and comments from supportive school board members as well as those complaining that Blue had been excessively negative.

"I'm like, OK, well, you are not a 15-year-old Native American boy, so I don't expect you to understand that negativity," Jessie said. "You've never had people want to know what will happen if they cut your hair off. You've never had people for five or six years of your life call you a little Indian girl. You've never been on a field trip to the museum, where they talk about everything in a historical context—like moccasins and roaches and buckskin dresses that you take the kids to see at the museum—*we have that in our house*."

The dust settled with the agreement that in the future, Blue would distinguish his own views from those of Operation Eagle. Meanwhile, the *Examiner-Enterprise* story had gone viral among Bartlesville High School students, many of whom began confronting Blue in class. When he got home from school, he armed himself with new facts to inform whatever debate he might find himself in the next day.

"They were like, 'Why should we have a day just for Natives when they don't have days for black people?'" Blue said. "And I'd argue with that, because they have a whole month: Black History Month. And they were like, 'Well, why isn't there a day for white people?' I'm like, 'That's almost every day.'"

A few weeks later, a former principal who'd reconnected with Blue at the school board meeting arranged a conversation between Blue, Jessie, and representatives of the high school, school board, and Operation Eagle. Now the executive director of Employment & Human Resources for the district, the former principal has become a key ally to Blue's push for Indigenous Peoples' Day. Operation Eagle also came around to officially endorse the effort.

To be clear, Bartlesville Public Schools doesn't celebrate Columbus Day in any formal way. However, the requirement to teach about Columbus Day appears multiple times in the Oklahoma Academic Standards, and Blue has interrupted more than one history lesson to provide more inclusive and historically accurate perspectives.

After a new superintendent joins the district this summer, Blue and his supporters will bring a formal proposition for Indigenous Peoples' Day before the school board. Initially, they intended to share the holiday with Columbus Day. After numerous conversations with family and friends, Blue and Jessie decided to push for the total replacement of Columbus Day with Indigenous Peoples' Day.

· · ·

Indigenous Peoples' Day is unseating Columbus Day in communities across the country. Last year, Anadarko became the first town in Oklahoma to reinvent the second Monday in October. Though Oklahoma City voted against the new holiday, the University of Oklahoma, Oklahoma City University, and Southeastern Oklahoma State University soon followed Anadarko's lead. The Muscogee (Creek) Nation, Choctaw Nation, and Delaware Tribe of Indians also adopted the holiday.

On October 9, 2015, as Indigenous Peoples' Day gained ground even here in the Plains, President Obama released a wistful proclamation reaffirming the observance of Columbus Day. The "[d]etermined and curious" explorer "inspired many," the article reads; "Columbus's legacy is embodied in the spirit of our Nation."

Even the proclamation's brief acknowledgment of Native peoples is flanked with borderline nostalgia for European colonialism:

Though these early travels expanded the realm of European exploration, to many they also marked a time that forever changed the world for the indigenous peoples of North America. Previously unseen disease, devastation, and violence were introduced to their lives—and as we pay tribute to the ways in which Columbus pursued ambitious goals—we also recognize the suffering inflicted upon Native Americans and we recommit to strengthening tribal sovereignty and maintaining our strong ties.

After landing in the Caribbean in 1492, Christopher Columbus and the Europeans who followed him decimated the Native peoples they encountered by means including rape, kidnapping, enslavement, beheading, butchering, and boiling. Though Columbus was far from the first outsider to "discover" the area, his expeditions paved the way for rampant European colonization of North, Central, and South America.

Columbus Day became a U.S. holiday in the 1930s. Ostensibly (and incongruously) celebrating discovery and progress, the holiday has also become an element of Italian-American heritage and identity. It has come under growing scrutiny since the 1970s.

· · ·

The Columbus mythology is just one piece of a complicated web Native kids navigate at school. Consider the grade school calendar: In October, kids learn about Columbus. When Halloween rolls around, they're blasted with rampant cultural appropriation in the name of trick-or-treating. Thanksgiving brings more fairytales, feather headbands and paper pilgrim hats. And more than likely, football season throws at least a few Native mascots[1] into the mix. Native American Heritage Day falls on the Friday after Thanksgiving—which you might have missed if you were at Walmart buying a new television set. And that's just the first semester. Come springtime, it's land run reenactment season.

A few years ago, Jessie filed away a Pocahontas worksheet her daughter, Kele Jane, brought home from school. Bookended with phrases including, "Whatever the real truth is," and, "Whatever

---

1 The problem of Native mascots persists at all tiers of the educational system and also among professional sports leagues, despite the American Psychological Association's insistence for more than a decade that this theft of Native imagery harms Native kids and does a disservice to non-Natives as well. Most notably in Oklahoma, the national championship-winning University of Oklahoma athletics program continues to cling to a mascot and chant that celebrate "the land run, anti-indigeneity, genocide and cheating," as a guest columnist put it recently in the OU Daily. Though the symbolism of OU's Sooners places them in a bizarre category all their own, the related use of Native imagery for mascots and logos remains an equally intractable, very slowly crumbling holdout in Oklahoma.

Blue Haase

A land rush in Oklahoma, 1889

you believe," the handout regurgitates popular notions of the Powhatan woman popularly known as Pocahontas.

"This is a very whitewashed version of Pocahontas," Jessie said. "This isn't what I tell my kids about Pocahontas. When I talk in terms of Pocahontas, it's rape and enslavement. This poor woman was taken halfway across the world to entertain the colonial fantasies of taming the savage, and died there, and was never brought home to her people. And for Native people, with removal and death and things like that, where our families are, it means something to us. She'll never be in her homeland. She'll never lay in rest. That's what we talk to our kids about—and then she brings home the little piece of paper that talks about John Smith and has the Pocahontas portrait with her in the colonial style clothing."

The Pocahontas Complex, as Jessie calls it, takes shape in her kids' lives in different ways. Kele Jane's peers fawn over her when she wears the feathers and furs of her traditional clothing, but Blue has been called a fag, a girl, and a pussy since he began growing out his hair in second grade. His braid now reaches his mid-back, and a girl once yanked it so hard that he fell to the ground. Aside from the *Twilight* wolf pack—itself rife with problematic stereotypes—popular images of Native boys are largely absent from American media. Native girls, on the other hand, were widely objectified in popular culture long before Disney made it official. As Kele Jane's classmates snap selfies with her, Blue's wonder aloud what might happen if they cut off his braid.

"They have their different experiences just based off of what we're teaching our kids when they're young," Jessie said. "What they're watching, what they're seeing, what they're reading."

. . .

Though Norman Public Schools discontinued land run reenactments in 2011, the Norman '89er Parade lived on despite burgeoning protests. Over the years, the parade has commemorated the Land Run of April 22, 1889, with everything from floats to fiddling contests to operas and, of course, covered wagons—the most conspicuous being the University of Oklahoma's Sooner Schooner, that iconic horse-drawn Conestoga that races across the field at every home and bowl game. After this year's '89er Parade, *The Norman Transcript* reported that organizers have announced a new name, Norman on Parade, due to growing pressure from protesters.

In Oklahoma City, the push to end reenactments hit a tipping point in November 2014 when White House representatives visited the city for a listening session with Native students. The event, one of nine gatherings in seven states, was part of the White House Initiative on American Indian and Alaska Native Education. The first effort of this kind and scope, the tour invited Native youth and other stakeholders to speak freely and candidly about bullying, discipline, mascots, and other challenges in their school environment.

For years prior to the listening sessions, Sarah Adams-Cornell, an advocate for social justice and Native American rights, had worked with Oklahoma City Public Schools' Native American Student Services to end land run reenactments. Adams-Cornell, a member of the Choctaw Nation who has two school-age daughters, even organized presentations to replace the activity. For her, rethinking the way we teach the Land Run is about checking blind patriotism.

"When you consider that for many Native people, the Land Run is a celebration of genocide and land theft, it makes you look at it a little differently," Adams-Cornell said. "...We certainly don't believe in ignoring our history—we want to talk about it. But we want to talk about it truthfully. Consider that not all of these events are worth celebrating. And especially for our kids—they're the ones who are usually doing these reenactments—so consider what you're teaching your children. Consider asking your Native friends to give their opinion on these subjects and to make that available to your children."

At the Oklahoma City listening session, Adams-Cornell's younger daughter, Gabby Cornell, gave the following testimony, which appears in the initiative's School Environment Listening Sessions Final Report:

> When I was in kindergarten, my class did a land run reenactment. We ran on the playground and put flags in the ground and claimed the land. I don't remember the teachers telling us it was Indian land and people were taking it from them. It makes me feel frustrated, mad, and sad that we had to do this. Why do teachers teach something that isn't right? I want land run reenactments to stop. My mom made a deal with the principal. She said we can do Native American presentations at the school to teach about Native history, language, dance, and the awesomeness of our culture if [the school] will stop doing land run reenactments, and my principal said yes! They promised to never do land run reenactments again, but not everyone can go to my school. I think all schools should do this.

Testimonies like Gabby's caught the attention of Aurora Lora, an administrator who had recently joined the district from out of state and was sitting in on the session.

"Because [Lora] wasn't from Oklahoma and

she hadn't been doing those her whole educational career, she was like, 'Why are we doing this? I don't understand why this is happening in our schools,'" Adams-Cornell said. "Within a couple of days, she sent a mandate out and said, 'Oklahoma City Public Schools are no longer participating in land run reenactments, from now on.' ...It took a six-year-old little girl at a microphone with somebody not from Oklahoma listening to it to go, 'Yeah, this is easy. Why are we doing this?' And that's how the change came about. It wasn't me going over and over again. It was little kids letting them know that this is hurtful."

The following April, Adams-Cornell and Native American Student Services rolled out Oklahoma History Day, a first-person storytelling curriculum they created. The interactive, hands-on program piloted in two Oklahoma City schools, teaching Oklahoma history from the perspectives of a freedman, a Native person, an immigrant, a pioneer, and the federal government.

The day far exceeded expectations and kept the kids engaged and asking a ton of questions, Adams-Cornell said. The catch was trying to fit all the activities and information into one day. This year, the curriculum returned as Oklahoma History Week in two different schools. Adams-Cornell plans to ultimately package it for use by any teacher in the state.

. . .

Change finds some Oklahoma districts more slowly than others. Though Jenks Public Schools discontinued land run reenactments more than five years ago, the neighboring and much larger Tulsa Public Schools deemed it unnecessary to take an official stance on the activity. Mary Jane Snedeker, academic coordinator for social studies, said the district reached this position (or lack thereof) with the input of its Indian Pupil Education program. Few Tulsa schools, if any, still reenact the Land Run, Snedeker said—though it's hard to actually know, because the district has no reliable method of accounting for what's happening in each school. The district influences curriculum through workshops and curriculum maps, which guide instruction throughout the year.

"In our curriculum map," Snedeker said, "we just put a note there that says, 'If you are going to do some reenactment of the Land Run, you need to make sure that it is holistic and fully historic.'"

In practice, site-based management in Tulsa leaves the particulars of teaching to individual schools. Aside from suggesting resources such as curriculum maps and sample lessons, the district provides very little targeted direction for teaching the state standards, including sensitive and traditionally ill-addressed topics such as the Land Run and Columbus Day.

"There's lots of gaps," Snedeker said. "It's like, 'What do I teach?' You might be teaching anything, really. It's wide open."

Under the leadership of Superintendent Deborah Gist, the district is moving away from site-based management toward a more cohesive culture. This includes developing a five-year curriculum management plan. In the next year, Snedeker said she's creating a committee to address the teaching of controversial topics.

"We [the state of Oklahoma] are just behind times here—we're 10 years behind times in education," Snedeker said. "...We've been failing them, really. We haven't done our job, and so that's why we're doing these things that we're doing now. We want them to have access to things that are meaningful, purposeful, personal, applicable to their lives."

Tulsa Public Schools' Indian Pupil Education program primarily serves Native kids in an advocacy and cultural enrichment capacity. Resource advisors work with individual schools, but they lack the standing to shape curriculum in any lasting way. Using this program to mitigate the effects of institutionalized racism—rather than to directly address institutionalized racism through curriculum—seems like a missed opportunity for the district. Coordinator Mitch McGehee said Indian Pupil Education is working toward gaining a stronger voice, but that this wasn't the program's original purpose.

"We're more of a supplemental program," McGehee said. "It's not our job to dictate the curriculum."

. . .

With education funding cuts in excess of $100 million, the pursuit of a less destructive school environment for Native kids in Oklahoma is likely to be met with increasing pushback. The resistance Blue and Jessie face in Bartlesville sometimes employs the following line of argument:

"It's like, 'Oh here's all those Indians protesting—they want to be treated different. We can't teach about all the cultures.'" Jessie said. "Well, why *not*? Why *can't* you? Why is culture not taught? Why are you only teaching for a math and reading test and not teaching culture or social skills?"

To that end, Operation Eagle is working with Bartlesville principals to enhance curriculum so kids are properly educated about Native history and peoples—and better prepared when it becomes age-appropriate to share the most difficult material with them.

"Life was ugly," Jessie said. "And if we always whitewash everything that we tell our kids, then they grow up and they're all like, 'Woe is me.' No, woe is not me. Rape is real. Murder is real. It's what our country was built upon. It needs to be taught as such."

Originally published
September 2012

by Spencer McCoy

THE HERITAGE TREES

On a rolling hill, wedged between downtown Tulsa and the mixed residential of Carson Heights, sits a small park with a well-manicured lawn surrounded by a low, wrought-iron fence. There are a few benches, some greenery, and a small set of statues frozen in action around a pole with an animal skull on top. Directly across the street, another sculpture—this one of a fire, large metal tendrils climbing toward the sky, cold brass forever burning. Odd though they are against the backdrop of cramped apartment complexes, these figures are not what make the corner of Cheyenne Avenue and 18th Street memorable. The memory lies in the Council Oak tree, the mature burr oak standing as a silent sentinel over the flames.

Around the U.S. there are many "heritage trees" marking the ceremonial and cultural importance of a specific place. Many of these trees—mostly over 100 years old—have beheld drastic overthrows of civilizations, often accompanied by bloodshed. As Michael Harkin, the chair of anthropology at the University of Wyoming, says, "The landscape bears traces, both physical and linguistic, of past events. In some instances this process alters the actual topography... in other cases, it is linguistic practice." Through the establishment, naming, and narrative of the Council Oak and its brethren, the trees are imbued with meaning, and affect the present.

Once, the Council Oak stood taller than almost anything in Tulsa—limbs spreading wide over the plains—but now it is overshadowed by middling office buildings and condos. From the base of the tree the Spirit Bank building is easily visible, with its neon green highlights and large American flag merrily waving high overhead. Cars drive by, hurrying home from work. Mere feet from the Council Oak, the light from a TV flickers through a window.

· · ·

Our soil is soaked in Native American blood. As the nation attempts to re-establish social and cultural roots, we encounter the severed roots of those that were here before us. And often we just attempt to thrust past them in our search for an unsullied heritage.

When I first heard of the Council Oak, my knowledge of the homeland was primarily experiential. In the acres of forest behind my house, I had pondered upon the best thinking rocks, gazed from the tops of the toughest climbing trees, scouted and built upon the hills suitable for fortifications. The base of my knowledge was physical and concrete; I did not comprehend the heritage of the land my feet ran and jumped upon. For me, Native American identity only resided in movies and the names of street signs. So, my first brush with the memories of the Council Oak created quite an impression.

My 9th grade Oklahoma history class was making a tour of the Art Deco buildings of Tulsa—remnants of an era commanded by oil barons—with a brief stop at the founding site of the city: a big oak tree. As the group began to gather in a semicircle around the teachers jointly guiding the trip, I didn't give the tree much thought. Beyond that it was pretty and climbable, my attention was elsewhere. The teachers talked a bit about something or another, but I was more interested in what my friends had to say. Still, certain words trickled down through my consciousness and began to resonate. Disease. Exhaustion. Death march. When they began to discuss the horrors of the Trail of Tears—which the tree in part commemorates—I was aghast. The abandonment of the Native American Creek tribe's traditional home in 1834, the spoiled meat "provided" by the U.S. government, the forced marches, the harsh weather, and the thought of seeing grandfathers and daughters and friends wither and die upon the trail sickened me. It was not as though I had not heard the tales before, but that day there was the tree—the tree that watched as the remnants of the Mvskoke tribe rekindled the live coals from their last fire from their home in Alabama into flames—commemorating their dead. The tree that saw the remaining 469, whittled down from 630 by affliction after affliction, tribe members promise not to forget their fallen comrades. The tree, swallowed up in the rumbling of cars, apartment doors opening and closing, and animated chatter of high school students, whispered even louder its recollections.

A common thread in the establishment and continuation of sacred sites, especially heritage trees, is described by Carolyn Prorok, a specialist in cultural geography:

> Many sacred sites were destroyed or built over by the conquering party, especially in the Western Hemisphere, and especially those of indigenous peoples whose lands were being absorbed or who were forcibly removed from favored lands. Add to this the inundation by foreign migrants who arrived by the hundreds of thousands and brought with them their own notions of what constituted a sacred place.

This concept is reflected in the devaluation of living memorials, like the Council Oak, whose branches almost brush against the apartments of downtown

Tulsa, whose memories are ignored by almost all but the Mvskoke, and whose sacred grounds are often used as a dog park.

But, there is hope. As in the case of the Treaty Oak, the power of the physical tree, a witness to a multitude of human interactions, can be appreciated. It is the last of the 14 oaks regarded as tree-gods and temples by the Comanche and Tonkawa of what is now Austin, Texas. The bands would gather under its widespread branches for sacred ceremonies; the tree was a witness to religious and tribal ritual. Legend goes that the Tejas Native American women would settle at the base of the tree and brew a tea to ensure the everlasting love and safety of the male warriors. The same Comanche bands that prayed under the tree would later be killed or driven from their home—their sacred places—to be quarantined in Oklahoma—forced to live cramped against other traditionally hostile tribes.

The Treaty Oak contains collective memory—experiences and meaning and importance, remembered and passed down from generation to generation. Yet, as in the tradition of our nation, those whom did not take time to appreciate the cultural significance—or did not want to appreciate—have threatened the tree again and again. The Treaty Oak has survived 13 of the original 14 trees in the sacred grove. But many who understood the importance have rallied around it, trying to save it from harsh, ignorant hands. The sacred land was up for sale, and the tree was almost cut down in the late 1920s. It was saved by pleas from women's and children's groups and other institutions. In 1989, in an act of vandalism, the tree was deliberately poisoned with enough herbicide to kill a hundred trees. Infuriated by the treatment, the Austin community came together in an act of solidarity and raised enough funds and supports to save the tree. Although half of the crown was lost to poison, the tree still stands, memories etched into its scarred bark.

Recently, I encountered a young man named Austin showing his very drunk older cousin the Council Oak site. They were the first people that I had met there on my many visits. Austin said that Creek tribe members, who were friends of his parents, had originally brought him to the tree when he was 12. He had been touched when they told him the tree was a peace tree, saying, "No war should take place here." While he explained this to me, his cousin pulled out a beer from his backpack, and opened it, spilling a good portion over the bag. The cousin stumbled over his words as he said, "I have a house right over there," pointing vaguely toward downtown, "and I have friends there," he gestured to the University Club apartments, spiraling over the landscape. "But I never knew this was here—I went by and thought it was not open to anyone—then he brought me here and I was like, cool!"

Austin patiently tolerated his cousin's drunkenness, trying to get him read to the brass placards relaying the history of the Mvskoke Creek that encircled the statue of the flame. His cousin said it was too dark, and commented aside to me, slurring, "by my choice I wouldn't be here."

. . .

The land we live in is drenched in blood. Every inch and acre of it has been the subject of conflicts, arguments, and wars. The heritage trees established by the indigenous peoples of America often commemorate this blood—blood that remains when all else fails. But often, less value is placed on these trees by a nation trying to forget than trees marking current catastrophes afflicting the United States.

One such case is the tree known as the Survivor Tree, an American elm that rests in the memory of the Alfred P. Murrah Federal Building in Oklahoma City. On that fateful day one cold April, glass from 258 nearby buildings was shattered, cars were torn apart, virtually everything in the vicinity was obliterated. Except the Survivor Tree.

Before the bombing, the Survivor Tree was the only shade tree in the building's parking lot. After the explosion, pieces of evidence were removed from the tree's branches, blasted there from the force of the bomb—thus marking the tree as a witness. The tree was blackened, torn apart, and heavily damaged, but a year later, the tree began to bloom, a sign of hope. Now, the tree is featured prominently in the memorial, its seeds are collected and sown each year to create hundreds of saplings. The tree has become venerated for the collective memory that dwells in its branches. Bits and pieces of glass and debris still scar its trunk, still denote it as a living witness of terrorism. The inscription surrounding the trunk reads "The spirit of this city and this nation will not be defeated; our deeply rooted faith sustains us."

The Survivor Tree is admirable, and worthy of commemoration. But many American people focus more attention on the trees denoting current catastrophes and less those trees whose roots dig deepest. Although the Treaty Oak served to unite the Austin community, it is only a mere shade of the symbol the Survivor Tree is to many people, although it holds more history in its trunk. It is too easy to overlook the living witnesses found in the heritage trees of the Native American culture preceding us.

It is a tragic and convenient forgetting.

The Council Oak is still standing on the corner of 18th and Cheyenne. Yet, as the condos and parking lots and cars and shadows of downtown Tulsa encroach ever closer, it is in danger of falling. Falling not to any physical affliction, but rather by the weight of unappreciated memories, tilting in blood-sodden ground.

CPSIA information can be obtained
at www.ICGtesting.com
Printed in the USA
FSOW04n1738040217
30313FS